DECONSTRUCTING RADICAL ORTHODOXY

Radical Orthodoxy is the most influential theological development in a generation. Many have been bewildered by the range and intensity of the writings which constitute Radical Orthodoxy. This book spans the range of the history of thought discussed by Radical Orthodoxy, tackling the accuracy of the historical narratives on which their position depends. The distinguished contributors examine the history of thought as presented by the movement, presenting a series of critiques of individual Radical Orthodox 'readings' of key thinkers. The contributors are: Eli Diamond, Wayne Hankey, Todd Breyfogle, John Marenbon, Richard Cross, Neil Robertson, Douglas Hedley, David Peddle, Steven Shakespeare, George Pattison and Hugh Rayment-Pickard.

Deconstructing Radical Orthodoxy

Postmodern Theology, Rhetoric and Truth

Edited by

WAYNE J. HANKEY
King's College and Dalhousie University, Canada

DOUGLAS HEDLEY
Clare College and the Divinity Faculty, Cambridge University, UK

ASHGATE

Published by
Ashgate Publishing Limited
Gower House
Croft Road
Aldershot
Hants GU11 3HR
England

Ashgate Publishing Company
Suite 420
101 Cherry Street
Burlington, VT 05401-4405
USA

Ashgate website: http://www.ashgate.com

British Library Cataloguing in Publication Data
Deconstructing radical orthodoxy : postmodern theology, rhetoric and truth
   1. Philosophical theology 2. Deconstruction
   I. Hankey, W. J. II. Hedley, Douglas
   230'.046

Library of Congress Cataloging-in-Publication Data
Deconstructing radical orthodoxy : postmodern theology, rhetoric, and truth / edited
by Wayne J. Hankey and Douglas Hedley.
      p. cm.
   Includes bibliographical references and index.
   ISBN 0-7546-5398-6 (hardcover : alk. paper)
   1. Philosophical theology. 2. Postmodern theology. I. Hankey, W. J. II. Hedley,
Douglas.
   BT40.D44 2005
   230'.046—dc22

                                                              2005003005

ISBN 0 7546 5398 6

Typeset by Express Typesetters, Farnham, Surrey
Printed by MPG Books Ltd, Bodmin, Cornwall

Contents

List of Contributors

Todd Breyfogle was a Rhodes Scholar at Oxford, studying Ancient and Modern History and Patristic and Modern Theology. His PhD is from the University of Chicago, where he wrote his doctoral dissertation on St Augustine's political theology. He is co-editor of a five-volume commentary on Augustine's *City of God* for Oxford University Press. At present he is Director of the University Honours Program at the University of Denver (email tbreyfog@du.edu).

Richard Cross is Fellow and Tutor in Theology at Oriel College, University of Oxford. Among his recent publications are *The Metaphysics of the Incarnation: Thomas Aquinas to Duns Scotus* (Oxford University Press, 2002), and *Duns Scotus on God* (Ashgate, 2004) (email richard.cross@oriel.oxford.ac.uk).

Eli Diamond is an MA from Dalhousie University with a thesis on Plato's *Sophist* and is currently writing a doctoral dissertation on Hegel's interpretation of Aristotle's *De Anima* at Northwestern University. His primary area of interest lies in the philosophies of Plato and Aristotle and their reception throughout the subsequent history of philosophy (email eli_diamond@yahoo.com).

Wayne J. Hankey, having studied Classics, Philosophy and Theology in Halifax, Toronto and Oxford, is Carnegie Professor of Classics at King's College and Dalhousie University and is Secretary and Editor of *Dionysius*. His *God in Himself: Aquinas' Doctrine of God as Expounded in the Summa Theologiae* was reprinted in 2000 by Oxford University Press in the series 'Oxford Scholarly Classics'. Most recently he published *Cent Ans De Néoplatonisme En France: Une Brève Histoire Philosophique* (Librairie Philosophique J. Vrin/Presses de l'Université Laval, 2004) (email hankeywj@dal.ca).

Douglas Hedley is a Fellow of Clare College, Cambridge, and a University Senior Lecturer in the Philosophy of Religion in the Faculty of Divinity (email rdh26@cam.ac.uk). He is the author of *Coleridge, Philosophy and Religion: Aids to Reflection and the Mirror of the Spirit* (Cambridge University Press, 2000), a Fellow of Clare College, Cambridge, and a University Senior Lecturer in the Philosophy of Religion in the Faculty of Divinity (email rdh26@cam.ac.uk).

John Marenbon is a Fellow of Trinity College, Cambridge. His most recent book is *Boethius* (New York: Oxford University Press, 2003) (email jm258@cam.ac.uk).

George Pattison is Lady Margaret Professor of Divinity in the University of Oxford. In addition to a number of books on Kierkegaard and various topics in modern theology, he is also author of *The Routledge Guide Book to the Later Heidegger* (2000). His new book, *Thinking about God in an Age of Technology*, is due to be published by Oxford University Press in 2005 (email george.pattison@theology.oxford.ac.uk).

David Peddle is an Assistant Professor of Philosophy and Chair of Humanities at Sir Wilfred Grenfell College, Memorial University, Newfoundland. He is co-editor of *Philosophy and Freedom: The Legacy of James Doull* (University of Toronto Press, 2003), and managing editor of *Animus* and of the James Alexander Doull Archives (email dpeddle@swgc.mun.ca).

Hugh Rayment-Pickard received his PhD from London University for a thesis on 'Derrida, God and Death' and taught the Philosophy of History and History of Philosophy at Goldsmith's College for several years. His publications include *Impossible God: Derrida's Theology* (Ashgate, 2003); *Myths of Time: from St Augustine to American Beauty* (Darton, Longman and Todd, 2004), and (with Robert Burns) *Philosophies of History: from Enlightenment to Postmodernity* (Blackwell, 2000). He is a parish priest working in West London (email hugh@clementjames.co.uk).

Neil G. Robertson is Associate Professor of the Humanities and Social Sciences at the University of King's College in Halifax, Canada. His publications include (as co-editor) *Philosophy and Freedom: The Legacy of James Doull* (University of Toronto Press, 2003), various articles on Montesquieu, Rousseau and early modern political thought generally, as well as on Leo Strauss, George Grant and James Doull. He is currently co-editing a volume entitled *Descartes and the Modern* (email ngrobert@dal.ca).

Steven Shakespeare completed his doctoral thesis on Kierkegaard at Cambridge University in 1994. His publications include *Kierkegaard, Language and the Reality of God* (Ashgate, 2001), and, co-edited with George Pattison, *Kierkegaard, The Self and Society* (Basingstoke: Macmillan, 1998). He is an Anglican priest and is currently Anglican Chaplain of Liverpool Hope University College (email sorenk@blueyonder.co.uk).

List of Abbreviations

Radical Orthodoxy

AW   Catherine Pickstock, *After Writing*: *On the Liturgical Consummation of Philosophy*, Challenges in Contemporary Theology, Oxford: Basil Blackwell, 1997.

JP   Catherine Pickstock, 'Justice and Prudence: Principles of Order in the Platonic City', *The Heythrop Journal*, **42** (2001), 269–82.

OT   John Milbank, 'Only Theology Overcomes Metaphysics', *New Blackfriars*, **76** (895), July/August 1995, 'Special Issue on Jean-Luc Marion's *God without Being*', 325–43; it is reprinted in *WMS*.

PA   John Milbank, '"Postmodern Critical Augustinianism": A Short *Summa* in Forty Two Responses to Unasked Questions', *Modern Theology*, **7** (3), April 1991, 225–37.

RO   *Radical Orthodoxy, A New Theology*, ed. J. Milbank, C. Pickstock and G. Ward, London/New York: Routledge, 1999.

TA   John Milbank and Catherine Pickstock, *Truth in Aquinas*, Radical Orthodoxy, London/New York: Routledge, 2001.

TST   John Milbank, *Theology and Social Theory*, Oxford: Basil Blackwell, 1990.

WMS   John Milbank, *The Word Made Strange. Theology, Language, Culture*, Oxford: Basil Blackwell, 1997.

Aquinas

ST = Summa theologiae
V = Quaestiones disputatae de veritate

Augustine

beata vita = De beata vita
c. Jul. = Contra Julianum opus imperfectum
c. litt. Petil. = Contra litteras Petiliani
civ. = De civitate Dei
Conf. = Confessiones
dial. = De dialectica

div. quaest. 83 = De diversis quaestionibus octoginta tribus
doc. christ. = De doctrina christiana
ep. (epp.) = Epistulae
ep. Jo. = In epistulam Joannis ad Parthos tractatus
Gesta coll. Carth. = Gesta collationis Carthaginensis
Jo. ev. = In Johannis evangelium tractatus
lib. arb. = De libero arbitrio
mag. = De magistro
mus. = De musica
nat. et gr. = De natura et gratia
ord. = De ordine
Retr. = Retractationes
s. Dom. mont. = De sermone Domini in monte
Serm. = Sermones
Simpl. = Ad Simplicianum
Sol. = Soliloquia
Trin. = De Trinitate

Derrida

A   *Aporias*, trans. Thomas Dutoit, Stanford: Stanford University Press, 1993.

C   *Cinders*, trans. Ned Nukacher, Lincoln: University of Nebraska Press, 1991.

Cir   'Circumfession', in *Jacques Derrida*, trans. Geoffrey Bennington, Chicago: University of Chicago Press, 1993.

D   *Dissemination*, trans. Barbara Johnson, London: Athlone Press, 1981.

Dem   *Demeure: Fiction and Testimony*, Stanford: Stanford University Press, 2000.

EO   *The Ear of the Other: Otobiography, Transference, Translation: Texts and Discussions with Jacques Derrida*, trans. Peggy Kamuf and Avital Ronell in McDonald, Christie V. (ed.), Lincoln: University of Nebraska Press, 1988.

G   *Glas*, trans. John P. Leavey Jr and Richard Rand, Lincoln: University of Nebraska Press, 1986.

GT   *Given Time I: Counterfeit Money*, trans. Peggy Kamuf, Chicago: University of Chicago Press, 1992.

H   'How to Avoid Speaking: Denials', in Toby Foshay and Harold Coward (eds), *Derrida and Negative Theology*, Albany: State University of New York Press, 1992.

LI   *Limited Inc abc ...*, ed. Gerald Graff, Evanston: Northwestern University Press, 1988.

M   *Margins of Philosophy*, trans. Alan Bass, Chicago: University of Chicago Press, 1982.

OG *Of Grammatology*, trans. Gayatri Spivak, Baltimore: Johns Hopkins University Press, 1976.
Par *Parages*, Paris: Éditions Galilée, 1986.
Pos *Positions*, trans. Alan Bass, Chicago: University of Chicago Press, 1981.
Psy *Psyché: Inventions de l'autre*, Paris: Éditions Galilée, 1987.
SM *Specters of Marx: the State of the Debt, the Work of Mourning and the New International*, trans. Peggy Kamuf, New York: Routledge, 1994.
SP *Speech and Phenomena and other Essays on Husserl's Theory of Signs*, trans. David B. Allison, Evanston: Northwestern University Press, 1973.
TP *The Truth in Painting*, trans. G. Bennington and Ian McLeod, Chicago: University of Chicago Press, 1987.
TS 'I have a Taste for the Secret', in J. Derrida and M. Ferraris, *A Taste for the Secret*, Oxford: Polity, 2001.
WD *Writing and Difference*, trans. Alan Bass, London: Routledge & Kegan Paul, 1978.

Plato

CW Plato, *Complete Works*, ed. John M. Cooper, Indianapolis and Cambridge: Hackett, 1997.

Scotus

Ord. *Ordinatio*
PW *Philosophical Writings: A Selection*, ed. Allan B. Wolter, Indianapolis, IN and Cambridge: Hackett, 1987.

Suárez

Disp. metaph. *Disputationes Metaphysicae Salamanca*, 1597.

Introduction

At the origins of modernity in the seventeenth century, picking up from beginnings in the Renaissance, there was a turn against scholastic theology, and a move towards the examination of the historical sources of the Christian theological declarations. The normative content given in Scripture and tradition was established by means of the developing historical and philological sciences. Historical narrative has been becoming the equivalent of, or the replacement for, metaphysics in theology and philosophy for Western Christians.

During most of the last two hundred years a consequence of the equivalence of history and metaphysics, or of history's displacement of metaphysics, was that Christian theology required the linguistic, philological, historical and exegetical disciplines at least as much as the philosophical. Nothing was more important to theology's work than the capacity to tell the truth about history, and to persuade critic, adversary and adherent that their stories were true. Precisely because of its *own* unmitigated reliance on metanarrative as a replacement for metaphysics, the construction of our philosophical and theological history told by Radical Orthodoxy demands vigorous and searching scrutiny.

The founding father of Radical Orthodoxy is John Milbank. His *Theology and Social Theory: Beyond Secular Reason* published in 1990 provides the account of modernity upon which what follows depends. There, Milbank argued that theology must no longer allow herself to be placed from outside by philosophy and by secular thought generally. He endeavours to persuade theologians to get over their 'false humility' in the face of modern secular reason whose challenge, he announces, 'is at an end, for it is seen that modernity was itself made in terms of metaphysics, and of a "religion"' (*TST*, pp. 1 and 260). He claims that postmodernism has freed Christian theology from having to 'measure up to ... standards of scientific truth and normative rationality'.

Milbank describes a 'Cambridge School' out of which Radical Orthodoxy grew. It consisted in Rowan Williams, Milbank's erstwhile teacher and mentor, and now the Primate of the Anglican Communion in Canterbury, Nicholas Lash, the then Norris Hulse Professor of Philosophical Theology, John Milbank, Graham Ward and Gerard Loughlin, all of whom were influenced by the work of contemporary French philosophers. Milbank situates this 'Cambridge School', and its reassertion of Christian Orthodoxy against the false religion constituting modernity, within a postmodern theology developed out of what some have called 'the theological turn' in French phenomenology. The leaders of this phenomenology, Jean-Luc Marion, Paul Ricœur, Jean-François Courtine,

Michel Henry and others, follow Heidegger in admitting 'the end of metaphysics' but attempt to avoid 'the nihilism of *la différance*' which Milbank associates pre-eminently with Derrida (Milbank, 2002, pp. 924–5).

Milbank, Graham Ward and Milbank's pupil Catherine Pickstock consciously formed a circle with the programmatic title 'Radical Orthodoxy' and publish together as well as separately. Radical Orthodoxy was centred at Peterhouse, where Milbank and Ward were Fellows until 1999. Milbank left Cambridge to become Professor of Philosophical Theology at the University of Virginia, and is now Professor for Religion, Ethics and Politics in the Faculty of Theology at the University of Nottingham. Ward has moved on to become Professor of Contextual Theology at the University of Manchester. The youngest of them, Catherine Pickstock, remains at Cambridge.

Radical Orthodoxy, A New Theology, edited by the trio in 1999, assembled essays by twelve authors of whom they tell us: 'Seven of the contributors …are Anglican, all of a High Church persuasion, five contributors are Roman Catholics. Eight of the twelve are British, four of them are American.' Their connections, as well as of those who influenced them, to Cambridge are listed, and the book is described 'as very much a Cambridge collection' (*RO*, Acknowledgements). *Radical Orthodoxy? A Catholic Inquiry*, which appeared in 2000, is devoted to exchanges with Roman Catholics, but some of the Catholic criticism is very sharp indeed. The Routledge Radical Orthodoxy Series edited by Milbank, Pickstock and Ward has just published *Speech and Theology: Language and the logic of incarnation* by the young and prolific Canadian Evangelical anti-philosophical philosopher and theologian, James K. A. Smith, who gained his PhD at Villanova University under John Caputo. In North America, neither Anglicanism nor Anglo-Catholicism provides a large platform, and Catholic reactions are divided. However, Evangelicals like Smith are attracted by the opposition of the movement to philosophy and by its assertion of the highest claims for the autonomy of theology. Enough headway has been made in the Anglo-American world to get the movement a short piece in *Time* magazine reproducing a claim that Radical Orthodoxy is the 'biggest development in theology since Martin Luther nailed his 95 theses to the church door'.[1] While this is certainly hyperbole, Radical Orthodoxy is the most controversial and influential British theological development since *The Myth of God Incarnate* in 1977, and is far more widely discussed – especially in North America and continental Europe. Yet unlike *Essays and Reviews* (1860) or *The Myth of God Incarnate*, this movement does not invite us to reflect upon problems which confront a faith demanding intellectual integrity, but presents itself as a radical subversion of secularity and a strident defence of Christian Orthodoxy. Because it claims that theology has overcome and can absorb philosophy, it attracts those rejecting liberal theology.

Notwithstanding the development of much commentary upon Radical Orthodoxy as a movement, the theology of Radical Orthodoxy remains deeply and self-consciously enigmatic. The style is oracular and opaque, its rhetoric combative; it refuses dialogue. Its resources, though recondite, are rich and varied, its cultural narrative sweeping. Its authors draw upon a wide reservoir of Platonic philosophy, patristic and medieval theology, and large parts of recent continental philosophy and theology, from contemporary phenomenology or sociology to liturgy. Many readers have been bewildered by the sheer range and intensity of the project of Radical Orthodoxy. Because most of the texts and authors for which it offers shockingly original interpretations are virtually unknown or much neglected in the Anglo-American philosophical and theological world, students are unable to offer alternative or critical readings of their own. The response has been dictated by scholars who have either been entranced or repelled; reviews have been either adulatory or dismissive. Much of the discussion has been determined by confessional questions, such as the legitimacy of the appeal to tradition, or the 'Catholicity' of the movement.

Essential to Radical Orthodoxy is a rejection both of philosophy as autonomous or foundational with respect to theology and of fideistic religion. As a result it altogether depends on its self-consciously subversive reinterpretation of the theological and philosophical tradition. This collection of essays approaches the movement resolutely from the perspective of the 'history of thought' and its pertinence for modern systematic theology and the philosophy of religion. Our volume provides interpretations of aspects of the thought of major philosophers or theologians treated by Radical Orthodoxy. Our aim is both to criticize the interpretations essential to the Radical Orthodoxy project and to offer alternative approaches to reading these authors. Building on the opening of the resources for philosophy and theology made by Radical Orthodoxy, the authors raise questions about the treatment of just these sources and provide more fruitful ways of engaging them.

A retrieval of Platonism is essential to the programme of Radical Orthodoxy and we begin with a consideration of Pickstock's Plato. Eli Diamond shows that her interpretation of the Platonic philosophy is intended to serve its anti-modern programme: the subordination of philosophy and reason to theology, myth and ritual, and the deconstruction of the modern subject. Pickstock's Platonism turns out to be a contradictory amalgam of the Hellenic and Neoplatonic, doing justice to neither. Further, consistent with the reduction of philosophy characteristic of the school, her liturgical mediation of divine and human destroys the philosophical mediation that Plato sees lying between the Good and the cave of human temporality. Anticipating the concluding chapter of this volume, Diamond shows that Pickstock's reading needs to be balanced by Derrida's. Derrida helps to draw out the *result* of Plato's thought, while Pickstock's interpretation of Plato, corrected for its ideological excesses, serves to bring out the *intentions* of the originator of metaphysics.

In Chapter 2, Wayne Hankey continues the examination of the philosophical school to which Radical Orthodoxy has self-consciously attached itself: Platonism as understood through its theurgic Neoplatonic development. He locates this attachment within the movements in contemporary French philosophy of which it is a subsidiary. He finds that Radical Orthodoxy misrepresents both the relation of Neoplatonism to the foundations of the

Western turn to the subject and also the way that philosophy, theology and religion preserve their difference, integrity and connection in Neoplatonism. Most importantly, the neo-Neoplatonism of this theological party shares the shape of other twentieth-century Heideggerian retrievals: it immediately joins the Transcendent and the material or sensuous, eliminating the hierarchy of intellectual forms which was essential to the historically actual systems.

No one is more essential to the Radical Orthodox project than Augustine. Todd Breyfogle engages its handling of this determinative thinker for Western subjectivity and finds that, by interpreting him within its polemic against modernity, it renders Augustine's thought almost unrecognizable or abandons it altogether. Breyfogle locates part of the problem in the denial of the independent role Augustine assigns to philosophy. Also, in accord with other contributors to this volume, he finds that, in its assault on modernity, Radical Orthodoxy goes both too far and not far enough, and so remains irrevocably implicated in the modernity it tries to overthrow. In particular it participates in the modern reduction of transcendence.

Chapter 4 by John Marenbon is the first of two examining Radical Orthodoxy's treatment of crucial medieval thinkers. He argues that *Truth in Aquinas* ignores the ordinary canons of scholarly enquiry, misrepresenting Aquinas's doctrine of being, his theory of knowledge, and his way of relating reason and revelation. He shows that *TA* does this by its use of Heidegger's history of metaphysics in terms of onto-theology, comparing *TA* unfavourably with how French scholars have dealt with the same questions. Richard Cross, in the second chapter examining the treatment of medieval philosophical theology, also looks at assertions by Radical Orthodoxy which arise out of its use of Heidegger's metanarrative of Western metaphysics in terms of onto-theology. It sees onto-theology as a central component of modernity, at the root of its destructive nature, and makes Duns Scotus and Suárez responsible for the shift in Western philosophical theology which transforms it into metaphysics. Cross accepts that there are metaphysical changes in the period between Aquinas and Christian Wolff, but he shows that Scotus does not play the role cast for him. Cross concludes that the processes of history are infinitely more complex than the sweeping metanarrative told by Heidegger and Radical Orthodoxy allows them to be.

Our consideration of how thinkers from early modernity – primarily Hobbes and Descartes – fare at the hands of Radical Orthodoxy appropriately follows on from Scotus and Suárez because, for Milbank and company, they determine modern metaphysics. Matching its anti-modern polemic asserted from the pre- and postmodern perspectives where they stand with Heidegger, Leo Strauss, Karl Löwith, Étienne Gilson and others, Neil Robertson stresses the difference between the late medieval/Renaissance and the modern, and undertakes to look out from inside, arguing for the integrity of early modernity on its own terms. He maintains that modernity has its own principle (self-consciousness), and, while concurring with Milbank that it is 'theological' in its origins, he argues that it is a form of Christian culture reflecting Augustinian and Chalcedonian orthodoxy. In Chapter 7, Douglas Hedley again takes up the claim of Radical Orthodoxy to belong within the tradition of Christian Platonism, examining it with respect to John Milbank's appropriation of the Cambridge Platonists. He finds that, because of the ways reason and religion are united for the Cambridge Platonists, their position is contrary to that of Milbank. Radical Orthodoxy seems better understood as an heir of the uncompromising critique of liberalism, 'rationality' and the 'secular', of the Catholic counter-revolutionary Platonism of De Maistre and others, as well as of the Protestant neo-orthodoxy of Karl Barth.

For David Peddle, examining *TST*, John Milbank finds anticipations of his own deconstruction of modernity in Hegel, but nevertheless argues that Hegelianism remains under the dominion of scientific politics and political economy, subscribing in its fundamental thought to a violent pagan theology. Finding much of value in Milbank's treatment, Peddle shows, none the less, that his assimilation of Hegel to Hobbes is untenable. Milbank misinterprets Hegel's concept of civil society as well as his conceptions of creation and providence.

Steven Shakespeare demonstrates that for John Milbank, Kierkegaard is the inaugurator and instigator of a new way of doing philosophical theology, whose vocabulary sets the agenda for contemporary poststructuralism. He seeks out and evaluates the influence the Dane has had in the key works of Radical Orthodoxy. Shakespeare finds that Kierkegaard does not offer a way of retrieving the lost age of patristic truth, although he does leave more room for genuine dialogue with contemporary culture than does the speculative metanarrative of Radical Orthodoxy.

George Pattison's penultimate chapter examines the resurgence of transubstantiation as a topic of fundamental philosophical importance. He shows that Pickstock's enthusiasm for it sits badly with her critique of modernity as committed to a wholesale project of spatialization. Professor Pattison shows that the doctrine of transubstantiation, seen as a historical and cultural event, is indissociable from a hierarchical and visualized spatialization of doctrine and ecclesiastical life. After exposing problems with taxonomic simplifications, he goes on to look at Lawrence Hemming's evacuation of the meaning of the doctrine, which subjectivizes it in order to keep it alive. Dr Pattison finds fundamental misunderstanding of Heidegger in the use Hemming makes of his thought. Proposing a way forward, Pattison locates areas of agreement with and difference from the approaches of Radical Orthodoxy.

The last chapter in our attempt to deconstruct the histories by which Radical Orthodoxy erects its narrative concerns a figure upon whose work it is entirely dependent but who is treated as a nihilist heretic guilty of 'necrophilia'. Dr Rayment-Pickard shows that its treatment of Derrida's writing does not intend to enter scholarly debate but is written from the perspective of a Hegelian end of philosophy aiming to 'reassert theology as a master discourse'. He examines the Radical Orthodox accusation of Derrida's nihilism and argues, perhaps fittingly at the end of this collection of essays, that deconstruction is not simply negative. Deconstruction undermines all simple alternatives and reveals complexity. It affirms life in all its flux, complexity and ambiguity. It appears ultimately that Derrida has something useful to contribute to the Christian understanding of the Eucharist.

The present volume has enjoyed the rare accolade of being reviewed a whole year before publication! John Bowlin in the summer of 2004, in his essay 'Parts, Whole and Opposites: John Milbank as Geisteshistoriker' in the *Journal of Religious Ethics* (vol. 32, no. 2, pp. 257–69) notes that the present volume attempts to address a genuine scholarly gap – John Milbank's use of historical materials and their place in 'his normative inquiries' (p. 258). However, Bowlin indicates that our emphasis is upon Milbank's use of historical materials in enquiries that interest philosophical theologians, metaphysicians and philosophers of language:

> It pays little attention to his use of historical texts and figures in his treatment of those issues that matter most to moral theologians and religious ethicists. In addition, the essays in the Hedley and Hankey collection largely ignore the critical and normative conclusions that follow from Milbank's historical inquiries. (p. 258)

Pace Bowlin, however, it is absolutely essential to the Radical Orthodox metanarrative that its polemic against modernity, with its very specific *Verfallsgeschichte*, and the project (including the success with which it treats 'those issues that matter most to moral theologians and religious ethicists', and so on) stands or falls with the accuracy of the historiography, which is inseparable from the interest and cogency of the arguments. For this reason the authors of the essays in *Deconstructing Radical Orthodoxy* share the conviction that a polemical misreading of the texts the Radically Orthodox handle has unavoidable and grave consequences for the cogency of their basic theses.

The present volume of essays aims constructively to critique Radical Orthodoxy by providing alternative and better established readings which reveal, notwithstanding the polemical force and imaginative ingenuity of the Radical Orthodox historiography, a much more complex and fertile relationship between philosophy and theology than John Milbank and his school dare countenance. We are not ourselves committed to a single judgement about modernity (or, indeed, about any of the other matters we treat). We are convinced, however, that philosophy and theology, and their histories and relations, are too important to be delivered so radically to polemic and rhetoric.

Wayne J. Hankey
Douglas Hedley

The Feast of St Augustine, 2004

Note

1. *The Chronicle of Higher Education*, quoted in 'Radical Orthodoxy, God as a Postmodern', *Time*, 17 December 2002, p. 61.

CHAPTER 1

Catherine Pickstock, Plato and the Unity of Divinity and Humanity: Liturgical or Philosophical?[1]

Eli Diamond

In *After Writing*, Catherine Pickstock offers a theological corrective to the excesses and evils of secular modernity. As part of the Radical Orthodoxy project, she engages in a rethinking of philosophical, cultural and religious traditions (*RO*, p. 2) in order to show the genealogy of our rise to and descent from what she calls the liturgical, or doxological, city. In this city, the diverse and dynamic character of material and temporal existence is invested with inherent worth through its manifestation of a supra-rational divine transcendence. The world is the site of the actual unification of the divine with nature and humanity. Yet because God is indeterminate and wholly beyond thought, the presence of the divine cannot be intellectually apprehended, but only ritually experienced. The first step towards a recovery of this insight is tracing the origins of liturgical theory and practice in pre-Christian times, and uncovering the process that has hidden this truth from our contemporary world.

Pickstock's reading of Plato plays a crucial role in this critical rethinking of the past. According to Pickstock, Plato's thought, formulated as a theological response to the scientific and sophistic nihilism of his day, offers an example of pre-Christian liturgical theory and practice, anticipating, if only incompletely (*AW*, p. 169), the liturgical unity of divinity and humanity/nature through his quest to show how the Good is intrinsically present in all reality as its origin and end. Her interpretation of the Platonic philosophy is intended to serve her anti-modern philosophical programme: the subordination of philosophy and reason to theology, myth and ritual, and the deconstruction of the modern subject. This essay aims to distinguish between what is genuinely illuminating in Pickstock's reading of the Platonic philosophy and what is merely a reflection of her own ambiguously post-modern and pre-modern position.

Her account is helpful in discerning the non-dualistic *intention* of Platonic thought, and she is right to argue that Plato wants sensible reality to have existence and truth as a manifestation, however imperfect, of the Good itself. She rightly argues that the spirit of Platonic philosophy should not be interpreted as an absolute rejection of temporal reality through a flight to abstract thought objects. Equally helpful is her comparison of the

Enlightenment and its post-modern critique with the intellectual revolution in the fifth century BC, which Plato simultaneously developed and criticized.

Yet Pickstock distorts the original meaning of Platonism in several ways in order to support her own essentially post-modern attack on subjectivity and autonomous philosophy and politics. First, her Platonism is a contradictory amalgam of Hellenic and Neoplatonic Platonism which does justice to neither. Second, Pickstock's liturgical mediation of divine and human destroys the philosophical mediation that Plato sees lying between the Good and the cave of human temporality. Placing the mediation in practical experience as opposed to thought abolishes the difference between pre-philosophical Athens and the Platonic state, thus neglecting the manner in which Plato preserves both the subjective power of sophistry and the Greek enlightenment's search for objective knowledge in his rationally mediated knowledge of the Good. By employing Findlay's interpretation of the movement from the middle to late dialogues (Findlay, 1974, p. xii), I will attempt to show how Plato is not satisfied with anything but a *logical* resolution of how God and the world are inherently related. We shall see by the end of this essay that while Pickstock's interpretation of Plato can, upon correction of its ideological excesses, help us to understand his philosophical *intentions*, Jacques Derrida's reading of Plato, by focusing on the *aporiae* of Platonism, draws out the *result* of Plato's thought. A perspective that can articulate what is positive in each of these readings can help us to appreciate the greatness and continued relevance of Plato's philosophy as a response to sophistry, and to understand why philosophy did not end with Platonic solutions.

Pickstock's Liturgical Platonism

Implicit in Pickstock's appropriation of Plato is an analogy between Hellenic Platonism and Radical Orthodoxy, in that both seek to recover our lost connection to the divine as a response to the secular excesses of scientific enlightenment and sophistic nihilism. Indeed, Pickstock's understanding of the movement from enlightened modernity to post-modern nihilism resembles Plato's own understanding of the Greek enlightenment and its necessary decline into sophistic relativism (see *Laws*, 888e–890d). She understands Plato's diagnosis of how a materialistic, pragmatic, relativist spirit caused a decline from the height of pre-philosophical Athens, tethered to the Good through immediate, unquestioning belief in and obedience to traditional myth, religion and political authority. Yet she wrongly portrays Plato's manner of reconnecting secularized society to the Good. Rather than seeking to recover the purely practical, mythical, pre-reflective and religious mediation between humanity and divinity, Plato seeks a relation that is philosophically grounded through knowledge.

Because she sees no positive development in the modern demand that everything other than the subject be comprehended by self-conscious reason, there is nothing inherently modern retained in Pickstock's return to the medieval liturgical city. Yet for Plato, the drive for a rational comprehension of reality is wholly retained within his critical relation to the abstract rationalism of earlier philosophers, and the scientific/mathematical approach is seen as a necessary precursor to true knowledge of non-mathematical entities. In both *Theaetetus* and *Phaedo*, the mathematical training of the interlocutors (Theaetetus, Cebes and Simmias) makes the respondents, who are part of the scientific enlightenment that demands mathematical proofs of everything, receptive to Plato's reflections on the Ideas and the Good. The movement up the line from the realm of sense-experience and opinion to mathematical objects is the move from the merely subjective into a world of objective principles. Mathematical objects, known through discursive thought (*dianoia*), are the first stage of objective knowing beyond the cave of sense-perception and opinion, since mathematical truths are not caught in a merely individual grasp of the unstable sensible world (*Republic*, 510d5–511a1). The sophist, designating himself the measure of truth beyond all authority or tradition, intensifies this demand that the individual know his relation to and difference from the Good. Through Pickstock's return to a pre-reflective, liturgical relation to the Good and to an unquestioning submission to tradition, enlightenment and the sophistic revolution take on a merely negative significance, having no *essential* import for a proper relation to the divine – in biblical terms, the Fall in Genesis is pure evil with no divine purpose.

As opposed to Pickstock's view, Plato sees that in Athenian life the immediate, intuitive sense of the primacy of the divine and the Good through adherence to custom and tradition has been thoroughly destabilized by the sophistic discovery that all reality is ultimately measured by our own subjective thinking. He seeks to restore our original identity with the Good by showing, through a rational grasp of reality, that the spirit of independent inquiry need not destroy society. Pickstock's view, in contrast with Plato's, resembles the perspective of the *Republic*'s Cephalus, who represents the ancient pre-philosophical relation to the Good of the *polis*. Cephalus does not let the fact that his definition of justice is destabilized by Socrates rupture his own intuitive sense of belonging to the ancient order. He merely walks away to attend the sacrifices, leaving the sceptical question for his son Polemarchus and the subsequent generation, since they are already possessed by the new subjective spirit. If Pickstock's liturgical interpretation of Plato were accurate, the *Republic* could end in Book I with Cephalus' rejection of the subjective demand for rational comprehension in favour of the performance of supra-rational liturgical rites. Pickstock's liturgical philosophy eliminates the difference between our original intuitive identity with the Good and a restored, rationally mediated identity.

Her liturgical reading of Plato diverges most clearly from Platonic thought in her conception of the mediation, or lack of it, between the Good and the cave. Pickstock suggests that divine and temporal human elements are 'bound together by the doxological or the liturgical – this is the secret middle term ...'

(*JP*, p. 280). We are raised to the divine through performance of 'repeated ritual patterns' (ibid.) that order the realm of sensible multiplicity so that through our harmony with the natural we can receive the divine mystery. Pickstock's Platonism relies upon a shortened version of the Platonic Line, in which one moves directly from the indeterminacy of knowledge in sense-perception and opinion, to the self-identical Good existing beyond the division of subject and object, and hence beyond any human knowing. The essential eidetic aspect of Platonism disappears from view, as Pickstock undermines the realm of mathematical objects and Ideas that mediate between the merely subjective character of material, temporal existence and the divine principle. While, on Plato's account, the intelligible realm provides a stable finitude for human thinking, Pickstock denigrates our relation to the Ideas to the level of a 'vision of an ineffable and ungraspable *eidos*' (*JP*, p. 276), and '*genuine* intellectual clarity is obtainable only when that which is to be "known" is allowed to remain open and mysterious' (*AW*, p. 20).

For Pickstock, creation is unknowable because God is unknowable. The nature of this infinite, divine realm permeates all of creation, and results in the 'indeterminacy of all our knowledge and experience of selfhood' (*AW*, p. xii). Neither the Christian nor the Platonic God is 'a simple objective presence *opposed* to supplementation' (*AW*, p. 21). Instead, God is the source of all language, and Plato offers 'an incipient account here of supplementation as the origin and possibility of language itself' (*AW*, p. 25). The divine is located in 'an ambiguous and shifting place beyond our own' (*AW*, p. 177). God exists prior to and beyond any rational consciousness of this ultimate reality, and is therefore completely other than thinking. Because everything originates from this unknowable Good, and can only be known through its divine origin, everything in the world remains mysteriously enigmatic and opaque to our rational understanding (*AW*, p. 12). In fact, responding to the materialist cosmology, Plato makes clear that thinking *nous* is at the origin of everything (*Laws*, 888e–890d). In this way, thought is not a later imposition upon the Good and the world, but their true nature.

Pickstock draws the correct conclusions from this revised Platonic ontology: with the supra-rational divine principle cut off from rational investigation, the apparent separation of finite and divine reality cannot be overcome in thought. Since our own existence is inextricably temporal and radically finite, our only access to this supra-rational principle is by going beyond human thinking through religious rituals that bring out the implicit divinity in our world. The identity of the two worlds is thus thoroughly immediate. We experience the Good only through its presence in sensible objects, not through an eidetic knowledge of a derivative sensible reality. Pickstock problematically associates this interpretation with Iamblichean–Proclean Neoplatonism.

While Neoplatonic influence is not explicitly mentioned in *After Writing*, Pickstock has since explicitly recognized the affinities between her liturgical Christianity and theurgic Neoplatonism in the more recent article 'Justice and Prudence: Principles of Order in the Platonic City'. In this essay Pickstock identifies two understandings of the soul's relation to what is above and below it, which she rightly characterizes as Plotinian and Iamblichean–Proclean (*JP*, p. 270). The first emphasizes the active side of the soul which can ascend towards intelligible realities, since the soul has, through its perpetual union with its highest rational faculties (*nous*), immediate access to the divine. The Iamblichean–Proclean understanding emphasizes the passive side of the soul's ascent, since the soul has no independent rational capacity to ascend due to the completeness of its immersion in the body and separation from intelligible realities. Independent human reason, completely embodied and historical, belongs wholly to the dividedness of the many (although, unlike lower realities in nature, it has the potential to rise above itself). So long as this reason remains autonomous, the undivided unity of the First Principle remains forever inaccessible. In his *De Mysteriis*, Iamblichus explains the necessity of theurgic rituals for the purposes of bringing the human into a proper relation to matter. Only in this way can the individual's inextricable connection to materiality be transformed from insurmountable obstacle into the only means of salvation. As a result, the whole individual, in both his rational and natural aspects, remains united throughout the soul's movement, and his materiality is not left behind as in the Plotinian ascent. For Pickstock, Iamblichus, as opposed to Plotinus, moves in a 'non-dualistic direction' (*JP*, p. 269). Pickstock writes that this dominant 'Plotinian' understanding of Plato must be supplemented by a 'Proclean doxological ("theurgic") and descending interpretation' (*JP*, p. 270).

There are several problematic features in Pickstock's appropriation of Neoplatonism. First of all, like many post-modern interpreters of Neoplatonism, she underplays the essential role of the noetic grasp of reality in Neoplatonic thought (see Hankey, Chapter 2 in this volume, and Hankey, 1998c, pp. 56–7). In its assertion that all knowledge is indeterminate as a defence of the Good's radical transcendence, Pickstock's 'Neoplatonism' is closer to Megarian thought (see Reale, 1987, pp. 281–5; Reale, 1985, pp. 45–54) than to the thought of Plotinus or Proclus. Second, due to her post-modern quest to escape modern subjectivity, Pickstock's Platonism mixes Hellenic and Neoplatonic Platonism in a fundamentally contradictory way. In order to emphasize the radically intersubjective character of her ideal community, she rightly points out that the Platonic individual is necessarily a political being, in no way complete apart from its civic engagements in the *polis* (*JP*, p. 271). Yet out of her liturgical interests, she defends a Neoplatonic version of Platonism which, as its starting point, assumes a free individual, complete in itself, and comparatively apolitical[2] in its flight from division to unity. Returning to Neoplatonism to overcome subjectivity is rendered incoherent by the fact that it is in Neoplatonic thought that one finds the origins of the modern subject (see Hankey, 1998c and Doull, 2003). The Neoplatonic discovery of the three spiritual hypostases does not begin with a self radically open to the divine element of the external world, but as a sceptical self wholly free and withdrawn from the otherness of appearances (see Plotinus, *Ennead* 5.1.10. 1–11). In contrast to Neoplatonism, Plato did not assume this free individual as a starting point: his entire political philosophy attempted to answer the question of the extent to which the individual had *any* existence apart from the whole.

In placing religion above philosophy, Pickstock unites all the themes of liturgy, myth and doxological language: '"Religion" here comprises the necessity of public ritual practice for the attainment of wisdom, and, in addition, the mediations of myth and continuous individual and collective praise of the divine' (*JP*, p. 270). In her attack on autonomous philosophy, Pickstock portrays Plato as having so thoroughly embedded *theoria* in liturgical *praxis*, philosophy in myth, and thought in doxological language, that they cannot be genuinely differentiated (*JP*, pp. 277 and 280). We must now examine how Pickstock's ascription of these three views to Plato constitutes a deeply flawed interpretation of Platonic thought.

Liturgy

The liturgical mediation appeals to Pickstock for several reasons. First, the liturgical union is felt rather than thought (*AW*, p. 4); second, as opposed to discursive reason, the defamiliarizing 'stutter' of liturgy prevents any pretension of having a total grasp of divine mystery, because the rituals themselves remain mysterious (*AW*, p. 178); third, liturgy is material and incarnate, with an embodied subject participating in the divine through material objects, thus exemplifying a non-dualistic embrace of the sensible, the temporal and the linguistic; fourth, liturgy undermines the sense of a closed, autonomous subject, due to its social and corporate nature. Drawing from the Greek concept of *leitourgia*, as evaluated by Levinas (see Levinas, 1996, p. 50), liturgy implies a public service, often burdensome, in which the self is subordinated to and only completed intersubjectively and dialogically with God and neighbours (*AW*, p. 170). Pickstock sees all these aspects exhibited in the liturgical city of Plato's *Laws* (*JP*, pp. 279–80). Unified through common song and dance rituals, the city outlined in the *Laws* acts and thinks as one soul, a soul which in turn imitates the structure of the world soul described in *Timaeus*. The division between public and private interests is overcome, since all individual consciousness dissolves into one liturgically united intersubjectivity. As we will see in what follows, Pickstock here demonstrates a limited understanding of Plato's *Laws* which emphasizes the theocratic elements of the dialogue at the expense of its undeniable quest to establish the self-conscious independence of human practical activity (see Diamond, 2002).

Myth

For Pickstock, Plato's philosophy does not criticize myth from a superior perspective, but rather occurs within the horizon of myth, which gives philosophy its content (just as Christian thinking occurs within the pre-given horizon of the Bible and liturgy). Pickstock asserts that it is myth, not philosophy, which first undermines the roots of nihilistic, pragmatic society in Athens (*AW*, p. 48). As Hankey remarks, Pickstock understands 'the Socratic dependence upon myth as modeling a Christian restoration of language as liturgical. Indeed, the myth about the origins of writing told by Socrates is treated as wisdom' (Hankey, 1998c, p. 19).

Pickstock rightly points out that the Platonic Socrates, as opposed to the sophists and the materialists of his age, does not reject mythical sources of wisdom whose origin and truth are not fully present. Oracles and mythic accounts are not merely falsifiable. While Plato certainly differentiates himself from the rationality of the Greek enlightenment which accepts nothing without empirical proof, he accepts myth only on the basis of its implicit rationality. He submits these sources to philosophical scrutiny, and only when he can understand their content philosophically does he accept them completely (see *Laws*, 644b9–645c6 and Gerald Naddaf's introduction to Brisson, 1998, pp. x–xi, xxi–xxxiii). The myths in the dialogues serve two central purposes. First, they illustrate the philosophical content through literary images. This verifies for the reader that he has understood the philosophical intention of the dialogue, since the content must be reconciled with the mythical representation. Second, in expressing Plato's philosophical intention, the myths allow the reader to verify the extent to which the dialogue has succeeded in fulfilling its philosophical intention logically. The myths do not, *contra* Pickstock, have a scriptural authority, but they are literary tools used to guide the reader's understanding of the dialogues.

Doxological Language

Pickstock characterizes the liturgical city as '*avowedly* semiotic' (*AW*, p. 169). In liturgy, one realizes that language is constitutive of our reality and is not to be escaped or superseded, in contrast to a theory of language which 'presupposes a supra-linguistic philosophical logos, independent of time and place' (*AW*, p. 4). For Pickstock, words as vocalized sounds only have meaning in a liturgical context, and fulfil the same role as music, vestment, bread and smoke (*AW*, p. 169). They are not merely signs that point beyond themselves, but have value in and of themselves; Pickstock understands Socrates' properly spoken words to be liturgical gifts and sacrifices to the divine (*AW*, p. 40). Words do not point beyond themselves to a clearer reality, but point towards a reality as mysterious as unexplained words (*AW*, p. 195). Thus the divine is present in words in such a way that one would never leave them behind, even if it were possible. Language and divinity are immediately related.

This is clearly opposed to the Platonic theory of language, in which being and language are mediated through a definition which expresses the thought of the thing. One of the primary goals of Platonic philosophy is to show that discourse is meaningful. One must show how the realm of language, in all its apparent contradiction, points beyond itself to the definition by which it is apprehended, and then to a thing which exists in itself. In the *Laws*, Plato makes this theory of language explicit. The Athenian points out that there 'are three points concerning each thing ... first, the being (*ousia*), second, the *logos* of the being, and third, its *name*' (*Laws*, 895d1–5; see also 669a7–b2, and *Sophist*, 218b6–c5). The thought of a thing mediates between its existence and its linguistic expression. The satiric treatment of inquiry through etymology in *Cratylus* is meant to demonstrate that the relation of language and reality is not immediate: words in themselves do not contain the truths they express. If word and thing were immediately related, there would be no criterion for judging which word actually carries truth (*Cratylus*, 438d2–8). As Socrates later states, 'it is far better to investigate [beings] and learn about them through themselves than to do so through their names' (*Cratylus*, 439b6–8 [*CW*, p. 154]).

Pickstock claims that Plato 'assumes the doxological character of all language ... language exists primarily, and in the end only has meaning as, the praise of the divine' (*AW*, p. xiii; see also *AW*, p. 177). This is certainly true in a qualified sense. Plato attempts to show, against the sophists, that the meaning of words does not have its origin in our own creative activity as human subjects. Words have significance in reference to divinely constituted objects, thus placing the divine on a qualitatively higher plane than the human. Through placing the origin of all meaning in himself as measuring subject, the sophist confuses himself with God. In contrast, the philosopher recognizes that the truth of the divine can, as Pickstock states, 'only be participated through a *sustaining* of its distance and otherness' (*AW*, p. 14).

If praise and abasement before the divine is recognizing that the true natures of things are not originally produced in the human subject, but were produced by the Divine Maker who establishes an order to be discovered by the philosopher, then Plato's theory of language can be thought to be doxological. In the *Sophist*, a hierarchy of three 'makers' emerges: God as maker in being, the philosopher as maker of accounts through a true apprehension of being, and the sophist as maker of accounts without apprehension, remaining at the level of speech without connection to what is. The sophist, through over-esteeming his own creative capacities and not recognizing, as the philosopher does, the inherently derivative character of human making in relation to divine making, forsakes the human's middle position between nature and divinity in the cosmos (*Sophist*, 264d10ff.). Yet Pickstock associates this praise and 'reverence' with leaving things mysterious. Plato would respond to Pickstock that rather than having doxology ground all meaning, meaning must ultimately ground all praise of the divine. Before praising God, we must have some understanding of the divine nature that is being praised. Praise of the divine conceived in the Homeric terms of gods who cause both good and evil, for example, is destructive of a well-ordered society. The piety of doxological language is dependent upon a prior philosophical grasp of the true nature of God (see *Laws*, X).

Plato's Intention: Non-Dualistic Teleology as a Response to Sophistry

Pickstock understands Plato's philosophy as an attempt to show how the universal and particular, spiritual and material, divine and human, theoretical and practical, critical and traditional are inseparably and internally connected. The task of philosophy is to show how the former is *in* the latter as implicit. She seeks to show, against an 'over-emphasis upon a dualism in Plato between matter and spirit, body and mind' (*JP*, p. 269), that for Plato, everything is contained within the divine. Pickstock shows how Plato is everywhere seeking to show how the world of becoming exists *in* the world of being. The opposite view, holding to the separation, belongs to a pre-Socratic, binary logic which sees the world either as an undistinguished mixture or as wholly separate contraries.[3]

One can perhaps most clearly discern Pickstock's point concerning Plato's non-dualistic intention through his representation of Socrates' enthusiasm and subsequent disappointment with the philosophy of Anaxagoras. In the *Phaedo*, Socrates states that he was excited by Anaxagoras' claim that mind orders and causes everything in the world, assuming that this meant that mind

> would direct everything and arrange each thing in the way that was best ... on these premises then it befitted a man to investigate only, about this and other things, what is best. The same man must inevitably know what is worse, for that is part of the same knowledge. (*Phaedo*, 97c4–d5 [*CW*, p. 84])

Plato sees that for a true, rational and objective understanding of generation, one must understand how the cause is *in* the caused, and how the latter is teleologically ordered to the former as its origin and end. Anaxagoras failed to produce an account that would satisfy this demand due to his inability to show how the self-identical, unmixed mind was related to the atoms which each contain all difference, and so appealed to mechanical and physical explanations of becoming. He was unable 'to distinguish the real cause from that without which the cause would not be able to act as a cause' (*Phaedo*, 99b2–4 [*CW*, p. 85]).

Against this abstract and external unity of identity and difference, we have in the *Phaedo* a clear statement of what Plato is attempting to accomplish philosophically: 'to investigate completely the causes of generation and destruction' (*Phaedo*, 95e9). One must seek an explanation of each thing by appealing only to teleological *necessity*, as opposed to 'arguments of which the proof is based on probability' (*Phaedo*, 92d2–5). The goal of this investigation is the discovery of 'what was the best way for it to be, or to be acted upon, or to act' (*Phaedo*, 97c8–d1 [*CW*, p. 84]). In other words, how is the Good actually present in every aspect of reality as the origin from which it came and the end to which its activity is ordered?

In Plato's search for an intrinsic relation between the Good and the world of which it is the cause, or the Good and what is other than the Good (its being and not-being), sophistic subjectivity is of the utmost importance. In order to bring out this crucial difference between Plato and Pickstock's un-Platonic acceptance of the post-modern account of the indeterminacy of all knowledge and selfhood, let us examine Plato's complex relation to sophistry. Plato recognizes that sophistry is, in a certain sense, more philosophically advanced than any previous position. Pre-Socratic thinkers had all been bound to a logic in which contraries either never combine, or always combine. In locating the measure of all things in the thinking subject, the sophist has discovered an activity that has a power over contraries, an underlying subject of the various appearances of a thing. By opposing finite determinations to one another, the sophist can show the mutual annulling of each in its independence. The sophistic subject becomes the unity into which all contrariety is resolved, the measuring limit who gives determinacy to the indeterminate being in the cave.

Plato sides with the sophist in recognizing the power of subjectivity and the demand that reason understand and recognize the truth of anything it accepts. Yet he denies, against the sophist, that contradictory appearances are exhaustive of the truth of things. Beyond the individual subject, Plato seeks an objective measure of the unity of these appearances in a rational realm of stable essence which does not violate the Law of Non-Contradiction. To move beyond the sophistic position, it must be shown how the measure is not merely externally related to the measured, as it is in the subjective measure of the sophist. The sophist, wholly satisfied with the indeterminate nature of the world and the absence of some external, objective measure, does not seek this objective measure, but places the individual subject as the measure of the being and not-being of everything (*Theaetetus*, 152a2–4).

The first Platonic response to this contradiction of sophistry lies in the second-best method (*Phaedo*, 99c8–102a1, House, 1981, pp. 57–61), in which one lays down the Good (or *Nous*), the unique stable Ideas and the sensible many as fixed beginning points and then follows out the consequences of this ontology. The stable Idea is wholly other than – yet as their cause is comprehensive of – its contradictory sensible appearances. Unlike the contradictory nature of sensible appearances, Plato sees this Idea as invulnerable to the sophistic activity of drawing out contradiction, because it is absolutely self-identical and unmixed, and thus excludes the distinction necessary for sophistic manipulation of contraries (*Parmenides*, 128e6–130a2). The relationship between sensible instance and its Idea as cause is one of *participation*. In participation, the caused both *is* and *is not* its cause.

Pickstock sees two worlds of divinity and humanity as satisfactorily connected by the image of participation (*RO*, p. 3; *AW*, p. 14). Yet in *Parmenides*, Plato, through the character of Parmenides, critically examines Socrates' connection of idea and sensible instance through the image of participation, in which the sensible instance both *is* and *is not* its Idea. Parmenides brings out against Socrates that the contradictory nature of the sensible instances exists at the level of the Idea itself: the Idea can either be seen as wholly self-identical or completely self-divided and different. One can look at the relationship either from the perspective of the many, or the perspective of the one Idea. Participation, by merely concealing this ambiguity, leaves the Ideas still vulnerable to a sophistic manipulation. The two relations must be brought into the object itself. It is with this goal in mind that Plato undertakes a revision of his principles in the late dialogues. Plato moves beyond considering various issues in relation to the stable Ideas, and considers the primordial principles out of which both Ideas and instances are composed: the One and the Dyad.[4]

Plato's Late Dialogues

Pickstock's liturgical account of Platonic thought depends primarily on certain aspects of Plato's middle dialogues (*Republic*, *Phaedrus*, *Symposium*). Her reading, aimed at showing how Plato's thought is receptive to temporality and natural difference, ironically depends upon certain features of the middle dialogues (the Good beyond the division of being and truth, participation as the link between the sensible and the divine), which are most restrictive of difference. Yet it is based on these very features of Platonism that Pickstock deduces a 'supra-philosophical place of religion in his thought' (*JP*, p. 270). While her interpretation can also be refuted through a close reading of the middle dialogues, I shall here briefly focus my response upon certain prevalent ideas in the late dialogues. In this late period, Plato undertakes a revision of the First Principles of his philosophy, realizing that his earlier formulation failed to escape the power of the sophistic argument.

In the middle dialogue ontology, the Good and its determinations, the Ideas, are wholly self-identical and beyond division, and hence they are also beyond the power of the sophistic dialectic and its manipulation of every contradiction. Yet having a principle that is beyond all division means that the particulars it comprehends must be stripped of their division in order to be truly comprehended by the self-identical unifying form. It is because the Good and each Idea are absolutely beyond distinction that citizens are stripped of their natural individuality in the three waves, so that they can be contained within the common life of the state. Differences of private property, gender and family, as features that distinguish the individual from the common identity of the whole, must be wholly eliminated by the logic of the *Republic*. These features through which the individual is different from the common identity of all citizens can be cautiously admitted into the *polis* only within the framework of the late dialogues, in which Plato demonstrates how what is different than self-same being is not wholly non-existent, but merely *other* than what is (*Sophist*, 256d11–e2; *Statesman*, 284a8–b2).

This revised ontology emerges in the *Sophist*. Instead of seeing the intelligible world as a realm of identity in contrast with the sensible world as a realm of difference, every object, whether intelligible or sensible, is constituted as a mixture of the First Principles of identity and difference (principles which Plato, following the Pythagoreans, will call Limit and Unlimited, which

Aristotle will refer to as the One and the Dyad, and which many modern interpreters, following Hans-Georg Gadamer, call 'the one and the two'). Having demonstrated in the *Parmenides* that identity and difference cannot exist separately from one another, Plato discovers in the *Sophist* how these two sides can be held together in one view by the *power* (*dunamis*) of a thinking subject. This power, common to both God and human, is itself neither identity nor difference, yet through its very activity of connecting (sameness) and dividing (difference) (*Phaedrus*, 265d2–7; *Sophist*, 252e9–254b5; *Philebus*, 16c5–17a5) is somehow both. Falling under the genus of *making* (*poetiken*) throughout the *Sophist*, it is identified with Being itself (*Sophist*, 247d8–e3) and is located *in the soul* (*Sophist*, 250b7). Though this third thing beyond rest and motion is initially taken to be wholly perplexing (*Sophist*, 249e7–251a3), it emerges clearly in what follows that Plato sees this as the power of a thinking which combines rest and motion, sameness and otherness. Using the example of letters, the Stranger demonstrates that there are two kinds of principles, one kind that is the cause of unity in everything, and one that is the cause of division.

Just as God produces things in nature as a mixture by imposing a limiting unity upon a principle of difference, and the philosopher apprehends these divine ratios in his production of a philosophical *logos*, so the statesman weaves together the state out of elements perfectly analogous to the principles of sameness (or rest) and otherness (or motion) in the *Sophist*, namely the passive principle of moderation, and the active principle of courage (*Statesman*, 305e3–4). Moderate souls are always ready to maintain peace through a quiet self-relation, avoiding deeds that might interfere or conflict with others (*Statesman*, 307e1–6). In other words, they manifest a principle of *rest* and *self-sameness* that *limits* the impulse in the courageous souls to constant motion and strife.

A stable state is thus woven from these principles out of the *dunamis* of the political *techne* in the soul of the ruler. Further, the ruler's creation of a political community, without reference to anything beyond his own spontaneous subjectivity, exhibits the same divine freedom of natural creation. Even his own previously instituted laws are not binding upon the political genius of the ruler, who only posits them as a second-best substitute for his spontaneous judgment in case of his inevitable absence. The ruler's judgment, in contrast to static laws, is able to adapt itself to the ever-shifting particular requirements of each situation (*Statesman*, 294a6–c8, 297d4–e6, 300c8–d2).

Thus from the perspective of the ontology in the *Sophist* and the *Statesman*, our proper relation to this divine power cannot be conceived, as Pickstock conceives it, as supra-philosophical. This is because the divine constitution of things shares the very same structure as the human powers of philosophical apprehension and political constitution-making, all of which are modelled upon the power of a *techne*. This amounts to the very strong position that absolutely *nothing* lies outside of thought. The structures of being and thinking are identical, not in the paradoxical Parmenidean form that excludes all difference, but as mediated through the differentiated character of the divine thinking itself. Previously irreconcilable distinctions such as rest and motion or being and not-being can only exist, be thought and be communicated as comprehended within the dynamic activity of dialectical thought. As a result, philosophy and theology are not separate activities, and Plato achieves a mediation of divine and human far beyond Pickstock's interpretation.

As we have seen, the manner in which identity and difference are related is not merely an ontological question concerning the structure of the First Principle, the Ideas and sensible objects. For Plato this relation has direct relevance for several important practical questions in his political dialogues: how the unity of the ruling element of the city is related to the multiplicity of the community as a whole; how the limiting force of reason is related to the unlimited character of natural pleasures; how the common characteristics that unify all citizens of a city are related to those individuating characteristics that distinguish them from one another. Thus, with otherness and opposition given a place within the ideas in the later political dialogues, many of the political tenets of the *Republic* are revised accordingly: the citizenry at large is given a role in governing the city, natural pleasures are permitted and encouraged within a certain rational limit, and individuating institutions such as private property and family are grudgingly allowed. Pickstock's claim that Platonic thought does not seek to repress or eliminate otherness is clearly substantiated by the new ontology of the *Sophist* and *Statesman*.

With the revised ontology of the *Sophist* and *Statesman*, Plato seems to have overcome the sophistic manipulation of contradictory perspectives, since the being and not-being of every object is fixed by divine thinking into a determinate ratio that measures the truth and falsity of our judgments. Yet in the last stage of his ontology, Plato addresses the concern that this location of limit and measure within the spontaneous activity of the soul is dangerously close to the sophist who claims to be measure of a world that is in itself indeterminate prior to his measuring judgment. As a response to this element of subjective arbitrariness in the *Sophist* and *Statesman*, in *Philebus* Plato subordinates the power of divine intellect to an objective measure that 'is the cause of the mixture' (*Philebus*, 65a3–5). Rather than occupying the highest place above the principles of limit and unlimited, the soul's demiurgic *dunamis* is subordinated to the three aspects of the Good (measure, beauty and reason), and remains above only the unlimited principle itself in the hierarchy of highest goods (*Philebus*, 66b8–c6). The demiurgic soul must now look to the authority of the Good beyond its creative intellect in order to determine the character of its mixtures, a change reflected in *Timaeus* by the fact that the demiurge merely imitates the Ideas in constituting the sensible world.

This lowered status of the agent who causes the interaction between the One and the Dyad is developed politically in the *Laws* by raising the law to the status of ultimate measure of right and wrong. The laws must all be established in extensive detail in order to allow as little room as possible for human tinkering. The lawmaker and the ruler occupy different positions in this society, and the ruler becomes a mere custodian of the pre-given laws. Yet having a measure existing independently of the subjective measure of the ruler opens the political structure of the *Laws* to a criticism of this model in favour of the dynamic measure of a knowing legislator–ruler made throughout the *Statesman*: a static law as absolute measure of right and wrong has no ability to conform itself to the particular requirement of individuals and their unique situations (*Statesman*, 294a6–c8). This is precisely what Pickstock opposes as sophistic: 'the grasping of a formula which can be mechanically applied to any given reality' (*JP*, p. 276). Yet the indifference of law to that which it legislates is the direct result of the ontological impasse of Plato's late ontology. By placing a self-identical measure above the measured, we return to the problem of Anaxagoras: a measure which must be imposed upon an indifferent matter by an external cause, due to the lack of internal relation between the limit and that which is limited. While Pickstock draws heavily on the *Laws* because of the legal orthodoxy of Book X and its frequent discussions concerning the importance of song and dance rituals, the fundamental character of this dialogue involves establishing the universal, static code as a way to stop the destructive emergence of individual self-consciousness in the community. Due to her own biases, Pickstock is unable to articulate how, in the 'tragic' political result of the *Laws*, Plato has already self-consciously fallen away from his quest, articulated in *Symposium*, to reconcile the tragic viewpoint of divine objectivity with the comedic emphasis on the natural subjective freedom of individual members of the community (*Symposium*, 223c6–d6; see Pickstock, *JP*, p. 279 and my discussion of Plato's renunciation of the earlier attempt to reconcile comedy and tragedy in Diamond, 2002, pp. 15–19, especially p. 19).

Conclusion: Pickstock, Derrida, and an Objective Approach to Hellenic Platonism

It is not the purpose of this essay to discuss the validity of Pickstock's interpretation of Derrida. Yet while Pickstock reads Derrida's 'Plato's Pharmacy' as a diatribe against Plato's repression of difference, I would suggest that by revealing the aporetic nature of Plato's logic, Derrida's primary aim is to restore the many possible, contradictory ways of interpreting Plato's texts (see *D*, pp. 62, 107). One way people have decided to interpret Plato is in the way Pickstock describes Derrida's reading as suppressing natural difference. Yet for Derrida, many readings remain possible due to the nature of the Platonic logic itself, in which the One and the Dyad, as opposed but equally necessary aspects of the Good, leave the possibility of seeing everything in two exclusive perspectives.

It will be remembered from what has been said above that in the *Phaedo*, Plato makes clear his overall intention, that is, to show how the activity of the Good is present in each thing as the teleological end to which everything is ordered, so that there is no need to appeal to external causes to explain why each thing is the way it is. Yet Derrida brings out two ways in which this intention is frustrated. First, Plato must constantly appeal to an unlimited, indeterminate principle in order for its cause to be a cause of something: the Dyad is needed to connect the One and the Forms, the receptacle of *Timaeus* is required to underlie Forms and sensible instances. The Dyad is as necessary for the production of Forms as is the One; as the receptacle it is as required for the generation of the sensible world as are Forms themselves (*D*, pp. 126–7). Second, since the One – as the cause of order – and the Dyad – as the cause of disorder – are inherently opposed, they have nothing which of their own nature would bring them together in one thing. For this reason, Plato must always appeal to an external agent, *an ancillary cause*, in order to bring the two sides together: the demiurge to bring the intelligible and sensible together, the charioteer to connect the rational and irrational sides of the soul (*Phaedrus*, 246b), the divine maker of the *Sophist* to bring together the One and the Dyad, the philosopher to comprehend the opposed aspects of sameness and difference in each object, and someone to forcefully drag the philosopher down from his vision of the Good back into the dividedness of the world.

Derrida argues, like Aristotle before him, that Plato did not completely overcome the sophistic power to manipulate contraries. If everything is a mixture of contraries that are only related through the perspective of a subject external to the mixture, one can still look at every object in two different relations – in its taming relation to identity, or in its independence as limitless difference. If this second perspective of indeterminacy emerges, the dyadic principle of difference must be wholly repressed in order to retain unity, lawfulness and rationality. The necessity that compels one towards the good, ordered life over the evil, indeterminate one is purely subjective, determined through the arbitrary choice of the soul's *dunamis*. Socratic/Platonic and sophistic dialectic thus differ principally in intention, not in technique (see Aristotle, *Metaphysics*, 1004b17–26). Derrida's treatment of Plato shows how it is possible, from within the Platonic logic itself, to emphasize the side of indeterminacy over order, the Dyad and the receptacle over the One and the Forms. While both sameness and otherness can be thought by the divine intellect, this is only possible through successive, separate perspectives of the one object, not through their genuine objective unification in one simultaneous perspective (this perspective would require the later Aristotelian distinction between potentiality and actuality). Thus Derrida tacitly repeats the Aristotelian critique of Plato: having started from contraries, Plato cannot show how there is ever one thing whose unifying principle is actually *in* the principle as its origin and end.

Must one look to two separate, antithetical interpretations of Platonic thought, balancing Pickstock's interpretation of Plato's intention with Derrida's interpretation of Plato's logical impasse, in order to discern the meaning of the dialogues? We have seen that Plato is fully cognizant of both these sides. While Pickstock's supra-rational mediation between the human and the divine opens the door to the sophistry of Derrida,[5] Derrida himself can only use the *aporiae* of the Platonic logic to illustrate the fundamental *différance* underlying all reality by abstracting the Platonic philosophy from its subsequent history, and assuming that the Platonic *aporiae* remain unsolved and unsolvable. Like the Platonic connection between human and divine, natural and rational, theoretical and practical, the intention of Plato's logic and its inherent problems can only be apprehended if one looks to them not in their abstract separation but in their internal unity. For in looking directly to the dialogues, we see the two sides together in their inherent connection, wonderfully expressed in one object. Pickstock is right in understanding that the Platonic argument is of great relevance to the conversion of secular modernity and post-modernity to a divine objectivity, yet in distorting Plato's philosophy to show how 'Platonism has a future in postmodern and postmetaphysical thought' (*JP*, p. 270), she robs this response to post-modernity of its full force and renders Plato's argument subject to the sophistry she would have it refute.

Notes

1   I thank Nicholas Thorne, Kieva Bearden, Wayne Hankey and Stephen Long for their helpful comments on an earlier draft of this paper. I gratefully acknowledge the financial support of the Social Sciences and Humanities Research Council of Canada.

2   While Pickstock wants to portray Iamblichean–Proclean thought as fundamentally political, she does not address the strictly hierarchical vision of the theurgic mediation, in which each person plays a definite role within a rigid hierarchy. She describes the inter-subjective communication of the Good's contagion as if it were a relationship among equal members of a liturgical community. She opposes the hierarchical society of the *Republic* to the liturgical society of the *Laws*, in which all citizens are guardians and philosophers (*JP*, p. 280). If Pickstock wishes to recover a theurgic version of Neoplatonism, she must explain the role of the rigid hierarchies essential to this perspective.

3   Pickstock correctly makes the (very Platonic) association between 'violence, manipulation, and sophistic exteriority' (*AW*, p. 28). In other words, a merely external relation of cause and caused demands violent, externally imposed force (see her brief description of the secular city, *AW*, p. 3). When the unifying form has no inherent relation with its content, the form must be indifferently imposed from without. Politically, this ontology represents a relation between ruler and ruled in which the ruler is indifferent to the will of the uncomprehending citizens, who have no inherent relation (through understanding) to that by which he rules. An external relation of the terms involves forced, uncomprehending obedience, while an intrinsic relation demands persuasion and agreement.

4   For the clearest discussion of the One and the Dyad in Plato, see Findlay (1974), pp. 61–6. Pickstock misunderstands the One and the Dyad as they are manifested politically in Platonic philosophy. She takes the One to correspond to the individual soul, and the Dyad to be the cosmos and the city (*JP*, pp. 271, 280). In truth, Plato understands *all* reality to be composed out of the One and the Dyad, including the city and the individual soul.

5   For an account of how Derrida's sophistry maintains a power over the distinction between post-modern theology and its apparent opposite, post-modern nihilism, see Diamond (2000), pp. 208ff.

CHAPTER 2

Philosophical Religion and the Neoplatonic Turn to the Subject[1]

Wayne J. Hankey

Introduction: a Heideggerian and French 'neo-Neoplatonism'

A retrieval of Neoplatonism is essential to Radical Orthodoxy. The same holds for other postmodern Christian theologians and philosophers with whom it is engaged, for example, Jean-Luc Marion, who returns to Dionysius the Areopagite, and Michel Henry, who draws upon Meister Eckhart (Hankey, 2004, pp. 203–10 and 224–38; Hankey, 1998c).[2] John Milbank is conscious of his debt to these French phenomenologists working in the wake of Heidegger's conquest of French philosophy and theology in the second half of the twentieth century (Janicaud, 2001). The thought of Heidegger himself, although it misrepresented Neoplatonism in absolutely fundamental ways, may be regarded as a kind of Neoplatonism, or at least as reiterating some of its most important gestures (Hadot, 1959, p. 542; Narbonne, 2001, *passim*; Hankey, 2004a). The French postmodern Christian theologians and philosophers upon whom Radical Orthodoxy depends reproduced Neoplatonic positions in order to get around Heidegger's critique of western metaphysics as onto-theology. This is also the concern and method of Milbank, although his post-Heideggerian Christian Neoplatonism differs importantly from that of any of his French models by refusing to give up the western Christian attachment to Being as the highest name of God. Crucially, however, the 'neo-Neoplatonism' of all these – Heidegger, the French phenomenologists and the Radically Orthodox – has a fundamental logic which characterizes Heidegger's alternative metaphysics. In contrast to the Neoplatonic tradition in its pagan and Christian, ancient, mediaeval, renaissance and modern forms, these twentieth century revivals eschew the mediation of intellect when relating the sensible, corporeal and psychic to the Absolute Principle. The present postmodern 'neo-Neoplatonism' unites the transcendent and the world of our experience immediately (for the Heideggerian and the old Neoplatonic logics, and their difference, see Narbonne, 2001, pp. 280–81).

Writing on 'Postmodernism', Milbank draws the work of 'the Cambridge school', out of which Radical Orthodoxy evolved, back to 'a certain number of French phenomenologists (J.-L. Marion, J.-L. Chrétien, P. Ricœur, M. Henry)' (Milbank, 2002, pp. 924–6). This group has been identified by Dominique Janicaud as belonging to 'the theological turn' in phenomenology (Janicaud,

1991).[3] According to Milbank these phenomenologists follow Heidegger in admitting the 'the end of metaphysics', but attempt to avoid 'the nihilism of *la différance*' which Milbank associates pre-eminently with Derrida. Indeed, Heidegger's end of metaphysics, limited to a modernity that is supposed to have given it birth – a limitation erected both by Radical Orthodoxy and by the French upon whom it depends for its representation of the history of philosophy – is essential to Milbank's position. Derrida's linguistic turn, from which the Radically Orthodox suppose their own subordination to Christian myth will eliminate the nihilism, is equally essential (see Cunningham, 2002). So much of what Radical Orthodoxy promises to give contemporary theology and philosophy derives from these French thinkers, and especially from Marion, with whom Milbank wrestles in one essay after another, that it seems parasitic upon them. A phenomenology turning toward theology is not, however, the only French contribution to Radical Orthodoxy.

France, during the twentieth century, has been the home of a vast retrieval of Neoplatonism not only as a work of scholarship but also as a philosophical, theological, spiritual and artistic force which, among other effects, either replaced or strongly modified the Thomism of French Catholics (Hankey, 2004). This retrieval has affected Radical Orthodoxy both by way of the French phenomenologists and directly. We must acknowledge that an English Anglican theological movement which draws on French phenomenology shows remarkable sophistication and courage. When Radical Orthodoxy adds to this a retrieval of ancient, mediaeval and modern Neoplatonism in its most theurgic forms, standing on the shoulders of the French retrieval, it extends this courageous breaking out from the narrow confines of the Anglo-American philosophical and theological world. In its Neoplatonism Radical Orthodoxy is almost alone in English-speaking Protestant theology which deleted from its memory the millennium between the sixth and the sixteenth centuries. Equally remarkable is its rebuke to what prevails as philosophy in the Anglo-American world, for which the millennium and a half of thought between the ancient and the modern Skepticisms is a black hole. The exuberant welcome given to Radical Orthodoxy in many parts of the English-speaking theological world is, in part, a delight in the riches of the past which the contemporary deconstructions of modernity have returned to us. The deficiencies in the retrieval lie in the same place. Neoplatonism bridges the epochs of the religious, theological and philosophical development of western culture. It can be authentically retrieved neither in a war against modernity or philosophy, nor in a denial of the turn to the subject that belongs to them (Hankey, 1998a, pp. 154–61; Hankey, 1999b, pp. 387–97).

While there are very many problems with what Radical Orthodoxy has made of Platonism generally, and of Neoplatonism specifically, in retrieving them as part of its anti-modern polemic, I shall concentrate on three: first, how the relations between philosophical reason and religion in Neoplatonism are misunderstood; second, how its role in shaping western subjectivity is forced out of view; third, how, in common with Heidegger and the French neo-Neoplatonists, the intellectual mediation essential to Neoplatonism is lost.

Fear and Hatred of Modernity and an Anti-Philosophical Platonism

The origins of Radical Orthodoxy in John Milbank's *Theology and Social Theory* remain determinative. There we find the account of modernity upon which what follows depends. In this work, Milbank argued that theology must no longer allow itself to be placed from outside by philosophy and by secular thought generally. He endeavoured to persuade theologians to get over their 'false humility' in the face of modern secular reason, whose challenge, he announces, 'is at an end, for it is seen that modernity was itself made in terms of metaphysics, and of a "religion"'. Milbank claims that postmodernism has freed Christian theology from having to 'measure up to … standards of scientific truth and normative rationality' (*TST*, pp. 1 and 260).

His subsequent works and those of his followers develop further a characterization of modernity, at base Heideggerian and Nietzschean. In a series of binary oppositions, modernity is reduced to 'bastard dualisms': faith versus reason, grace versus nature, *theoria* versus *poiêsis*, substance versus *praxis*, the spatial versus the temporal, closed objectifying subjectivity versus self-transcendent openness, philosophy as metaphysics versus theology, secular humanism versus divinity, the immanent versus the transcendent, isolated individualism versus community, mind versus body, and so on (*RO*, p. 2). Milbank, Catherine Pickstock and Graham Ward assert that, by way of 'a return to patristic and mediaeval roots, and especially to the Augustinian vision of all knowledge in divine illumination', Radical Orthodoxy gains for itself both sides of what it accuses modernity of opposing. Its 'central theological framework' for this radical overcoming 'is "participation" as developed by Plato and reworked by Christianity, because any alternative configuration perforce reserves a territory independent of God' (*RO*, pp. 2–3). As Eli Diamond has shown in Chapter 1, this is a Plato altogether strange both to the Platonic tradition and to philosophy generally.

In contradistinction to the Plato of the dialogues who opposes *mythos* and *logos*, who uses a sceptical dialectic to criticize the lies of the poetic theologians about the gods and human virtue, and who composes new philosophical myths to replace the old, this Plato writes a kind of liturgical theology. In their determination to attack the roots of philosophy, Pickstock and Milbank reduce Plato to the later, theurgic Neoplatonism. In fact, the leading scholar of the relations of myth and reason in Plato, Luc Brisson, contrasts him with the Neoplatonists, who derived their allegorizing strategy from the Stoics. Plato rejects the central assumption of allegorization that myth conceals truth 'since for him truth can only be revealed in philosophical discourse' (Brisson, 1998, p. 127; Nicholson, 1998). In opposition to a Plato who founds philosophy, Catherine Pickstock claims: 'the theological interim of dialogue is crucial since we are led through it *into* doxology, which for Plato is our principle [sic] human function and language's only possibility of restoration' (*AW*, p. 43). The reduction of philosophy to theology determined by myth so that reason will have no 'territory independent of God' forces a break with French phenomenology. Criticizing Marion's use of 'phenomenological donation to rethink it as Christian charity', Milbank gives an account of philosophy, its origins and the place of Plato in it:

> An independent phenomenology must be given up, along with the claim, which would have seemed so bizarre to the Fathers, to be doing philosophy *as well as* theology. ... [P]hilosophy as autonomous, as 'about' anything independently of its creaturely status *is* metaphysics or ontology in the most precisely technical sense. Philosophy in fact *began* as a secularizing immanentism, an attempt to regard a *cosmos* independently of a performed reception of the poetic word. The pre-Socratics forgot both Being and the gift, while (*contra* Heidegger) the later Plato made some attempt to recover the extra-cosmic vatic *logos*. Theology has always resumed this inheritance, along with that of the Bible ...

This picture determines what theology must do to philosophy: 'if it wishes to think again God's love, then it must entirely evacuate philosophy, which is metaphysics, leaving it nothing (outside imaginary worlds, logical implications or the isolation of *aporias*) to either do or see, which is not – manifestly, I judge – malicious' (*OT,* pp. 340–41).

Despite the criticism of Marion, Milbank shares with him something fundamental in an anti-modern shaping of the history of philosophy. This picture, deriving for both from Étienne Gilson, which locates a fatal turning in philosophy with Scotus and Suárez, has become increasingly general among Christian postmodern theologians, although its efficacy for overcoming Heidegger has been recently questioned by Adrian Pabst (Pabst, 2002; Courtine, 1990; for a survey, see Miner, 2001). In accord with this shaping, John Milbank judges that 'it is arguable that recent researches suggest that "modernity fulfils metaphysics" should be radicalized as "modernity invented metaphysics" ' (*OT,* p. 328). By this shift to modernity as inventing metaphysics, Marion and Milbank are able to use features of Heidegger's critical analysis of the modern while retrieving the pre-modern in a way he would not allow. In fact, Milbank goes further with Gilson than Marion does by attempting to resuscitate 'Christian philosophy'. However, Milbank reforms Gilson's notion by a subordination of philosophy to myth which he identifies as Neoplatonic. This would chagrin Gilson, who waged war against Neoplatonism as a form of idealism (Marion, 1995, p. 56, note 60; p. 58, note 63; p. 60, note 70; Marion, 1980; Hankey, 1998b; for Marion's relation to Heidegger, see Janicaud, 2001, ii, *Entretiens*, pp. 210–27).

For both Marion and Milbank, getting beyond secularizing modernity requires reducing or eliminating the autonomy of philosophy. It is in this context that Radical Orthodoxy retrieves its theurgic Neoplatonism. In replying to an article of mine, Milbank affirms that he and Pickstock are 'rightly linked' with 'the Dionysian legacy of theurgic neoplatonism' (Milbank, 1999, p. 485, responding to Hankey, 1999a). Following the French, these neo-Neoplatonists are moving away from the traditional English enthusiasm for Plotinus to Iamblichus and his successors. However, Milbank's creation of a 'Postmodern Critical Augustinianism' within English 'Radical Orthodoxy' (see *PA* and Milbank, 1997), reminds us that the twentieth-century retrieval of Neoplatonism may either work to establish an alternative to a Porphyrian–Augustinian kataphatic onto-theology or, instead, may reinterpret Augustine in such a way as to draw him toward an apophatic Neoplatonism realized in charity and *poiêsis* (Hankey, 2001, pp. 72–4). John Milbank takes the second course and refuses my 'contrast of a Porphyrian Augustine and theurgic Dionysius'. For him 'Augustine also places the soul within the cosmos and in the *Confessions* finally realises his own self-hood through losing it in cosmic liturgy' (Milbank, 1999, p. 497, note 142). Thereby Milbank tries to keep the ontology which Marion refuses.

Saving ontology is undertaken by the total reduction of philosophy to theology – a reduction attributed to theurgic Neoplatonism – so that ontology replaces it. Whereas Marion refuses the Neoplatonic One for the sake of the Good and charity (Marion, 1977, p. 185; Janicaud, 2001, ii, *Entretiens*, p. 216), Radical Orthodoxy supposes that its theological ontology subject to Christian myth allows it both to have God as Being, and also to embrace enthusiastically the theurgic religion that went with strongly henological Platonism. Milbank's postmodern Neoplatonism, refounded in Christian myth, consists in

> notions ... [which] remain essential for a Christian theological ontology: these are those of transcendence, participation, analogy, hierarchy, teleology (these last two in modified forms) and the absolute reality of the 'the Good' in roughly the Platonic sense. The strategy, therefore, which the theologian should adopt, is that of showing that the critique of presence, substance, the idea, the subject, causality, thought-before-expression, and realist representation do not necessarily entail the critique of transcendence, participation, analogy, hierarchy, teleology and the Platonic Good, reinterpreted by Christianity as identical with Being. (*TST*, p. 296)

I shall have more to say about this passage because Milbank's exclusions from authentic Neoplatonism make evident that the restrictions placed on what can be accepted from ancient and mediaeval Neoplatonism derive from the Nietzschean, Heideggerian and Derridean criticisms of metaphysics. In common with them, Radical Orthodoxy seeks to deconstruct the western subject.

Philosophy in Augustinian and Iamblichan Neoplatonism

Our postmodern theologians are correct to link apodictic philosophy with the construction of the western subject, but they are wrong to delay both until modernity, and Radical Orthodoxy is mistaken in eliminating both from

Augustine and Neoplatonism. For Augustine the indubitable unity of thought and being in the human mind has content, and this content, known in philosophy, is absolutely essential to his representation of how he came to Christian belief. Moreover, his rational certainty determines the character of his Christianity. The first seven books of Augustine's *Confessions* – significantly the first autobiographical construction of a self – recount the steps by which he came to a Platonism mediated to him through Plotinus and Porphyry, because, as he makes explicit in Book Seven, Augustine cannot become a baptized Christian until he can conceive incorporeal substance, that is, until he knows not just that it is but positively grasps its nature. In Book Seven, the centre of the *Confessions*, Augustine tells us that knowing his own nature, the nature of God, the origin and nature of evil, and his responsibility for his own sinful deeds, all depend on what he learned from the Platonists. Instructed by them in the art of introspection and the ascents it enables, he shows us in Book Seven and in subsequent books how he has learned to experience the unity of thought and being through reflection on his own thinking as incorporeal and indubitably existing. He equally displays how well he has learned to rise from world and self by reiterating repeatedly the Plotinian mystical ascents. Nor is the *Confessions* by any means the only place where Augustine demonstrates that his Christianity depends on a knowledge possessed by philosophers from whom he must learn.

Another work central to the construction of his Christianity, the *De Trinitate*, is a step-by-step deepening of the understanding that we are essentially rational, what this means, what it makes possible and what it requires (*Trin.* 2.16.27, 2.17.28, 3.2.8; Hankey, 1999a, pp. 118–19). Book 10 is occupied with self-presence. Here too, within his own thinking, Augustine finds again the required knowledge both that incorporeal substance exists and what it is (*Trin.* 10.10.16). Using the resulting unity of incorporeal thought and being as a place from which to perceive both what is above and what below himself, and practising the disciplines of Plotinian spirituality, Augustine arrives at and locates his *mens* within a hierarchy where God is the true identity of thought and being, like the Plotinian *nous*. So far as it is mutable, the human *mens* lies between true being above him and sensible 'almost non-being' below. In the *De Trinitate* as well as in the *Confessions* the knowledge that the human *mens* is indubitably existent incorporeal substance is thus necessary to Augustine's Christianity.

The unbreakable self-reflexive unity of remembering, understanding and loving in the Augustinian *mens* has, and must have, for Augustine a truthful basis. Not only does it involve an indubitable certainty (*Trin.* 10.10.14, 15.12.21), but establishing that we are rational is, from the beginning to the end of the *De Trinitate*, required to lead us to God. When Augustine finally reaches the consideration of the inner and superior reason and of the image of the Trinity which belongs to it, he makes his principle explicit. The image of the Trinity has been impaired by sin but not lost: 'Behold! the mind … remembers itself, understands itself, and loves itself; if we perceive this, we perceive a Trinity, not yet God indeed, but now finally an image of God' (*Trin.* 14.8.11). If the essential incorporeal rationality of the human soul could be denied, nothing in the whole argument would work. This is why Augustine returns to his refutation of the Skeptics in the final book of the *De Trinitate* (*Trin*. 15.12.21).

When Milbank interprets Augustine so as to draw him toward a theurgic Neoplatonism, he denies that 'the Augustinian *cogito* [is] Cartesian ... no *res cogitans*, enclosed upon itself, is here reflexively established' (Milbank, 1999, p. 497, note 142). His refusal to allow any real connection between the Augustinian and the Cartesian *cogito* is part of his endeavour to overcome metaphysics by means of theology. Milbank equally interprets Aquinas so as to collapse the theology which is part of philosophy into sacred doctrine. In fact, Augustine's Platonism does *not* stand against a philosophical reason which, in accord with its own logical necessities, reaches certainly established conclusions. Just the opposite. This reason is essential to the knowledge by which the rational self is established as a foundation for the knowledge of God and of all else. In consequence, Augustine's Platonism not only confidently borrows from his predecessors in the tradition, but also looks forward to the rigorous reasonings of the mediaevals and of Descartes. For him, as indeed for Plato and Plotinus, conceding to rationality its proper self-certainty does not involve reserving a territory which excludes God. Indeed, the contrary holds (Hankey, 2001, pp. 65–88; Hankey, 2003). The same is true for Iamblichus and for his successors in the Neoplatonic schools.

One of the unifications made by the Christian theologians of antiquity and intensified by their mediaeval successors (who simultaneously distinguished them more clearly and united them more closely) was between philosophy, theology and religion. In this, the Christians were interlocutors and successors of the later Neoplatonists, especially the Neoplatonic hero of Radical Orthodoxy, Iamblichus (Hankey, 2001a). The 'divine' Iamblichus is all at once a priest, a theologian and a philosopher. He knows the difference between these roles and their necessary mutual interconnection. The central purpose of his system is to maintain the difference, the integrity and the connection of: (1) diverse religious practices in which the gods and humans cooperate (among these are what is called theurgy, which at some levels requires the use of material means and thus was recognized by Augustine as the pagan equivalent of Christian sacraments); (2) human moral discipline; (3) the rational and human work of philosophy; and (4) our passive yielding to the gracious activity of the divine toward us (Hankey, 2003a). The loss of the proper subject, discipline and autonomy of philosophy to theology and religion is altogether contrary to the intention and practice of Iamblichus. In fact, Iamblichus is concerned with keeping the levels of reality separate. Philosophy works with what the human can do within the limits given to it. Gregory Shaw writes:

> There is in Iamblichus's Platonism a willingness to *identify* with the humiliation of the human condition ... Damascius's companion Isidore once remarked, after meeting a pretentious philosopher: '*Those who would be Gods must first become*

human!' For the hieratic Platonists the limits of our humanity must be fully realised in order to recover our lost divinity. (Shaw, 1996, p. 41)

For Iamblichus, the human and the divine are not to be confused. Right doctrine

separates the Soul off ... following upon Intellect, representing a distinct level of being ... subsisting independently on its own, and it separates the soul from all the superior classes of being and assigns to it ... [a] particular definition of its essence. (Iamblichus, 2002, 7, p. 31)

Soul is in the middle, communicating life and being from the Intelligible realm to what is below. The soul 'cannot become divine but only attached to the divine. It is permanently inferior' (Iamblichus, 2002, p. 219).

What moved Iamblichus to theurgy, namely, the conviction that the individual human soul is altogether descended into the realm of becoming, requires him to embrace both religion and the work of philosophy for ascent toward the One. The *Protrepticus* is an exhortation to the philosophical life with all its intellectual disciples and moral virtues. The *De Mysteriis*, an answer to Porphyry's criticism of theurgy put by Iamblichus in the mouth of an Egyptian priest, contains both that upon which philosophy depends and what is beyond it. Philosophy presupposes 'an innate knowledge of the gods [which] is co-existent with our nature, and is superior to all judgment and choice, reasoning and proof' (Iamblichus, 2003, 1.3, p. 11). Moreover, theurgy surpasses philosophy as a way of union, which is 'intellectual and dependent upon us' (Iamblichus, 2003, 2.11, p. 115). Contact with the gods beyond where philosophy, limited by the bounds of what the discursive mind could reach, must be initiated by the gods themselves.

For Iamblichus, philosophy is for the human as human; it activates the best powers of the soul. By it we contemplate beings, and attain knowledge and understanding of all things. The soul is capable of philosophy because she has in herself the 'system of universal reason' (Iamblichus, 1989, 4.5–7). Philosophy is a striving for contemplation for which education, in the fullest sense and with all its means, prepares us. Truth is the highest operation of the highest part of the soul; therefore, our ultimate human goal *qua* human must be contemplation (Iamblichus, 1989, 7.6). As with Aristotle, whose arguments he repeats, intellectual activity is an end in itself; it is 'a part of virtue and felicity: for we affirm that felicity either is from this or is this' (Iamblichus, 1989, 7.8). Iamblichus repeats Aristotle: 'In a perfect and free activity itself there is a pleasure, so that theoretic activity or contemplation is the most pleasant or delightful of all' (Iamblichus, 1989, 11.7). Philosophy has its own foundation in what we are, its proper sphere of operation, methods, powers, satisfactions and end.

There is, however, a yet higher union with the divine. Precisely, as power or act of the human as human, philosophy is denied the capacity to bring about true union. Although philosophy reaches true contemplation, it is moved by a further desire, one that draws the soul closer to God, yearning for a contemplation where its activity and end are no longer divided. Philosophy is the way to that higher end and anticipates it, but the human activity which reason is and requires must finally give way to an activity toward us and in us of the gods. The ultimate goal is beyond theoretical knowledge and lies in the soul's association with the gods, in returning to being and revolution in communion with them, as she was before her incarnation (Iamblichus, 1989, 3). The ultimate union is by a divine gift beyond philosophy and human capacity, but this union and its means are established relative to and are dependent upon philosophy, upon the leading of intellect, and upon the human effort which life in accord with intellect requires.

For Milbank, in contrast, after its modern decadence, philosophy can only be restored so far as it is debased, 'contaminated', by Christian myth. For him metaphysics and ontology have two senses. One, 'the post-Suárezian attempts to have a prior "general" metaphysics and ontology, wherein being can emphatically be treated in its supposed own integrity, before one goes on to treat God in "special" metaphysics as the highest instance of being' (Milbank, 2001b, p. 487). Metaphysics in this sense he totally rejects. The second sense, which he applies to patristic and mediaeval theology, is looser and wider. Here 'the inherited general categories for being were both contaminated and revised by the consideration of narrative event' (ibid.). In virtue of a 'gnoseological circularity between ontology and narrative ... the event of revelation both interrupted and completed ontology itself' (ibid., pp. 486–7). In consequence, metaphysics, in the second looser and wider sense, is restored to Christian theology; indeed, it becomes total. Milbank judges: 'Beyond metaphysics, then, there is only metaphysics, intruding into all knowledge, all lived cultural existence' (ibid., pp. 488–9). Metaphysics, both necessary and possible, returns so completely that 'we are right to trust in a limited intellectual insight into the structures of being' and correct to affirm, with Hegel, that 'to choose this speculation is therefore to choose reason itself' (ibid., p. 489).

By the contamination in which philosophy loses its proper integrity and is confused with what is prior and beyond it, Milbank thinks that he overcomes the 'bastard dualisms' of modernity. What the Neoplatonists judged to be the labour and divisions consequent upon our finitude have been surpassed. Milbank supposes that (1) having correctly diagnosed the problem to be philosophy as immanentizing reason, he then (2) exempted Platonism from this judgement, and, (3) radically surrendered philosophy, so that (4) he gets philosophy back on his own terms.

Deconstructing the Western Self

As we have already noticed, among other criticisms of its past forms, Milbank requires a critique of the Neoplatonic 'subject' before it is ready for rehabilitation within Radical Orthodoxy. According to Milbank's account, ancient philosophy sought objective substantiality and modern philosophy sought subjective substantiality (both of which are to be opposed), because they remained 'inside the horizons projected by the Greek *mythos*, within which the Greek *logos* had to remain confined' (*TST*, p. 295). In her *After Writing*, Catherine Pickstock seeks to open the self-closed objectified subject, which results from the modern division of subject and object. Theurgical Neoplatonism provides the opening. It is essential that liturgy transform language so that material things are treated as numinous and are addressed as if personal (*AW*, pp. 195ff.). Pickstock hopes thereby to effect the restoration of a 'genuine subjectivity', a 'living subject', with 'a substantive, though not completed identity', having 'a definite but open identity' (*AW*, pp. 95, 114, 118, 192, 199, 211–12, 214). Smashing the autonomy of philosophy and of the subject go together.

The basic project and its means (if not its rhetoric) are those of the so-called 'spiritualisme français', whose origins reach back to the positivism, realism and Neoplatonism of Schelling. This 'spiritualisme français' was also deeply critical of the closing of the human subject which it attributed to modern metaphysics. In the twentieth century the French retrieval of Neoplatonism, and yet another of the many neo-Augustinianisms created by the French, were the means by which this metaphysics and its closure of the subject were combated (Schmutz, 1999, pp. 169–200; Janicaud, 1969; Hankey, 2004, pp. 138–9). Michel Henry and Jean-Luc Marion, whose phenomenology is anticipated in Maine de Biran, are heirs and continuators of this 'spiritualisme' and its aims (Henry, 1965; his fidelity to de Biran is examined in Lemoine, 2000).

The French philosophers on whom he is dependent are accused by Milbank of retaining an unredeemed philosophy because, against their own intentions, he has detected that they continue the Cartesian and Kantian subject. For example, of Lévinas he writes: 'The Kantian vision has today been radicalised by Lévinas. ... Lévinas ... produces a bizarre inverted egoism, which conserves a mode of Cartesian dualism, and indeed perhaps accentuates it into a mode of manicheanism' (Milbank, 2001a, pp. 341–2). Marion is also accused of continuing Cartesian dualism. Associating Marion and Michel Henry in the doctrine of subjective auto-affection, Milbank judges of Marion that his 'new restored Descartes is a yet more solipsistic Descartes' (ibid., p. 356). Henry is also guilty of manicheanism and of a 'hyper-Cartesianism' (ibid., p. 360). For John Milbank, against these, Derrida is employed to deconstruct the identity of the modern subject and its constitution of a matching rational object: 'the reduction of being to the "object" whose existence does not exceed the extent to which it is known by the subject' (*AW*, p. 70). Derrida is mingled with Eriugena. The old ontology has been replaced with a post-Derridean 'logontic' in which the divine and human are interchangeable. Man creates his linguistic world so totally that, as Milbank puts it, 'man as an *original* creator' participates 'in some measure in creation *ex nihilo*' (Milbank, 1997a; *WMS*, p. 79; *PA*, §42).

Milbank's war against the modern subject is largely fought with weapons borrowed from Heidegger. Crucial to Heidegger's history of metaphysics is a move from substance to subjectivity as characterizing the move from the ancient to the modern metaphysics; for example 'the change of *idea* from *eidos* to *perceptio*' (Heidegger, 1977, p. 72). This change is associated by Heidegger with Descartes and Leibniz. Placing the change where he does is important to Heidegger's argument because it becomes the basis of the shift to the will to power as the consummation of modernity. Milbank, who largely follows Heidegger in his characterization of modernity, but wants to retrieve pre-modern forms, needs to place this fatal move as late as possible. This involves a misrepresentation of Hellenistic philosophy generally and of Neoplatonism particularly. As a matter of fact, the shifts to the subject as the fulcrum, and to *perceptio* as constitutive of reality, occur already in late antiquity and are fundamental to Neoplatonism, both pagan and Christian.

The Move to the Subject

The move to the subject is already a development within ancient Stoicism and Skepticism. The skeptical schools are only answered by the Neoplatonists in so far as they proceed to God and the world from within the self. This turn to the subject, and to the forms of objective reality as fundamentally determined by the perspectives of diverse subjects, are the fundamentals of Neoplatonism, and of the philosophies and philosophical theologies of its Jewish, Islamic and Christian heirs, even those called 'Aristotelian'. Philosophy, as the care of the self, and its *exercices spirituels* are inherited from the Platonists and Stoics by the Christians; they become essential to the orientation of Christianity to personal salvation, and they are its spiritual means (Hadot, 1998; Hadot, 1981; Hankey, 2003a).

One case must serve to indicate something characteristic of Neoplatonism and its heirs. The last book of the *Consolation of Philosophy* refutes a divine determinism which threatened to destroy the argument of the work just at the point when the consolation of Boethius as condemned prisoner was positively successful. By a formula about the relation of the subject and object of knowing, Lady Philosophy dissolves a necessity which had threatened to destroy the ladder by which he had climbed out of despair. Philosophia saves him yet again by declaring: it is not true that all things are known 'by the power and nature of the objects known. Totally the contrary, for all which is known is comprehended not according to the power of the thing itself but rather according to the capability of those who know it' (Boethius, 1973, 5.4, p. 411).

This formula by which subjectivity is centralized, and by which the proper differentiation of its forms becomes essential, had a two-hundred-year history before Boethius used it. His likely source was a commentary of Ammonius where this Neoplatonist solves the problem of determinism by a position which he ascribes to Iamblichus: 'knowledge is intermediate between the knower and the known, since it is the activity of the knower concerning the known' (Ammonius, 1998, 135.14; p. 98).

Despite ascribing it to Iamblichus, Ammonius would also certainly have known the doctrine from his teacher, Proclus. In common with Ammonius and Boethius, when Proclus is treating Providence, the doctrine serves to dissolve a determinism seemingly required by divine knowledge of the future; contingency is saved for the sake of human freedom. The ultimate source for both Ammonius and Proclus is probably Porphyry *Sententiae* 10, where we are told that everything is in a subject according to the mode of its substance. From Proclus the doctrine is picked up by the *Liber de causis*, a product of Arabic Islamic philosophy, and Dionysius. For Aquinas, the doctrine is hugely important (Henle, 1956, pp. 328–33; Aquinas, 1996, p. xxvi).

Boethius shifts from the objective to the subjective side in order to prevent confusions between diverse forms of knowing and being and thus to save human hope and prayer. The purpose of the shift to the subject is salvation for the soul. Employed more radically, the turn to the subject has enormous consequences for the creation of the cosmos, for its structure, and for the activity by which its various intelligences are related. Eriugena works out these consequences in the most radical possible way. In the *Periphyseon*, human apprehension in its diverse modes actually causes the varied forms of being. Ineffable non-being, before all definition, being and multiplicity, comes into definite, varied and perceptible being by passing dialectically, or 'running through', intellect, reason, imagination and sense, faculties all contained in the human *mens*. Human *mens*, at the middle of what is and of what is not, unites all the created kinds as diverse forms of unity and division. What knows all makes all. Therefore, 'in the human everything is created' (Eriugena, 1865, 4.8, *PL* 774A: 'in homine … universaliter creatae sunt').

The recentring of knowledge and creativity in the character of the subject and its perspective is central to post-Plotinian Neoplatonism and to its Greek and Latin mediaeval heirs (Hankey, 1998c; Hankey, 2002, pp. 126–50; Hankey, 2002a, pp. 308–9 and 321–2). There is no need to wait for Descartes and Leibniz to find the roots of the modern subject. Neoplatonism becomes unintelligible when we fail to attend to its origin in and radicalization of the Skeptical turn to the subject. Augustine knew this, understanding that the Skeptics were 'Academics'; following Plotinus he made Skepticism the essential precondition to his own path inward and upward (*Conf.* 5.10–14).

Neoplatonism as the Immediate Union of Life and the Absolute

Iamblichus held that philosophy is the properly human activity, preserving its difference from the religiously participated action of the gods toward us. He judged that it belonged to the human subject from which he distinguished other spiritual substances and to which he attributed a unique character and a specified place in the cosmos. When philosophy and the human subject are eliminated, we do not so much 'transcend' the 'modern bastard dualisms' as destroy the preconditions of mediation and collapse its structures. With Heidegger, with the French Christian phenomenologists who are heirs of the 'spiritualisme français', and with Radical Orthodoxy dependent upon both, the mediatorial structures which are essential to Neoplatonism disappear. The 'neo-Neoplatonism' of our time joins life and the Absolute immediately. The metamorphosis undergone by figures from the history of philosophy, as they suffer a 'colonization' within the Radical Orthodox empire in what James Hanvey calls a sophisticated postmodern 'strategy of deception' (Hanvey, 2000, pp. 155 and 164), displays the logic of this 'neo-Neoplatonism'.

As we have seen, the retrieval of Neoplatonism by Radical Orthodoxy is undertaken to reduce the modern subject and philosophy. Ancient and mediaeval thinkers are rehabilitated to become figures in the neo-Iamblichan Platonism it uses and transforms in order to accomplish this reduction. As we have observed, Augustine is reconciled to Iamblichus, so that union with the divine for both is by way of joining in the cosmic *poiêsis*. In common with Marion and Michael Henry, but more radically, for Radical Orthodoxy the First Principle and sensual life are immediately united, that is, without the mediation of soul or mind. Milbank, Marion and Henry reduce autonomous and objectifying reason, identified with modernity, and replace it with an incarnational Neoplatonism. However, only Milbank presents his project in precisely these terms. It may be doubted whether Milbank's own position is coherent, or his representation and use of other philosophers is just to them, but no one is more determined than he to overcome the modern subject by means of what he regards as a Christian (and Augustinian) Neoplatonism.

Seeking the philosophical logic at work here we may turn to Jean-Marc Narbonne, who exposes the most radical form of such an immediate union of the experienced and the Absolute in Heidegger. Narbonne concludes his *Hénologie, ontologie et Ereignis (Plotin–Proclus–Heidegger)* with a comparison between the verticality of the Neoplatonic metaphysics and the *Seyn* of Heidegger's *Ereignis* as immediate horizontal ground and points to the grave problems with the Heideggerian alternative:

> Despite a certain communality in the will to pass beyond objectification … we have ascertained that Neoplatonism is set out along an axis opposed to that of which Heidegger has an inkling. The Neoplatonic way is erected vertically; it is ordered upward along a mediation notably by way of soul and intellect. … The Heideggerian horizontal approach is totally different. … In place of the steps of reality he substitutes a pure process which begins from an event (the *Seyn* as *Ereignis*), with which no mediated connection is permitted. … In place of the Neoplatonic theme of the 'beyond' (*epékeina*), it seems to me that he proposes the theme of the 'on the contrary side', that is to say of that which happens without mediation, if not in opposition, at least as something done behind its back, and as a kind of crossing-over from everything else. (Narbonne, 2001, pp. 280–81)

It is ironic, but not surprising, that a 'neo-Neoplatonism', created in large part by a fundamental acceptance and partial rejection of the Heideggerian critique of western metaphysics, should so deeply reproduce what is most problematic about the structure of his alternative metaphysics.

Notes

1   I thank Ian Stewart, who generously provided the encouragement this project needed, and his critical eye.
2   For a critical treatment of Marion and Henry by Milbank, exposing some of what is common and what different in their retrievals of Neoplatonism, see Milbank (2001a and 2001b).
3   Many of those Janicaud identified as part of this 'theological turn' published Courtine (ed.) (1992) in response. These are translated in *Phenomenology and the 'Theological Turn': The French Debate*, Dominique Janicaud, Jean-François Courtine, Jean-Louis Chrétien, Michel Henry, Jean-Luc Marion, Paul Ricœur, Perspectives in Continental Philosophy (New York: Fordham University Press, 2000). In 1998, Janicaud added another volume to this controversy, *La phénoménologie éclatée*, Collection 'tire à part' (Paris, Éditions de l'Éclat). See also Schmutz (1999).

CHAPTER 3

Is There Room for Political Philosophy in Postmodern Critical Augustinianism?

Todd Breyfogle

Radical Orthodoxy is a determined stand against modernity. Like Augustine in his own day, Radical Orthodoxy aims to topple the household gods in defense of a unique and decisive Christian narrative of history. Indeed, insofar as it represents a coherent position, Radical Orthodoxy places Augustine at the center of its enterprise.[1] Yet, at many crucial junctures, Radical Orthodoxy renders Augustine's thought almost unrecognizable or abandons it altogether. By neglecting the even-handedness of Augustine's analytical and descriptive method, Radical Orthodoxy loses its equilibrium and in so doing loses both its radical character and its orthodoxy. In failing to follow Augustine's thought to its logical conclusions, Radical Orthodoxy loses its nerve. As an assault on modernity, Radical Orthodoxy goes both too far and not far enough, and so remains irrevocably implicated in the modernity it tries to overthrow.

In this essay I aim to chart some of Radical Orthodoxy's excesses and shortcomings in its treatment of Augustine in three particular areas: epistemology and the self, history and ontology, and politics and desire. I conclude by suggesting ways in which Radical Orthodoxy's failures with respect to Augustine undermine important aspects of its attempt to position itself as a critique of modern thought.[2] To reap the benefits of Radical Orthodoxy's critique of modernity and to foreclose the risks that same critique entails, we must inquire whether there is room for political philosophy in 'postmodern critical Augustinianism'.

Epistemology and the Self

Radical Orthodoxy posits a non-autonomous self, embedded in communities of language (primarily) and cultural traditions, over and against the autonomous Cartesian, Enlightenment self which constructs, from indubitable premises, a rational philosophical system of clear and distinct ideas. In so doing, Radical Orthodoxy puts itself in step largely with that post-Enlightenment philosophical tradition of the hermeneutics of suspicion in which all modes of discourse are understood to be subordinated to and formed by the will to power (*TST*, p. 401;

31

see also Burnaby, 1960, p. 87). This Augustinian impulse recognizes that knowledge is colored by desire and that the self is always already embedded in cultural and linguistic narratives of the collective and individual past, and sees all rational knowledge as subject to what Augustine calls the *libido dominandi*, the lust for domination. The hermeneutics of suspicion is only a special, if dominant, case of the grounding of all epistemology on love. Too great an embrace of the hermeneutics of suspicion, however, constitutes an assault on Augustine's theory of knowledge, his notion of the human person and, correspondingly, the pedagogy appropriate to free (if contextualized) moral agents.

In articulating his understanding of knowledge, Augustine consistently maintains the fundamental unity of the true and the good. The fact that the interpretation and articulation of truth are always mediated and contingent does not relativize or foreclose the possibility of truth or render truth a narrative creation of the human intellect (*Conf.* 10.23.33; also O'Daly, 1987, pp. 178–89). For Augustine, philosophy and scripture are unified under the aegis of truth.[3] As an aspect of human cognition, truth signifies an adequacy of our understanding of the things themselves. As the scriptural name of the Son, truth is an aspect of the Divine which signifies a certain transparency of being, despite the opaqueness of human cognition (*Trin.* 6.11; *ord.* 2.19). In both its philosophical and scriptural aspects, truth, for Augustine, is begotten not made, though we struggle in words to articulate and understand the world as we encounter it (*lib. arb.* 2.38; Augustine's *De magistro* treats the topic extensively). In holding that the 'linguistic turn' contextualizes both the self and truth itself (*WMS*, pp. 27ff; *TST*, pp. 425ff.), Milbank has separated good from truth and, in so doing, eliminates truth (an inversion of Enlightenment philosophy's separation of truth from good, which eliminates the good).

A more consistent appropriation of Augustine's own engagement with philosophy would grant a greater (if still measured) degree of autonomy to human reason. Augustine famously makes use of 'pagan' wisdom insofar as it accords with truth, just as the Israelites appropriated Egyptian wealth as they embarked upon their own pilgrimage (*doc. christ.* 2.40.60), and never abandons his conjoint appeal to reason and the authority of scripture (*ep.* 23.7, *ep.* 93). Moreover, he often reaffirmed his debt to Platonic philosophy and philosophy's completion in Christianity (*Conf.* 7.24; *ep.* 118.17). In arguing that it is impossible to articulate a reified Christianity while at the same time trying to purify Christianity of its 'secular' accretions, Radical Orthodoxy betrays a fundamental logical weakness. The attempt to theologize the linguistic turn notwithstanding, Radical Orthodoxy appropriates a host of non-Christian philosophical material (by what consistent measure can Milbank criticize Reinhold Niebuhr's borrowings from Stoicism yet justify his own appropriation of, say, Derrida?). Augustine's reservations are not about pagan (or 'secular') philosophy *per se* but about the object and mode of intellectual love – the soul's gaze is rightly directed toward truth and God in an attitude of worshipful humility (*beata vita* 10, *Serm.* 150.4, *civ.* 8.8, *Trin.* 13.7–12).[4]

What Augustine observes as the fundamental human desire to know – our thirst for truth (*Serm.* 306.9) – cannot be understood as a mere 'desperate device' masking the linguistic construction of reality (*WMS*, p. 27). The desire for God is not a linguistic construction, however halting and conditional our attempts to articulate that desire may be. Augustine understands the desire to know as both an empirical and moral commitment to an ever more adequate apprehension of things. For Augustine, the intellect (*intellectus, ratio superior*, or *sapientia* – the 'mind at worship' [Burnaby, 1960, p. 155]) is the power of inner sight which judges the data of sensory perception according to their likeness to intellectual forms (*Jo. ev.* 15.19–20; *Trin.* 15.10.17; *div. quaest. 83* 46; *civ.* 11.10.; Breyfogle, 1999a, 452–4; O'Daly, 1987, pp. 189–99). To see truth is to learn to see truly 'in some sort of incorporeal light' the divine light; to abandon truth as a merely linguistic construction is to deny grace and defy the ordered intelligibility of divine creation (*lib. arb.* 2.9.26, *Trin.* 9.6.9, 14.15.21; O'Daly, 1987, pp. 204–7).

Augustine's illuminationist theory of knowledge is grounded in an intelligible rational order; one cannot retain Augustine's illumination theory while denying the metaphysical understanding of truth on which it is based. Yet a recognition of the indeterminacy of language need not abolish truth altogether. Augustine recognizes quite acutely that no single sign, or constellation of signs, can exhaust the reality of the thing it is intended to signify; words mislead, obscure and reify at the same time they disclose a thing's intelligible reality. Augustine's is not a definitional correspondence theory of language, and the rejection of the correspondence theory of truth does not require rejecting Augustine's belief that we can have a *qualified* apprehension of things as they are.[5] Augustine would fault Radical Orthodoxy for transposing indeterminacy from epistemology (the realm of knowing) to metaphysics (the realm of being).

The contextualization of truth substantially erodes Augustine's notion of the human person – a rational being made in God's image and participating intelligently in the divine order of things. For Augustine, the contextual self is not the determined self. Though subject to language, culture and history, the human person is always his own agent fundamentally responsible for his own actions, responding freely and intelligently to the situation in which he finds himself as an initial (and culpable) cause, not as the victim of an external efficient cause (*c. Jul.* 1.101 with *Retr.* 1.22; *civ.* 14.6, 14.9, 14.13). Significantly, Augustine speaks not of the self but of the soul, and particularly of the rational soul (O'Daly, 1987, pp. 7ff.). To speak of a 'soul' rather than a 'self' is to recognize a spiritual singularity (an individual in the strict sense, distinct from a species) defined primarily in reference to God.[6] The soul's moral autonomy (understood as free action and consequent responsibility) need not be reduced to mere unfettered, selfish individualism. Augustine sees the human person as acting out his loves, formed in the tension between intellect and will, neither of which is primary (Burnaby, 1960, p. 81). 'My love is my weight,' Augustine writes; the soul is carried in the direction of its love (*Conf.* 13.9; *ep.* 55.10). To historicize the human person and to view the rational soul as contextually *determined* wrongly subordinates intellect to will, undermining the human person's moral freedom and precluding the possibility of rational persuasion.[7]

Philosophy is, then, for Augustine, the love of wisdom (knowledge plus judgement) directed toward understanding both one's soul and God, its origin and end (*ord.* 2.18.47). Interpretation and dialectical reason are not merely intellectual but spiritual exercises which always include a moral component and in which the rational soul grows in its understanding and participation in the divine order (*Conf.* 12.30–32).[8] Radical Orthodoxy's critique of philosophy ignores the spiritual dimension of antique philosophy (including Socratic dialectics) both by letting Enlightenment philosophy stand for philosophy as such and by viewing antique philosophy through an Enlightenment lens (for example, *TST*, pp. 262–3). The rejection of dialectics in favor of rhetoric has profound pedagogical and political consequences, for each employs quite different attitudes toward the human person.

Augustine recognized (especially in *De doctrina Christiana*) the propensity of rhetoric and narrative to be un-self-critical unless they derive from the authority of truth arrived at through dialectical reasoning and a standard of rational intelligibility. Dialectics both helps purify the soul's gaze by freeing it from false opinion and by affirming its own limits as a mode of intellectual inquiry (*Sol.* 1.6.13). Dialectics so understood is an occasion for learning from that inner *magister*; the most important things cannot be taught, only learned (*mag.* 1.1 and the fragmentary *De dialectica*). Despite Augustine's rhetorical sophistication, his major works exhibit a fundamentally dialectical movement which aims not at proof but to bring hearers and readers to the point at which truth discloses itself. Rhetoric lacks the deliberative, self-critical engagement appropriate to the formation of persons who think, love and worship freely; the abuse of rhetoric, Augustine saw (especially in *civ.* 1–5), risks the worst forms of coercion and political ideology. Much of the *City of God* is an exposure of the earthly city's own propensity to use rhetoric to deceive others and itself; Rome, no less than our own age, witnessed the deadly tyranny of regimes that sacrificed dialectical truth to rhetorical enthusiasm. Dialectics, more than rhetoric, is bound by the principle of justice – rendering unto each what is due – because it aims not just at persuasion but at persuasion by doing justice to the truth (*civ.* 4.2.3; *dial.* 1.7–8; *doc. christ.* 2.31–2.34).

The unit of Augustinian political analysis is the spiritual love of the individual soul. To reject the possibility even of a minimal universal truth which can be apprehended by human beings apart from Christian revelation is to deny the rational structure of the created order and man's participation in it.[9] Moreover, such a rejection reduces politics to competing rhetorical formulations and factions, and pits demagogue against demagogue in a scramble to place both rhetoric and coercive force firmly in the service of the *libido dominandi*. Radical Orthodoxy over-radicalizes the effects of the Fall in maintaining that language and culture outweigh our participation in God; and it under-radicalizes the effects of the Fall in immanentizing ontological harmony.

The effect of Radical Orthodoxy's approach to epistemology and the self is to undermine, rather than champion, Augustine's insistence on truth, the human person, and the political pedagogy appropriate to rational beings made in the image of God.

History and Ontology

Augustine would find in Radical Orthodoxy a double confusion: in the realm of epistemology, Radical Orthodoxy emphasizes the priority of history over ontology; in the realm of politics and ecclesiology, Radical Orthodoxy emphasizes the priority of ontology over history. This formulation inverts Augustine's understanding of the relation between ontology and history. Milbank's articulation of a 'Counter-Ontology' yields three major components of a Christian counter ethics, incorporating: the celebration of difference as the proper fulfillment of charity and forgiveness; the reconciliation of difference with virtue; peace as a primary reality (*TST*, p. 422; *WMS*, p. 263). Radical Orthodoxy's misconceptions about ontological peace radically and mistakenly elevate history over nature and revelation and, in so doing, render history theologically incomprehensible.

Milbank is correct to argue that Augustinian Christianity 'denies ontological necessity to sovereign rule and absolute ownership' and seeks 'to recover the concealed text of an original peaceful creation beneath the palimpsest of the negative distortion of *dominium* ... by means of forgiveness and atonement' (*TST*, p. 417). That Christianity 'can scarcely claim to have resolved' its compromise with worldly *dominium* presupposes that the compromise can be resolved in this world, something that Augustine steadfastly denies (Markus, 1970).[10] Augustine always views *dominium* simultaneously in both its historical and ontological aspect. To see Augustine's assertion of 'the ontological priority of peace over conflict' as 'firmly anchored in a narrative, a practice, and a dogmatic faith, not in universal reason' (*TST*, p. 390) fails to retain this double aspect. For Augustine, the ontological priority of peace is rationally discerned as the logical consequence of understanding conflict as a privation of peace (just as evil is a privation of good). What is discerned by faith is the salvific remedy to the privation of peace, a remedy disclosed in history through the narrative of creation, fall, redemption (recounted in the last twelve books of *City of God*).

Augustinian political theology always weaves two contradictory yet complementary narratives. The ontological priority of peace is always juxtaposed with the mysterious historical reality of violence in the two intertwined cities whose narrative undergirds Augustine's political theology (see *civ.* 15 in particular). The narrative of the Fall mediates between (and is expressed in) the two complementary narratives of ontological peace and historical violence by rendering intelligible two natures: a first nature, the perfection of original creation; and a second nature, the historical creation conditioned by original sin. The failure to distinguish between created nature and historical nature in Augustine's thought (or what Richard Hooker later called primary and secondary nature) creates considerable confusion in Radical Orthodoxy's understanding of the status of law and sovereignty. The Augustinian pilgrim lives in the necessary tension between the ontological and historical narratives; to seek a synthesis of the two, or to reduce one to the other (utopianism and nihilism respectively) is a dangerous fallacy which threatens to yield both civil and ecclesiastical imperialism. By privileging ontology over history, Milbank transposes Augustine's eschatological vision of politics into the realm of history; history fulfills eschatology rather than the other way around. It is important to recall that book 19 of *City of God* falls, by Augustine's own organization, outside of the narrative of human history (O'Donovan, 1987). The peace for which we strive is not perfected in time (*Jo. ev.* 104.1).

Politics understood as a project for progressive earthly transformation is, for Augustine, a deficiency of patience with divine providence (Markus, 1970, pp. 22–44). Radical Orthodoxy collapses ontology and history precisely because it fails to recognize history as always implicated in between ontology and eschatology. Augustine would see Radical Orthodoxy's desire to be a partner in the progressive, visible realization, in time, of the universal community as a dangerous immanentization of the eschaton (Voegelin, 1952). This danger might be ameliorated by the articulation of a counter-counter-history. Milbank notes that Nietzsche's *Genealogy of Morals* is the *City of God* written back to front. In a similar vein, Milbank's *Theology and Social Theory* is, to an extent, only the first ten books of Augustine's *City of God* – the critique of contemporary ideology (both philosophical and political) – without a scriptural and historical exegesis comparable to books 11–22. One could never be faulted for failing to match Augustine's masterpiece, but the absence of a counter-history leaves Radical Orthodoxy in a mode of critique which collapses history and ontology.

It is not the case, then, that Augustine believes that 'the realm of absolute *dominium* can progressively recede in time.' Augustine's vision may be a 'more mitigated form of resignation' to the effects of sin and the need for its regulation, but the 'bare "compromise" between competing wills' always, for Augustine, gives way to submission to divine sovereignty (*TST*, pp. 401–2). Augustine would not likely disagree that salvation from sin 'must mean "liberation" from political, economic and psychic *dominium*, and therefore from all structures belonging to the *saeculum*' (*TST*, p. 391). Yet Christian liberty, for Augustine, is meaningful precisely because it transcends and wells up within (and despite) the structures of the *saeculum*. For Augustine, the liberation wrought by Christ is a liberation from one's own desiring participation in the *dominium* of the age; it signifies a release from bondage to the *saeculum* in favor of divine service. Only a changed and liberated love can change and liberate the structures of the *saeculum*.

Augustine's consistent distinction between ontology and history reinforces with greater clarity Radical Orthodoxy's attention to harmony. Perfection is not of this world; the harmony of the soul is a tempered ordering toward eternity *in time*. In Pickstock's elegant formulation, 'harmony is not our possession, but our borrowing from eternity' (Pickstock, 1999, p. 268). In appealing to Augustine's '*musical* ontology' for a resolution of historical difference and ontological peace, Radical Orthodoxy advances an epistemological–political model of baroque harmony which admits 'the peaceful transmission of difference' in dissonance together with structure and grace (*TST*, p. 417). Augustine indeed views politics and virtue against the backdrop of a musical ontology, understood as a series of different and differing 'intensities' in which one 'must pass beyond the suppression of passion towards the rectification of desire, and a peaceful order that is pure consensus' (*TST*, p. 410). This understanding of Christian ethics transcends the compromise of reason and feeling in *phronesis* to embrace a unity of thought, feeling and being: '*Honestas* and *decorum*, therefore, approximate the ethical condition much more to an aesthetic one, and make of the instance of ethical decision a matter of *theoria* as well as *praxis* …' (*TST*, p. 413). The 'pure consensus', however, ironically smacks of the rational propositional agreement of modern procedural liberalism, as distinct from Augustine's 'concord' (*concordia*) which is only approximated in time with the coming together of hearts despite, not because of, a lack of propositional consensus.

Moreover, for Augustine, the elastic responsiveness of musical charity cannot be the realm of infinite openness and radical equality. Absolute openness is a nihilistic freedom from everything; freedom for the beautiful and the good is a freeing limitation (*civ.* 10.32). Augustine's account of harmony in *De musica* postulates a realm of infinite possibility, but does not embrace an infinite openness. Music and poetry are governed by laws and rules which cannot be transgressed (though mere slavish obedience to rules produces wooden, unvirtuosic poetic lines). Laws both restrain and direct, but can never dictate that free poetic or moral action which accords with what is beautiful or good, with what is in harmony with the divine will (*Conf.* 3.7.14; *mus.* 6).

While the ethical order may be understood as 'an aesthetic relation of the different,' ethics cannot be only a subjective apprehension (*TST*, p. 428). Aesthetic (and, with it, ethical) judgement, for Augustine, remains an act of reason which entails knowledge of individual objects and the whole into which they fit. Peace is itself an order of reason, a conformity of things 'subject to the spirit of man' who is himself subject to God (*s. Dom mont.* 1.11). The beauty of truth and wisdom intrinsic to aesthetic judgement, for Augustine, is inseparable from teleology and justice as criteria of appropriateness. Justice is both 'giving each his due' and 'the perfect ordering of all things' (*civ.* 19.4; *lib. arb.* 1.27, 1.15, 2.38). Similarly, virtue is 'the order of love' (*civ.* 15.22). The proper freedom of Augustinian virtue (as with baroque music) lies in the virtuosity of its discovery of the possibilities of a rational order and their articulation in charity – the Christian is indeed, ideally, a kind of virtuoso of the moral life. Musical ontology, for Augustine, is not merely a feature of the knowledge of truth, but a principle of justice (a subject on which Pickstock's provocative recovery of the ethics of music in Augustine's thought is strangely silent [Pickstock, 1999]). Rendering unto each what is due, and striking the appropriate note at the appropriate time, for Augustine, go hand in hand. And while the virtuosic life of virtue does not admit of dialectical resolution, the relationality of music (and poetry) for Augustine does find its resolution in *logos* or *ratio* (*Conf.* 12.28–29; *mus.* 6).

The beauty of music or a virtuosic life of charity lies in its *modus* – its ordered proportion, mediated by the one Mediator of heaven and earth. In *modus*, justice and beauty become one in love; the rationally ordered concord of different instruments in harmony have an analogy, for Augustine, in the rationally ordered concord of the different elements of the city (*civ.* 2.21, quoting Cicero). In the realm of ontology, the '"musical" harmony of infinity' may be most fittingly articulated in terms of the 'infinite series of differences' of inner-Trinitarian relations (*TST*, pp. 422–3, following Williams, 1990). But political existence is a feature of time, and in the realm of history Augustine's appeal is to the Incarnation as the mediation of harmony. In the Incarnation God becomes God with us. Whereas the Trinity is characterized by timelessness, the Incarnation embraces and discloses the possibility of harmony in the intersection of the timeless with time. The Incarnation is a reminder that the fragility of order – in the soul and the *polis* alike – requires the maintenance of both the earthly body and the *corpus mysticum*.

Viewing the temporal life of the city and the Church in terms of the Incarnation maintains the distinction between ontology and history. The marriage of Bride and Bridegroom models the pilgrim's love and the unity of the Church visible and invisible (Burnaby, 1960, p. 101). The exemplary form of truth, the '*participation* of the beautiful in the beauty of God', is the Incarnation (*TST*, pp. 426–7; *Trin.* 8.7). The Incarnation, not the Trinity, reminds us that strength is made perfect in weakness.[11] The Incarnation stands as the beacon of the soul's defiance of the material depredations of the earthly city's *libido dominandi* because it reminds us that while we take our bearings from eternity, we remain in this life always implicated in the tragedy of history.

Politics and Desire

Radical Orthodoxy strives to rearticulate our conception of politics in three related ways: first, reconceiving politics not as the limitation of violence but as the positive instantiation of an ontology of peace; second, the resacralization of the sphere of politics – the recognition of politics as a religious (especially false religious) sphere which can never be neutral (secular) with respect to the divine and to violence; third, the advocacy of a positive model of a 'complex space', a web of intermediate associations, in a hierarchical structure of subsidiarity, based upon modern theorizations of specifically Christian (if underdefined) socialism (*WMS*, pp. 268–92). The central question may be formulated in this way: how are we to form an inclusive, diverse, non-coercive polity with a substantive collective vision of human flourishing while remaining simultaneously skeptical about the epistemological foundations of that substantive collective vision? Radical Orthodoxy's answer undervalues Augustine's assessment of the earthly peace, the positive valence of law as a wellspring of Christian virtue, and the complex relationship between the Church and temporal rule.

Radical Orthodoxy's critique of the lowered horizons of modern political liberalism dismisses what Augustine sees as one of the chief accomplishments of fallen political society: peace under the rule of law. Milbank rejects both the rational artifice of modern political liberalism and the naturalness of antique politics (*TST*, p. 407). This dual rejection leaves unclear how either the origins or ends of politics are to be determined apart from subjective will (precisely what Milbank is trying to avoid). Augustine does not love the earthly city unduly, but neither does he, like Radical Orthodoxy, despise the earthly peace for being minimally the limitation of violence. The earthly peace is 'in its own kind, better than all other human good' and is to be enjoyed in this life and used for divine ends (*civ.* 15.4, 19.26, also 19.10, 19.17; *Jo. ev.* 11.13–14).[12]

The denigration of the earthly peace derives from an understanding of law as irrevocably violent: 'no return to law, to the antique compromise of inhibition of violence, remains possible' (*TST*, p. 432). This unequivocal rejection of law is simply shocking. All political foundings are indeed rooted in historical violence, but for Augustine the ideals of justice expressed in law form a counter-narrative to that of brute force. Law is not the legitimation of violence but its negation in reason and dispassionate justice. Early liberal theorists (including Hobbes and Locke) understood full well that a civil peace (understood indeed as the suspension of violence) was predicated on the fraternization of souls at peace with themselves. To insist on going beyond the 'violence of legality' and 'the arbitrary limitation of violence by violence' under-represents the significance Augustine accords to the triumph of law over vengeance (*TST*, p. 391; also *WMS*, pp. 236–7, 249).

Punishment, as distinct from vengeance, is not the 'curbing of sin by sin' for, Augustine says explicitly, it is not the return of violence for violence.[13] Coercion exercised dispassionately, in the attitude of *caritas*, is the discipline which we rightly owe to others and to God. Fidelity to community requires fidelity to truth (*epp.* 93, 211; *ep. Jo.* 10.7). The law's primary moment is directive – instructing by eliciting rational assent – and is only secondarily coercive – correcting us and enjoining punishment when we go astray (*c. litt. Petil.* 2.84.184, *Conf.* 10.37).[14] Before the law punishes wrongdoers it marks boundaries not to be transgressed and so helps direct souls in virtue. Even then, legal punishment serves as a reminder of our spiritual estrangement.

Part of Milbank's rejection of law is grounded in his contention that law is increasingly private and that the 'abstractness of law' is a mark of impersonal generality (*WMS*, p. 227). On the contrary, the whole movement of law, both theoretically and historically, is away from the violence of private, subjective will to the relative peace of a public, reasoned order – the collective rendering in *lex* of individual *ius* (for example, *lib. arb.* 1.5.; Berman, 1983). Law is abstract and general in its directive moment only, for the execution of law always requires a judge to apply it to a specific person in a specific case.

Significantly, Augustine sees the origin of law not in violence but in divine command.[15] For Augustine, all political rule is authorized by God, whose moral governance of the universe is accomplished in part through human law (a position Milbank eccentrically attributes to eighteenth-century political theology [*WMS*, p. 236]). God's authorization of all political rule is not to say that all rule is justified. Earthly rule is measured according to divine standard and the witness of revelation; the political act is always an act referred to God (O'Donovan, 1996, pp. 20–21). Divine *lex*, properly speaking, is the articulation and promulgation of what is right, just, peaceable and orderly (*ius*). Only in God are *ius* and *lex* indistinguishable; the unity of *lex* and *ius* in God is, for Augustine, the ontological root of law (*Jo. ev.* 6.25.15). To speak, as does Radical Orthodoxy, of the ontological violence of law is therefore to attribute violence to divine command.

Ultimately, Augustine views law as dependent upon the authority of reason rather than the threat of coercive force. Obedience to the law has its origins, ideally, not in the threat of violence, but in the desire for the ends expressed by the law (*div. quaest. 83* 31; *ord.* 1.2.4; *beata vita* 1.4.25; it is for this reason that St Paul can say that those who have grace have no need of the law, for they possess a right directedness which comes from within, from the law written on the heart). Law binds us, both in theory and in practice, because it is freely assented to (*ord.* 2.9.26).[16] Law enjoins a peaceful positive and negative liberty; Augustine's concise account of the law reads: first do no harm; second, do good as you are able (*civ.* 19.14). To deny legitimacy to political authority as such is to cast all political relations into the realm of pure force and so to reject the possibility of voluntary relations.

In noting the visible and invisible punishment of legal constraint and the natural order, Augustine does not make an ontological 'mistake' (*TST*, p. 419), but acknowledges the pedagogical value of a tragic historical reality. Far from denying a person's 'freedom and spiritual equality' (*TST*, p. 421), legal punishment holds all persons equally accountable for the freedom of their actions. Christianity, for Augustine, does not 'seek to reduce the sphere' of punishment's operation, but to reduce its abuse. Law and political rule are historical, artificial responses to contingent evil, though they are not themselves essentially evil. While evil has its origins in history (not ontology), law takes its bearings from eternity, not as a necessary, artificial evil but as a necessary and authorized response to evil. To imagine political rule without power is to imagine a world with no evil; law regulates the exercise of power in defense of the possibility of freedom and spiritual equality.[17] Law, for Augustine, does not produce Cain; it condemns him.

Alongside law, Augustine places the habits of virtue, yet these too Milbank understands as 'damage control' in response to the 'original conflict' of ontological evil (*WMS*, pp. 236–7). What separates Christian from pagan virtue, for Augustine, is not a different ontology (peace vs violence) but a different teleology (right worship) mediated by grace, both formally (in law) and informally (in virtue). The problem of ontological violence, for Augustine, resolves itself into the teleology of the earthy and heavenly cities and their loves (the movement of the whole of *civ.* 21–2; see O'Donovan, 1987). Without 'the virtue of worship,' Milbank rightly insists, 'there can be no other virtue' (*WMS*, p. 231). As complementary mediators of grace, law and virtue counteract rather than express the violence of evil.

Radical Orthodoxy rightly places much weight on the decentralization of temporal rule in theorizing the notion of a 'complex space' consisting of a variety of intermediary associations in the spirit of Christian socialism. That said, Radical Orthodoxy unduly conflates the soul, the household, the city and the Church, rather than preserving their distinctive scope and modes (*WMS*, pp. 268ff.; *TST*, p. 402). First, civil rule is not the rule of the household writ large.[18] For Augustine, household and city are related analogically, shaping each other reciprocally while aspiring to related but distinct ends. The formal relations of citizens to ruler are not properly, for Augustine, those of household to *paterfamilias*, neighbor to neighbor, or friend to friend.[19] Second, in making the right ordering of the city dependent upon the right ordering of the souls of its citizens, Augustine is not guilty of embracing an isolated individualism (*TST*, p. 371). *Polis* and *psyche* are mutually reinforcing reflections of aggregate loves; the spiritual and analogical relationship between *polis* and *psyche* is an expression of both individual and interpersonal ends (*civ.* 19.24). 'If there is, in such an individual, no justice,' Augustine writes, 'there certainly can be no justice in a community' (*civ.* 19.21, also, for example, *doc. christ.* 1.7).

Third, in advocating the spatial co-extension of the Church with society, Milbank conflates the respective teleologies of Augustinian earthly and heavenly cities. The good Augustinian ruler may indeed 'reduce the scope of the political' and render 'extremely hazy' the 'bounds between Church and state,' in ways that expanded the role of the Church in the public square beyond the present restrictions of the strict doctrine of the American separation of Church and state (Milbank, 1990, pp. 419, 408).[20] But it is simply not the case that 'Augustine himself implies that the Christian emperor will make the empire recede into the Church,' nor is it at all certain that 'Augustine certainly understands that salvation [*sic*!] *means* the recession of *dominium* (of the political, of "secular order")' (*TST*, pp. 419, 421). While Augustine sees the Church playing an intercessory role in civic matters, his vision of the earthly city is not the progressive replacement of civil with ecclesiastical rule as a Christian emperor increasingly 'treats his political function as an inner-ecclesial one, or as an exercise of pastoral care' (*TST*, p. 407). The Augustinian recognition of distinct (though not separate) complementary political and ecclesiastical spheres is more conducive to the notion of a complex space than is Radical Orthodoxy (Deane, 1963, pp. 172–220).

There are two fundamental tensions in Radical Orthodoxy's vision of the Church. First, it demands that the Church be pure from any ontological violence and yet advocates the use of coercion (*TST*, p. 418). Second, Radical Orthodoxy wishes to see the Church expand to embrace an infinite openness to difference while contending that the Church should be a 'community of virtue' rather than a 'community of rights' founded upon 'liberal indifference' (*WMS*, p. 154). How can the Church be rendered visible in its progressive expansion into civic life, yet remain invisible in an embrace of a virtually infinite openness to difference that makes it 'a space whose boundaries are properly ill-defined' or an institution without walls (*TST*, p. 422)? The root of this confusion is Milbank's un-Augustinian contention that the Church on earth is 'the realized heavenly city ... [or] the *telos* of the salvific process' (*TST*, p. 403).[21] By contrast, the heavenly city is formed historically (not ontologically) over and against the city of human sin; it is defined eschatologically and realized only eschatologically. Insofar as the Church, for Augustine, contains both wheat and tares and exercises its responsibility to discipline its members, it cannot embrace infinite difference or relegate institutional adherence as 'a secondary and incidental matter' (*TST*, p. 402).[22] The Church's status as a 'political' reality derives from its presence in history, not because it is the heavenly city realized on earth.

Radical Orthodoxy's account of the Church derives less from Augustine than from Rousseau in its embrace of a mythical natural peace disrupted by the contrivances of property and law.[23] Milbank's modified Aristotelian virtue ethics proceeds on the fundamentally Rousseauian premise that all acts of virtue presuppose some initial evil or deficiency. (For Augustine, not every lack is an evil though every evil is a lack.) Radical Orthodoxy's laudable prophetic call for civil excellence nonetheless sets dangerously utopian expectations for what civil associations can and should attain and, by conflating household, *psyche*, *polis* and Church, gives considerably more scope to coercion in temporal rule than Augustine himself would allow.

The dilution of Augustine's complex account of the intermixedness of the two cities leads Milbank into some perplexing contradictions: infinite openness cannot be compromised yet coercion is sometimes salutary; the earthly Church is the *telos* of the salvific process and yet has no *telos*. As the Church expands to encompass civil government, both state and Church will, it is alleged, resist the temptation to appropriate the other's sovereignty. Milbank approximates the sanguine, progressive, Pelagian spirit of John Stuart Mill rather than the Augustinian analysis of wilful and persistent human blindness.

This conflation is patently unrealistic as a practical engagement with an ever more pluralistic world, particularly in an age on the verge of renewed religious violence. The natural limits of our imperfectibility are not, for Augustine or for Niebuhr, excuses for complacency covered over by an appeal to tragedy; rather, they are the inoculations against the desire to achieve too much.[24] Milbank's politics are, simultaneously, a recapitulation of the Pelagian's vision of individual perfectionism and the Donatist's insistence on the purity of the institutional witness.

Our ability to imagine and practice a less possessive political rule depends upon the possibility of the transformation of earthly desire into divine love, a cultivation of 'the spontaneous life of creative charity' (*WMS*, p. 239). Whether we can imagine or practice a non-possessive political rule depends upon our ability to move beyond desire manifest in the *libido dominandi*. 'The law of liberty is the law of love' (*ep*. 167.6.4). 'Perfect charity is perfect justice' (*nat. et gr.* 70.84). With these two phrases, Augustine sets the standard for conceiving a non-possessive political rule. Love, in Burnaby's memorable words, 'breaks the line between the here and the hereafter, between change and the changeless, time and eternity. It is peace in conflict, contemplation in the midst of action, sight piercing through faith. For in love the divine meets the human: heaven comes to earth when Christ is born, and man rejoices in the truth' (Burnaby, 1960, p. 82).

The structure of politics follows the structure of desire – this is at the root of Augustine's considerations of politics. But the structure of desire – and so of politics – is supported by hope. Is it enough to live in anticipation of the not yet? Or does hope sustain us by subsuming and transforming our desire? Desire defers to the not yet. Love expands to fill the what is, and in so doing unites authority, order, justice and humility in charity.[25] The test of any political theology – and theological expression – is whether it yields the expansion of love beyond desire.

The Modern Predicament

Radical Orthodoxy's quarrel with modernity is both intellectual and moral. This quarrel proceeds on four fronts: (1) a return to medieval roots, especially 'to the Augustinian vision of all knowledge as divine illumination'; (2) deploying this recovered vision 'to criticise modern society, culture, politics, art, science and philosophy with unprecedented boldness'; (3) an imperative to 'rethink the tradition'; (4) an insistence that only transcendence celebrates what secularity claimed to celebrate but which it had actually ruined: 'embodied life, self-expression, sexuality, aesthetic experience, human political community' (*RO*, pp. 2–3). In the realm of thought, Radical Orthodoxy denies the pretensions of positivistic philosophy and science to account for the whole of human experience and meaning. In so doing, it rightly exposes theology's self-immolation in correlating itself to the godless theology of (late) modern natural and social science. In the realm of politics and morals, Radical Orthodoxy decries the autonomous individual and the individual's participation in the purely procedural relations of market and democratic associations. Modern liberalism, for Radical Orthodoxy, does not simply set its sights too low, it prostitutes itself irredeemably to an ontology of violence. In both the intellectual and the moral sphere, Radical Orthodoxy sees itself responding to the linguistic turn, the recognition that the inescapable mediating function of language renders all human experience and judgement unstable by subjecting experience and judgement always to interpretation.

In short, Radical Orthodoxy's baroque–aesthetic epistemology and gothic political theory refuse the reduction of intellectual and moral life to mere matter, resist modernity's consequent dismissal of the world of the spirit and transcendence, and abandon all efforts to offer either normative or procedural judgements in grounding intellectual and moral order. On the first two points, Radical Orthodoxy remains Augustinian in spirit; on the third, it parts company with Augustine and so implicates itself more deeply in the modern milieu. By denying an independent role to philosophy, evacuating politics of a natural end, and diluting charity in a solution of infinite openness, Radical Orthodoxy exposes itself to the intellectual and moral haemorrhaging of the late modern age. At stake is nothing less than an understanding of the individual person, how and what that person knows, how that knowledge is expressed in political community, and how political community itself is transcended in the worship of God.

Unlike Augustine, who acknowledges the achievements of the earthly city, Radical Orthodoxy's impatience with present arrangements fails a measure of justice in refusing to acknowledge the goods of liberalism alongside its faults. Radical Orthodoxy's rejection of political philosophy renders it incapable of adequately criticizing liberalism or giving liberalism its due, while exposing itself to the philosophical and political excesses of the postmodern will to power. For Augustine, the body politic – and Augustine's insight is especially applicable to the modern nation state – risks always being theorized as an earthly instantiation of the transcendent *corpus mysticum*. Modern secular ideology is marked not by religion's disappearance but by its metamorphosis. Radical Orthodoxy, like our present age, is preoccupied with an earthly project, with doing rather than being. A 'movement' *does*; a Church *is*.[26]

Ours is an age which has lost its bearings largely because it has lost a sense of transcendence and a vocabulary with which to articulate it.[27] Yet, if renewing a sense of transcendence is the essential and most appropriate response to our age, Radical Orthodoxy has failed to fulfill the task it itself identifies. Should not writing itself be doxological? Does Radical Orthodoxy give us either a vocabulary for articulating transcendence or a literary form from which our soul may launch into praise? Insofar as Radical Orthodoxy is neither exegetical nor liturgical in its literary form, it remains firmly implicated in the modern–postmodern morass, the thick mist of which obscures the full possibilities of an embrace of pre-modern reason as a spiritual way of life. And despite its attention to aesthetic beauty, Radical Orthodoxy's expression lacks the clarity, beauty and worshipful character that marks Augustine's work. The greatest doxological writing describes and nourishes simultaneously, as does Augustine in his *Confessions* (but by no means only there). Augustine writes always to show rather than tell, to lead the soul vicariously to the moment of realization of the intelligibility of the parts within the whole. 'The aim is not to demonstrate theological propositions,' Burnaby writes of Augustine, 'but to *show* God, to bring Him into the heart so that He may be "felt"' (Burnaby, 1960, p. 65). Despite its appreciation for aesthetic harmony, Radical Orthodoxy remains an almost singly inelegant example of didactic propositional assertion. The invocation of indeterminacy, the mimicry of postmodern instability and linguistic play, and the coy flirtations with nihilism are insufficient substitutes for simplicity, beauty and grace. In taking flight to return to God, the soul has no need for a theology burdened with footnotes.[28]

The Incarnation reminds us that the expansion of love beyond desire is an expansion of our humanity in the fullness of the *imago dei*. The fundamental question in the resurrection of political theology is not, 'What is theology?' or 'What is social theory?' but rather 'What is Man?', specifically the 'man' behind '*modern* man'.[29] This is the question Augustine's work continues to ask us to ask ourselves; it is the central unasked question of modernity and now of postmodernity.

My observations are, I hope, ultimately a defense of the Augustinian humanistic spirit – a corrective both to modernity's discontents generally (together with their postmodern expressions) and to the dangers Radical Orthodoxy in particular poses to the possibility of political philosophy. For in abandoning philosophy, Radical Orthodoxy sacrifices human reason to the will to power; in replacing politics with the Church, Radical Orthodoxy suppresses the temporal necessity of political rule and sets itself on the quixotic course of ameliorating the effects of sin and the Fall. In contrast to Radical Orthodoxy's postmodern impulses, an Augustinian response to the present age suggests a pre-modern, self-critical Christian humanism, an Erasmian reforming moderation against the budding Luthers of our age.

Radical Orthodoxy is ultimately a salutary reaction against the idols of modernity, but one which fails to forestall a precipitous slide into becoming an overreaction to modernity. In its rejection of philosophy, its recasting of politics, and its failure to free itself from disordered desire, Radical Orthodoxy abandons Augustinian moderation, and so abandons itself again to the remnant idols of the modernity it rejected. The voice crying in the wilderness protests too much and, without correction, risks becoming a further contribution to the white noise of the present, demonic age. Augustine's vision of political philosophy remains an articulation of the reality of the Incarnation and the hope of the Resurrection, both of which sound, in time, always in a minor key.

Notes

1   The final movements of *TST* and *RO* are forthright appeals to Augustine. In an early manifesto between these two works, Milbank describes his project as 'post-modern critical Augustinianism', *PA*.

2   Radical Orthodoxy's neglect of the various accounts of modernity offered by Michael Oakeshott, Leo Strauss, Eric Voegelin, Hannah Arendt, Pierre Manent and Jacques Ellul leaves it inordinately subject to the intellectual thrust of continental critical theory.

3   *div. quaest. 83* 9; *civ.* 8.1; *lib. arb.* 2.9.26, 2.13.37; on truth and the unity of the Church see *ep. Jo.* 6.10.

4   See further *Conf.* 3.4.8; *Jo. ev.* 15.19–20; *Trin.* 15.10.17; *ord.* 1.1.2, 2.18.47; *Sol.* 1.2.7.

5   Milbank's conclusions (*WMS*, pp. 90–91) are in part a consequence of a strange
    misreading of *De magistro*.
6   On the self and self-love, see Burnaby (1960), pp. 116–26 and O'Donovan (1980).
7   Hanby (1999), pp. 109–26 rightly points to the tension between intellect and will
    and its proper expression in doxology, though the political implications of this
    position (and its consistency with radical historicism) are left coyly undeveloped.
    Hanby (2003) appeared too late for me to address it properly here, but corrects
    many of Radical Orthodoxy's excesses with respect to Augustine. Milbank steps
    back from his apparent prioritizing of will over reason in *TST* when (in *WMS*, pp.
    187–8) he argues for the simultaneity of understanding and will in the receptivity
    and judgement of an image.
8   See also Pierre Hadot (1995), Martin (2000). *AW* offers important, if unaccentuated,
    correctives to Milbank though there has been little attempt to reconcile Pickstock's
    position with Milbank's earlier critique of antique philosophy. The absence, in the
    main works of Radical Orthodoxy engaged here, of more than a single passing
    reference (*WMS*, p. 51) to the seminal work of Pierre Hadot on antique philosophy
    is astonishing.
9   *WMS*, p. 251 offers a more balanced account of rhetoric than Milbank's earlier
    work.
10 For a thoughtful exposition of Milbank's position and comparison with Markus's
    work, see Hollerich (1999).
11 For example, *civ.* 10.24, 10.29, with 9.15, 9.17, 10.6, 10.19–20, 10.32. For the
    Incarnation in Augustine's thought more generally see Bonner (1984) and Gilson
    (1947).
12 For the use/enjoy distinction see *doc. christ.* 1; *civ.* 11.15 and O'Donovan (1982).
13 *TST*, p. 406. See Augustine, *ep.* 89 on the way in which law corrects evil custom;
    in *ep.* 86 he speaks of the law healing the tumour of crime 'by warning' rather than
    removing it after the fact by punishment.
14 On the restrictive, corrective and directive features of law, see also Keating (1958)
    and Brown (1964), with Breyfogle (1999b), pp. 688–90.
15 See O'Donovan and O'Donovan (1999), pp. 104–13; Deane (1963), pp. 143–7;
    more generally in Augustine, see for example *epp.* 87, 135.5.19. Retributive justice
    for Augustine is an act of God (*Simpl.* 1.2.16).
16 Law properly concerns itself with action, not with belief. See also *ST*, 1–2.91.6;
    Simon (1980), Morrison (1969) and Arendt (1954).
17 See Deane (1963), pp. 116–53; *TST*, p. 400. For the relation of rule and power see
    Oakeshott (1991), pp. 363–84; Manent (1994), pp. 178–85.
18 The passage in question comes at *civ.* 19.12. Milbank is simply incorrect in
    asserting that 'every household is now a little republic' (*TST*, p. 403). See
    O'Donovan and O'Donovan (1991), p. 112 and Breyfogle (2004).
19 See Burnaby (1960), pp. 127ff. The contrasting interpretations (focused on how to
    understand, *civ.* 19.16) of the relation of the household to the city are best
    articulated in O'Donovan (1987), p. 104 and Williams (1987), p. 64. Radical
    Orthodoxy follows Williams on this point.
20 The phrase, as is well known, though enshrined in many twentieth-century judicial
    decisions in the US, is nonetheless not a constitutional doctrine, but has its origin
    in Jefferson's letter to the Danbury Baptist Association.
21 How Milbank reconciles this idea with his ascription of no *telos* to the Church on
    p. 405 I cannot see; see also *TST*, pp. 410–11 and *WMS*, p. 154.
22 In formulating his account of the visible and invisible Church, Milbank asserts an
    interpretation of Augustine's battle against Donatism which is simply bizarre. See
    Gesta Coll. Carth. 3.261; *ep.* 265; *s. Dom. mont.* 1.20.
23 See, for example, *WMS*, pp. 241, 220; Rousseau (1997).
24 See Niebuhr (1955), pp. 27–46 for a spirited Augustinian analysis which

nonetheless does not succumb to disengaged stoicism or political Augustinianism (cf. *WMS*, pp. 233–54) and Oakeshott (1996).

25   'The Augustinian faith in its essence is at the same time adherence of the mind to supernatural truth and humble surrender of the whole man to the grace of Christ; the mind's adherence to the authority of God implies humility, but humility in its turn implies a trust in God which is itself an act of love and charity.' Gilson (1947), pp. 294ff., quoted in Burnaby (1960), p. 79.

26   The spirit of what Oakeshott calls 'rationalism in politics' infects theology as well; see Oakeshott (1991), pp. 6–42.

27   See Pieper (1999) and Voegelin (1987).

28   For reflections on the paradoxes of genre and contemporary academic theology, see Breyfogle (1996), pp. 77–81.

29   See Manent (1998).

CHAPTER 4

Aquinas, Radical Orthodoxy and the Importance of Truth

John Marenbon

Veritatem meditabitur guttur meum, et labia mea detestabuntur impium

Truth in Aquinas, by John Milbank and Catherine Pickstock, appeared in 2001.[1] I shall begin (Sections One and Two) by looking in detail at some parts of it, arguing that it offers a blatant misreading of Aquinas that ignores the ordinary canons of scholarly enquiry. In a number of his writings, however, and even in part of the one essay he wrote on his own for the book on Aquinas, Milbank advances ideas about Aquinas and his place in the history of thought that may indeed be highly questionable, but which, nonetheless, deserve to be considered in earnest, since they are initially plausible and have a currency wider than the narrow circle of the Radically Orthodox (Section Three). In particular, Milbank considers that Aquinas held a view about God and being sharply different from that which became widespread in the later Middle Ages, even among Thomists (Section Four), and he argues that Aquinas did not, as is commonly accepted, make a separation between reason and faith (Section Five). Both of these views are very important as foundations for Radical Orthodoxy. They merit examination, but, as developed by Milbank, they turn out not to be convincingly supported.

Milbank and Pickstock's failure to follow accepted procedures for discerning an author's meaning is no accident nor even, on their own terms, a failing. Their methods here give a striking illustration of the principles of Radical Orthodoxy in practice, and the failings of their work on Aquinas have wide implications for their view as a whole. I end, therefore (Section Six), by asking some larger questions about the coherence of this position.

Section One: Pickstock on Aquinas on Being and Truth

Pickstock offers what seems, at first sight, to be a close reading of some important texts from Aquinas' *De veritate* and the *Summa theologiae*. The best way to see the qualities of her work is, therefore, to look in detail at a sample of her interpretation, and the beginning of the book is as good a place as any. After some discussion about modern theories of truth, Pickstock turns to Aquinas and points out (*TA*, p. 6) that he opens his treatment of truth in *De veritate* by looking at its relation to being. She is quite correct to do so, and to add that Aquinas considers that truth and being are both 'transcendentals' and so they are 'convertible'. What Aquinas is in fact saying, though in terms unfamiliar to modern readers, is sober and straightforward. According to Aquinas (*V*, 1.3; *ST*, 1.16.2), the basic sense of 'true' is that which applies to thoughts, and the sentences that express them, when they conform to how things are, have been or will be in fact: that is to say, the sense in which 'John is writing now' is true. He also, however, considers that everything not only exists – that is to say, is a being – but that it can be called 'true' because every being is in principle knowable (*ST*, 1.16.3 resp.) and so a thought that is true in the basic sense can be formed about it. But from these comments of Aquinas Pickstock immediately draws some outlandish consequences. She tells her readers, wrongly, that

> From the very outset, then, Aquinas shows us that he does not intend to *refer* truth to being, as if it were at a kind of static speculative epistemological remove from being. Rather, he is asking about truth as a *mode of existence*. (*TA*, p. 6)

Truth is not a 'mode of existence', but rather something that any thing can be said to have precisely because it is a possible object of knowledge. And it is silly for her to go on and state that

> Truth, like Being, shatters the usual hierarchy of categorical priorities in such a way that the humblest creature equally shines with the one light of Truth as the most exalted, and is just as essentially disclosive of it. (Ibid.)

This comment does not correspond to anything Aquinas says – not surprisingly since, stripped of the dramatic language, it amounts to very little: no more, in fact, than saying that every thing that exists does indeed exist, and every true statement is true.

The danger of being bewitched by small words with supposedly big meanings – like 'Being' – becomes clear in the next paragraph, when Pickstock writes that

> Being's equal proximity to everything, whether genus or species and so forth [! – how would Pickstock continue this list?], seems to indicate a maieutic [!] or private closeness of Being to each thing, and hence of that thing to itself, so that under this aspect, all things appear to remain in quietude, distinct from one another and in some sense rather self-absorbed. (*TA*, p. 7)

From the point that what exists exists, Pickstock draws out the charming but ridiculous idea of Being with a capital 'B' sneaking up to, for instance, my toothbrush and helping it to give birth or be born (this is the meaning of 'maieutic'), with the result that (why?) my toothbrush is distinct from the tube of toothpaste and 'rather self-absorbed'. But these are not supposed to be Pickstock's own ruminations, but Aquinas', and we must ask why she attributes them to him. The only note to this paragraph refers to a page in a study by Rudi te Velde (Velde, 1995, p. 273). There is nothing there to give a textual basis to these ideas, but the reference is useful because it enables the reader to track the sequence of thought in the following paragraph.

Here Pickstock talks about a triad of Being, Life and Knowledge: living things move outwards from themselves towards 'one another and their ends', and those living things that have understanding are able to have the forms of other things within themselves. These ideas (with one exception) are taken straight from te Velde, as is the remark by which Pickstock ends the paragraph. She says that Being, Life and Knowledge

> form a circle. As a being, a thing remains in itself; as living, it opens itself through the operations of life towards others; and as *known* or knowing it returns from others to itself. (*TA*, p. 7 = Velde, 1995, p. 273, except for the two words in italics, on which see below)

The first, and least serious, problem about this discussion is that te Velde is basing himself on parts of Aquinas other than those supposedly being considered here.[2] Second, Pickstock adds to what she takes from te Velde the idea that living involves things in moving not just towards others, but to their ends: it 'concerns the Good (or teleological ends) of those things' (*TA*, p. 7). For Aquinas, however, *everything*, whether living or not, moves to its end.[3] This problem is related to the third, and most serious, one. When he talks about his triad, te Velde is emphatically *not* discussing the transcendental properties of things – properties every thing has by virtue of existing. Only some existing things are alive, and only some living things have knowledge. Pickstock tries to paper over this difference by adding to te Velde's sentence that as 'knowing' a thing 'returns from others to itself' the words 'known or' – because it is as known, or rather knowable, that every thing is true. But, of course, there is no way in which by being known, as opposed to knowing, a thing can be said to make this return.

Pickstock now momentarily takes the reader back to Being and Truth, but then immediately introduces another, unexpected idea – that of Beauty:

> In these three stages or aspects of our modus, we see the interpenetrations of Being and Truth. But, more mysteriously still, one might say that this circle traces the mediations of a further transcendental, namely, Beauty, which seems to bestow itself obliquely on each of these three stations. Beauty, because it is to do with harmony, fittingness and proportion, including that between being and knowing, is at once invisible and hyper-visible for Aquinas; it is oblique yet omnipresent. (*TA*, p. 7)

Beauty is, indeed, like Goodness and Truth, a transcendental property for Aquinas, but it is one in which he takes very little interest: he does not mention it when he discusses transcendentals in *De veritate*, and in the *Summa theologiae* he mentions it as a transcendental only in passing, in reply to an objection (*ST*, 1.5.4 ad 1).[4] Still, Pickstock would be perfectly justified in saying that, according to Aquinas, every thing is not just true but beautiful. But she wishes to make a much more intimate connection between beauty and truth. Beauty, she says, 'is to do with harmony, fittingness and proportion, *including that between being and knowing*'. And, she adds, 'insofar as Beauty is linked with desire (Beauty being defined by Thomas as that which pleases the sight), it is crucial to the outgoings or ecstases (*sic*) of the will and the Good'. Why does the proportion involved in beauty include 'that between being and knowing'? Pickstock says by way of explanation that

> when [Aquinas] speaks of a *proportio* between Being, knowledge and willing (of the Good), and not mathematical *proportionalitas* which would denote a measurable visible ratio, it is clear that Aquinas alludes to the ineffable harmony between the transcendentals, whereby in the finite world they coincide and yet are distinguished. (*TA*, p. 8)

As a footnote to this passage, she gives a (not entirely correct) translation of the one passage (*ST*, 1.5.4 ad 1, though she wrongly cites it as art. 5) in the *Summa theologiae* on beauty as a transcendental. But in this passage Aquinas says nothing about a *proportio* between Being, knowledge and willing. Rather, he says that both the goodness and the beauty of things concern their form, but – whereas the good is related to desire, and so should be seen as a final cause – beauty is related to the ability to know. Aquinas then introduces the idea of proportion to explain why we delight in seeing beautiful things. Beautiful things are justly proportioned and so they are similar to our cognitive powers, which are themselves 'ratios'. Aquinas, then, mentions both a proportion in things and a sort of proportion in our powers of cognition, but not a proportion between things (to say nothing of 'Being') and our cognitive powers. And he explicitly contrasts the way in which things are seen as an object of desire (a final cause), with how they are seen as beautiful (in respect of their formal cause). The conclusion to which Pickstock now brings this section, that for Aquinas 'every judgement of truth ... is an aesthetic judgement', is without foundation. And it would labour the point to continue the close examination of Pickstock's work. Every paragraph contains similar or worse misreadings.[5]

Section Two: Milbank in *Truth in Aquinas*

The reader may hope for something better in the chapter that follows, 'Aquinas on Vision', the only one in the book entirely by Milbank himself. Yet Milbank engages in a similar distortion of the texts. He claims that, according to Aquinas, even the natural powers of thought 'operate through participation in the uncreated and intelligible light of the divine intellect', so that

> the *intellectus* or 'higher reason' enjoys a certain very remote approximation to the divine intuition or immediate intellectual vision, which operates without recourse to discursive unfolding. Hence it enjoys some vision of the pure divine form without

matter only known to our *modus cognoscendi* as the diverse transcendentals of Being, Unity, Truth, Goodness and Beauty. By way of this vision it permits the 'lower reason' in its higher scientific aspect (as identified by Aristotle) to discern by judgement in some measure the 'simple essences' of finite substances as (literally) conveyed into the human mind by way of the senses. Concerning those essences it cannot be deceived, in such a way that here it partakes infallibly of the divine power of intuitive recognition. (*TA*, p. 22)

If what Milbank says is right, then Aquinas does not, as usually thought, explain intellectual cognition in mainly Aristotelian terms, as working by abstraction from what is sensibly perceived. Rather, the Aristotelian account would fit into a broader framework in which the 'very remote approximation' to divine intuition enjoyed by the intellect provides the foundation for our knowledge.

But what is Milbank's evidence? To support his first point, that our natural powers of thought operate through participation in the light of the divine intellect, he quotes from *ST*, 1.12.2 resp. What Aquinas says here, however, is not that our natural powers of thought operate *through* participation in the light of God's intellect, but that they *are* 'derived' from this light.[6] Aquinas is not, then, saying – as Milbank suggests – that some sort of illumination along Augustinian lines is required for individual acts of knowing, but rather that each human's intellect derives from God and bears some resemblance to God's intellect.

Milbank's next point, about the intellect enjoying 'some vision of the pure divine form without matter' is supported by a long footnote citing texts from the *Summa theologiae* and the commentary on Boethius' *De Trinitate*.[7] The passages from the *Summa* do certainly bring into prominence an aspect of Aquinas' account that is sometimes overlooked: how the role of *intellectus*, which abstracts universal forms and grasps the first principles of each branch of knowledge, provides a link between the discursive process of human reasoning and the non-discursive, immediate grasp of the truth enjoyed by angels. Yet these passages also make it clear that Aquinas, though paying lip service to Augustine's authority, is intent on avoiding any suggestion that, in this life, we gain any sort of knowledge by looking at how all things are in God. So in *ST*, 1.84.5, he answers in the affirmative the question, 'Does the intellective soul cognize material things in their eternal reasons [which are in God]?', apparently because he does not wish to contradict completely the passage from Augustine given as the *sed contra*. But in his reply, Aquinas draws a distinction between two senses of 'I know *x* in *y*'. In Sense 1, *y* is the object known – as when I know a face by seeing it in a mirror. In Sense 2, *y* is the *principium cognitionis*, that which enables the cognition – as when I see a building in the sun (which I would be unable to see if it were dark). Aquinas then explains that in this life we do not see things in their eternal reasons in Sense 1, but rather in Sense 2, because our intellectual light is 'a certain participated likeness of the uncreated light [God] in which the eternal reasons are contained'.[8] Aquinas therefore explicitly rules out the interpretation advanced by Milbank (*TA*, p. 118, n. 8), according to which 'participation in the divine light must amount to' 'participation in divine intuition'. Milbank himself gives an excellent summary of his general position about Aquinas' theory of knowledge in an earlier article:

> In the case of Aquinas, for reason to be reason, it must aspire to the complete knowledge of the beatific vision, yet such aspiration, as exceeding finite nature, must somehow receive some dim glimpse of that vision in advance if it is recognized as a possibility. Reason ascending, therefore, is an inchoate and relatively non-discursive anticipation of the final end, and in consequence reason ascending is already grace descending. (Hemming, 2000, p. 35)

The analysis fits neatly with Milbank's claim (see below) that Aquinas' thought is entirely theological and has no place for philosophy. The problem is that it simply does not fit with Aquinas' texts. In the earlier article Milbank wisely offers no references in support of his view. And when he does try to support it, in *TA*, he has to misrepresent the texts he cites.

I shall not try to look at the remaining chapters of *Truth in Aquinas*. It is enough to say that they are worse than the first two. They have been well discussed by Anthony Kenny.[9] On the basis of a simple misreading of Aquinas' text, the authors develop the idea that Aquinas gives special priority, among our ways of achieving knowledge, to the sense of touch. Aquinas' theory of the Eucharist is then presented from this extraordinary perspective. In the Eucharist 'the *Logos* descends into tasting' and 'such tasting itself becomes instructive of the intellect' (*TA*, p. 97). It is easy to see how this view fits with Milbank and Pickstock's wish to make Aquinas (contrary to what he everywhere holds) found human knowledge on some sort of immediate, non-discursive intuition. But, as Kenny points out, their interpretation entirely ignores the point that, on Aquinas' view, what the Christian sees and tastes in the Eucharist are the accidents of the bread and wine, whereas what Christ takes the place of in this miracle is their substance.

Section Three: Scotus and Aquinas on the Univocity of Being

Milbank developed his two, linked central contentions about Aquinas long before he collaborated with Pickstock on *Truth in Aquinas*, and they are central to the story about the history of thought on which Radical Orthodoxy is based. Radical Orthodoxy seeks to recover a tradition in theology lost, it claims, by 'modernity'. In particular, it looks to the idea of participation 'as developed by Plato and reworked by Christianity', which 'refuses any reserve of created territory, while allowing finite things their own integrity' (*RO*, p. 3). According to Milbank and his followers, this tradition was, at least in most respects, brought to its highest point of development in the 1250s and 1260s by Aquinas. Just forty years later, we are told, Duns Scotus (very much the evil genius in Radical Orthodoxy's tale) went against the main tenets of Aquinas' thought and introduced the characteristic ideas of modernity.

The contrast between Aquinas and Scotus – which Milbank considers of almost inestimable importance: 'the turning point in the destiny of the West' (*WMS*, p. 44)[10] – rests on their different theories about being. Scotus argues for the univocity of being: that is to say, that there is an element of common meaning between 'being' as used of any thing whatsoever that exists. When I say 'God is a being' and 'This lump of dirt is a being', the word 'being' has the same meaning (although qualified in different ways: God is an infinite being, whereas the dirt is a finite being). By contrast, Aquinas considers that no word describing God preserves the meaning it has when used of creatures: the only relation between the meanings is one of analogy. For Scotus, therefore, on Milbank's view, God has become one being among others, and so by the seventeenth century 'no longer is there any question of God as "most being"; rather God is simply a different type of being, infinite as opposed to finite' (*WMS*, p. 41).[11]

In the view of Radical Orthodoxy, by turning away from Aquinas' view, which sees everything from a theological perspective, Scotus and the modernity he harbingers try to 'define a zone apart from God', constructing an independent metaphysics. But, instead of safeguarding the worldliness of 'phenomena such as language, knowledge, the body, aesthetic experience, political community, friendship, etc.', as they seek to do, they end by making even that worldliness 'dissolve' (*RO*, pp. 3–4).

Section Four: Milbank on the Onto-theological Constitution of Metaphysics

Milbank's stance on Aquinas' theory of being is neither novel nor distinctive. As Milbank's own references indicate, its context is the discussion of 'onto-theology' begun by Heidegger. Heidegger was not responsible for this unwieldy neologism: that honour goes to Kant, who used the word to describe that branch of natural theology concerned with proving the existence of God through the ontological argument (*Kritik der reinen Vernunft*, A632/B660). For the later Heidegger, however, all metaphysics has an 'onto-theological' constitution.[12] There is, Heidegger considers, a fundamental difference between being and beings. Metaphysics, the subject that studies being as such, has throughout its history been occupied by this difference, without taking the step back needed to see the difference itself clearly and so – as Heidegger himself wishes to do – investigate the basis of metaphysics, which lies outside metaphysics itself. The reason why this difference has eluded our grasp lies in how being and beings are tied together. Being provides the ground for beings, but beings, as what most are, ground being (Heidegger, 1969, pp. 137–8). Heidegger spells out this idea in terms of a distinction between beings in general and a highest being (but still *a* being, not being): beings are grounded, but the highest being grounds all other beings as their cause. When metaphysics thinks about beings in general it is engaging in a logic of being (onto-logic); when it thinks about the highest being, it is engaged in theo-logic. The constitution of metaphysics is onto-theological because it requires both activities: metaphysics considers beings in general as grounded by being, and then looks to the highest being as providing the ground both for beings and for being itself. The highest being must, therefore, be its own cause (*causa sui*) and it is this which is the name, says Heidegger, for the God of philosophy – a God to whom we can neither pray nor sacrifice (Heidegger, 1969, p. 140).

Heidegger's characterization of metaphysics as onto-theological allows of no exceptions – indeed, he ends *Identity and Difference* by asking whether the onto-theological nature of metaphysics arises from the very nature of Western languages. For Heidegger, therefore, Aquinas' metaphysics, like all metaphysics, is onto-theological. But there have been various writers from the 1950s to the 1970s who have accepted much of what Heidegger had to say about onto-theology, but have argued that Aquinas' approach to being is not onto-theological.[13] More important, though, than any of them for understanding the (mostly French) background to Milbank's position is a writer who was not a Heideggerian, but a distinguished historian of medieval philosophy, Étienne Gilson. By the middle of his life, Gilson had come to the view that Aquinas was unique among philosophers because of his grasp of the notion of being. Aquinas founded his metaphysics, Gilson thought, not on essence or on entities, but on the very act of being – an insight unknown to his predecessors in the ancient and medieval world and lost by subsequent philosophers.[14] Gilson's reaction to Heidegger's discussion of being was nuanced. Strains of irony show through, but Gilson seems for the most part to feel genuine respect for Heidegger as a thinker who has made much the same, distant and arduous philosophical journey as Aquinas but who – in a way that a follower of Aquinas cannot but help find puzzling – wishes to situate the discovery of being outside metaphysics altogether (Gilson, 1962, Appendix II, pp. 365–77).

Whilst, for Gilson, Aquinas was unique in his attitude to being, by the late 1960s popular French philosophers were, though in passing, singling out Duns Scotus as the figure whose theory of univocal being changed an earlier approach which Aquinas had *shared* with his predecessors.[15] Then, in 1990, the historian of philosophy Jean-François Courtine argued in a learned and careful study that, between the time of Aquinas in the mid-thirteenth century and Suárez at the turn of the seventeenth, a fundamentally new approach to being was developed, with Scotus taking a major part in its development (Courtine, 1990). Though Courtine himself says nothing quite so crude, his history supports the idea that onto-theology characterizes, not all metaphysics, but metaphysics since the later Middle Ages, after the time of Aquinas. In the last decade, the view that metaphysics became onto-theological only with Scotus has received some powerful scholarly support. Olivier Boulnois has declared so explicitly, in an article dedicated to determining when onto-theology began (Boulnois, 1995, p. 107).[16] Géry Prouvost, in a study of different Thomisms, has also supported this conclusion (Prouvost, 1996, pp. 57–73). The recent views of the theologian and interpreter of Descartes, Jean-Luc Marion, are particularly striking. Taking his cue from Heidegger, in his earlier work Marion condemned the whole metaphysical tradition of onto-theology, Aquinas included, and sought to present a 'God without being' (Marion, 1991 [1982]). But gradually Marion came to change his view so far as Aquinas is concerned, and in 1995 he published an article examining point by point the charge of onto-theology against Aquinas and urging, in a formal retraction of his earlier views, that it does not stand (Marion, 1995, p. 33, n. 2 for the gradual change of view, and p. 65 and n. 82 for the retraction).

Milbank's interpretation of Aquinas' views on being belongs, then, to a debate conducted by respectable and learned scholars. He was certainly not the first to think along the general lines he follows, although he can claim to have reached a view about Aquinas that Marion – one of the influences on his own thinking – would come to share. Should Milbank therefore be credited, at least on this topic, with making a genuine contribution to the understanding of Aquinas, especially since he has introduced into Anglophone discussions ideas and approaches that were previously the preserve of Continental scholarship?

The answer must be negative. The reason has to do with method. Suppose – what is open to question – that Heidegger's ideas about onto-theology are a valuable piece of philosophy within the context of Heidegger's work. Nonetheless, to base an understanding of the *history* of philosophy and theology on them, or on a revision of them, is quite contrary to good historical method. Many philosophers make general, and often very sweeping, statements about the history of philosophy, and these statements may well serve a useful function within their philosophical argumentation. But their readers will sometimes be seriously misled if they take these statements as accurate accounts of how philosophers in the past really thought. Original philosophers do not always engage in the extensive, precise, detailed and dispassionate investigation of texts from the past that would enable them to reach an accurate understanding of the arguments they contain. They should not be blamed for this deficiency, for such scholarly investigation is not their job: it is the job of an historian of philosophy. When they make general statements about the past of philosophy, often philosophers might do well to put the names or general designators they use into inverted commas and talk about 'Plato', 'Aquinas' and 'Western metaphysics', for instance, rather than about Plato, Aquinas and Western metaphysics, so that it is clear to everyone that they are not making unsupportable claims about what real thinkers of the past actually thought, but advancing a hypothetical position useful for setting out their own arguments, and giving to it as a tag the name of some thinker or thinkers whose ideas perhaps had something in common with the position in question. (There may indeed be some philosophers whose arguments require that the apparently historical claims they make be genuinely historical. If their claims turn out to lack historical support, then they are most certainly blameworthy, and their arguments should be rejected. The charitable assumption to make for the present discussion is that Heidegger does not belong among them.)

Few examples of an apparently historical statement made by a philosopher are so poorly supported, if taken as history, as Heidegger's claim that all Western metaphysics has an onto-theological constitution. In his explicit treatment of the question, Heidegger offers no historical evidence whatsoever, but rather a piece of loose armchair reasoning to show why metaphysics must be onto-theological. The adapted version of Heidegger's claim advanced by Milbank and others, that from a certain time onwards (say, that of Duns Scotus) all Western metaphysics began to have an onto-theological constitution, is no better grounded. Milbank provides a few observations, simplified and/or distorted, about a few thinkers whose views, he claims, bear out his thesis; he says nothing about the thousands of thinkers who might provide counter-examples. But it is not merely that Heidegger and Milbank's claims about onto-theology are dubious history, because they have not been given the necessary backing of historical evidence. They are obviously false claims. The history of thought, as anyone knows who has studied any period of it even in a little detail, is not susceptible to such vast generalizations. Statements about all Western metaphysics, or of all metaphysics since Scotus or whoever, must either be vapid or false.

Of course, granted that Heidegger is talking about 'Western metaphysics', then perhaps he is being the profound philosopher for which his followers take him, and which perhaps he is. And why, then, is not Milbank also entitled to a supply of inverted commas, the most precious resource for philosophers too involved in the profundities of their own thought to interest themselves in what really happened in the past? Let him have them! Who will then continue to read his writings? Although Radical Orthodoxy does not involve a simple return to the past, the greater part of its exponents' concern seems to be in putting forward the views of thinkers who lived in various centuries long ago. True, the Radically Orthodox are not interested in these views merely as history. They wish to take them as their own. But, since they do not argue for them independently, they need the *authority* of those who originally, they claim, proposed them in order to support their reassertion of them. The force and appeal of Radical Orthodoxy, for those who feel them, consist in the way it allows modern Christians to believe that they are at the cutting edge of modern philosophy by accepting as gospel the claims of postmodernism, and yet also to make their own the positions of Plato, Augustine, Aquinas and others. Clothe these eminent figures in inverted commas, and Radical Orthodoxy will begin to seem very bare. 'Augustine' and 'Aquinas' do not carry any authority, and Radical Orthodoxy lacks the arguments that would make the positions represented by these labels independently convincing.[17]

Section Five: Philosophy and Theology in Aquinas

'In the most usual interpretations', writes Milbank (*TA*, p. 19), 'Aquinas is seen as espousing a sharp distinction between reason and faith, and concomitantly between philosophy and theology.' Milbank goes on to say that he will 'argue that this dualistic reading of Aquinas is false'. There is indeed good reason to endorse what Milbank says here, in the light of the historiography of scholarship on medieval philosophy, and more general considerations of historical method.

There is a certain 'separationist' approach to Aquinas (and to medieval philosophy more generally) that grew out of the neo-scholastic project of reviving medieval philosophy in order to challenge nineteenth-century philosophical movements, such as Kantianism and Hegelianism, which seemed inimical to Catholicism. It was essential to this approach that Aquinas, who was considered the medieval philosopher *par excellence*, be seen to have a *philosophy*, distinct from his theology, constructed purely rationally, without the benefit of revelation. As a result, 'separationism' has been the approach to Aquinas and other medieval philosophers favoured until recently, especially by clerics and those trained in church institutions (Marenbon, 2000, no. XVII, pp. 5–8).

Yet, as an approach to history rather than a tool in an ideological conflict, there is little to recommend separationism. Certainly, there are passages in Aquinas separationists can cite to show that Aquinas distinguishes between discussions based on revealed premises and those that are not. But Aquinas' overall project was a theological one, and any historically accurate account of Aquinas' thought must recognize that he worked as a theologian in a theology faculty. Aquinas' conception of his role as a theologian allowed an important place for individual projects that centred on the works of the ancient, non-Christian philosophers – his scrupulously detailed commentaries on Aristotle and others – or on topics posed in an avowedly philosophical manner – as in his early *De ente et essentia* and his late *De unitate intellectus*. Nonetheless, even these philosophical enterprises were part of a wider professional life as a theologian. Historians must, if they are to write about Aquinas, and not 'Aquinas', recognize this wider context, even if their guiding interests are philosophical.

These historical considerations show how well founded is Milbank's opposition to the separationists, but they do not support the positive view that he himself advocates. To simplify a long, winding, and far from clear exposition, Milbank discerns (*TA*, p. 40) a contradiction within the Aristotelian claim that metaphysics is at once an architectonic subject, laying down just an abstract ground-plan, and that it deals with being transgenerically. From the deconstruction for which, he says, this contradiction opens the way, Milbank derives the idea that God's self-knowledge 'corresponds to the transgeneric status of esse ... in a way that metaphysics ... simply cannot' (*TA*, pp. 40–41). 'It follows that', Milbank continues a little further on

> there can indeed be no secure, immanent, Aristotelian consideration of either being or substance for Aquinas, since metaphysics will not answer to the transgeneric manifestness of being ... Only God's own science, and then *sacra doctrina*, can so answer. Thus *sacra doctrina* as meta-architectonic is really only architectonic as also artisanal and bumpkin-like. (*TA*, p. 42)

One result is that 'Philosophy as metaphysics ... because of its inadequate response to its own subject-matter ... does have a tendency to be "evacuated" by *sacra doctrina*' (*TA*, p. 42).[18] Milbank, then, believes that reason and faith cannot be separated in Aquinas because, in his view, Aquinas will not grant a place for an independent philosophical metaphysics, and because both metaphysics and *sacra doctrina* are supposed somehow to be based on God's own self-knowledge. So, far from representing a sound, historically based rejection of separationism, these two ideas are even less well founded than those of the neo-scholastics and their followers. Although Aquinas' work is, as a whole, that of a theologian, he clearly articulated different aspects of it, and one of the sharp distinctions he made was between metaphysics as practised by the ancient philosophers and continued by men such as himself in their reading and interpretation of the ancient texts, and *sacra doctrina*. Milbank – against Aquinas' obvious intention – wishes to remove the distinction. Wayne Hankey has already argued forcefully against this aspect of Milbank's theory and pointed out how, by contrast, Marion manages to save Aquinas from (what he regards as) the charge of onto-theology precisely by emphasizing the contrast he makes between metaphysics and sacred doctrine (Hankey, 2001a, pp. 341–5).

Section Six: Is the Radical Orthodox Narrative True?

Might it be, however, that in the light of the more fundamental principles of Radical Orthodoxy the methods and conclusions singled out above for criticism can be vindicated, at least as the consistent working out of a coherent and plausible intellectual view?

The clearest statement by Milbank of his fundamental position is in an article written twelve years ago, before he had become leader of a movement and when he styled his position as 'postmodern critical Augustinianism' (*PA*, and Hemming, 2000, pp. 33–45). He began by declaring that

> The end of modernity ... means the end of a single system of truth based on universal reason, which tells us what reality is like ... In postmodernity there are infinitely many possible versions of truth, inseparable from particular narratives ... Outside a plot, which has its own unique, unfounded reasons, one cannot conceive how objects and subjects would be ... (*PA*, p. 225)

Surprisingly, Milbank believed that this dawning of 'postmodernity' provides a valuable opportunity for Christian theology. As he wrote later, 'back in the 1980s, I certainly saw postmodernism as a moment of opportunity for theology, because it seemed to qualify and diminish secular claims to truth' (Hemming, 2000, pp. 41–2). The modern (though not the pre-modern) 'way of securing universal reason' involved, he wrote, a 'fixed notion of the knowing subject', and 'this caused problems for theology, because an approach grounded in subjective aspiration can only precariously affirm objective values and divine transcendence' (*PA*, p. 225). But now that 'the epistemological approach from the subject is shown to be as foundationalist as pre-modern metaphysics, the latter makes a strange kind of return ...'; 'Christian theology, by contrast to nihilistic modernity ... imagines temporal process as, in its very temporality, reflecting eternity ...' Of course, as Milbank's initial remarks on postmodernity indicate, there is a price to pay for this new opportunity, and Milbank did not, at least at first, shrink from it. Christian theology has (merely) 'equal validity' to nihilistic postmodernism; it is only 'just as valid or invalid as claims about supposedly universal human needs'. The speculation of Christian theology 'is utterly unfounded, is inseparable from a narrative practice of remembering'. The return made by pre-modern metaphysics is strange indeed: it comes 'as a necessary "fiction" concerning the unseen relation of time to eternity, not as a record of "observation" of this relationship' (*PA*, p. 225).

In short, Milbank advanced the hypothesis that now, in the age of what he calls 'postmodernity', no account of the world can be correct by virtue of showing how things really are. Philosophical and theological positions are merely narratives, none more 'valid' – whatever this is supposed to mean – than another. Christians can put forward their own particular narrative, and unashamedly use pre-modern metaphysics, so long as they acknowledge that what they are saying is merely a necessary 'fiction'. All this raises an obvious question, which Milbank had the honesty to put directly in this article: 'If Christianity is just one of many possible perspectives, then why believe any of them?' Of course, no satisfactory answer emerged in the remainder of the piece. Rather, Milbank went on to talk about Christianity as a 'discourse' that is open to 'difference' and seeks a peace in which difference is acknowledged. At best, these considerations might be used to advertise Christianity as a narrative to be chosen because of the psychological satisfactions it will give. Milbank's views about the validity of an infinite number of narratives, about necessary fictions (with or without inverted commas), make it hard for him to offer any good reason why we should believe Christianity, or anything else for that matter.

Ten years later, writing another general account of his programme – now called 'Radical Orthodoxy' – Milbank tries to draw the contrast between postmodern thinking and his own position more sharply. After acknowledging the opportunity with which postmodernity had provided him, he continues:

> At the same time, I considered that its claimed exposure of the arbitrary assumptions of all discourses *itself* made the assumption of an ultimate ontological violence, an assumption which might be relativised in turn by theology (though by theology alone). The latter, I considered, might be regarded as the discourse making a wager on the possible harmony of all discourses in a universe that might be harmonised, since it rested on an ultimate harmonious source, now obscured. I noted the unfounded character of the nihilist demonstration of the truth of untruth ... I thought that ... theology might once again, as with Plato and Augustine, assert the reality of truth. (Hemming, 2000, p. 42)

What does this new position amount to? Milbank seems still to accept many of the presuppositions of postmodernism: he still regards the world in terms of multiple discourses of which theology itself is one, although a special one. He does not – and cannot, in view of his starting point – give any reason why we should choose to be led by theology, or rather his version of theology. Rather, he talks of a 'wager' and, aware that it would be at variance with his initial principles to hold out the prospect of a solid reward for those who take it up, he resorts to the idea of 'the possible harmony of all discourses', although his postmodern starting point should rule out there being any criterion to distinguish the harmony of discourses from their discord. He wishes, as he says at the end of this passage, to 'assert the reality of truth', but he has left himself no consistent way of doing so (see *RO*, pp. 1–2).

Milbank and Pickstock are left trying to pull together two quite irreconcilable lines of thinking, the one which acknowledges 'the secular demise of truth', the other which asserts 'theological truth' and seeks to give it postmodern credentials by talking about indeterminacy and interpersonal harmony, instead of about real things and their relations. It is hard to see how, in the end, their position amounts to more than fideism in the face of the unbearably nihilistic conclusions of the postmodern thinkers that, to a large extent, they uncritically accept. They talk Jekyll-like at one moment, unquestioning in their orthodoxy, the heirs to Augustine and Aquinas and to the liturgical tradition of the Catholic Church; at the next, they come out like Mr Hyde, in the jargon of postmodernity, without foundation or rational principle.

The split personality of Radical Orthodoxy helps to explain its strange treatment of Aquinas. What Radical Orthodoxy reads Aquinas himself as proposing is the orthodox, Christian view it wishes (as Dr Jekyll) to espouse. But the methods it must use to give this reading are the Hyde-like ones of postmodernism. For, although Aquinas was, indeed, an orthodox Christian thinker, his thought did not run along the lines that Milbank, Pickstock and their followers have chosen as *their* orthodoxy. He was *not* fundamentally a Platonist and, so far from trying to base human knowledge on some grasp, in this life, of God's way of knowing, he strove to give an account of our cognition in the light of his Aristotelian account of what human beings are – bodies informed by rational souls. The Aquinas of Radical Orthodoxy is a fine monument to the arbitrary power of postmodern hermeneutics: a totem, erected by Milbank and Pickstock for their own ideological purposes, which has almost nothing to do with the Aquinas of history.

Notes

1 Of the four chapters, all but Chapter 3 had been previously published.
2 Te Velde's main source is Aquinas' commentary on the *Liber de causis*, prop. 18; see Velde (1995), pp. 269–70, nn. 28–20.
3 Pickstock's note cites Velde (1995), p. 273 again – but he does not connect life with the teleological end of things – and *V*, 1.1, resp. – a text which brings up Good as a transcendental as that which *every thing* seeks, not just living things.

4   H. Pouillon (not 'Poullion' as Pickstock has it; *TA*, p. 113, n. 24) makes it very clear how incidental beauty is to Aquinas' thought: Pouillon (1946), pp. 308, 313–14.

5   I am happy to supply further detailed examples to anyone who is interested.

6   '... since the intellectual power of a creature is not the essence of God, it remains that it is a certain participated likeness of him – he who is the first intellect. And for this reason a creature's intellectual power is called an intelligible light, because it is derived from the first light: this applies to both our natural intellectual power and to any extra perfection added by grace or glorification.' (I give my own translation; the ones printed by Milbank are not wholly accurate.)

7   The passages cited from *ST* are those mentioned below and 1.79.4 c (which is about the need to posit an active intellect in each of us that abstracts universal forms) and 1.79.9.

8   Exactly the same point is made in another passage cited by Milbank: *ST*, 1.12.11 ad 3.

9   *Times Literary Supplement*, 5 October 2001, p. 14.

10   See also AW, pp. 121–31, for an even more exaggerated account along the same lines.

11   Milbank had already developed a view along these lines in *TST*, pp. 302–6.

12   Heidegger develops his notion of onto-theology in his Introduction of 1949 to his *Was ist Metaphysik?* (1929). His most important exposition of it is in *Identität und Differenz*, Chapter 2: 'Die onto-theologische Verfassung der Metaphysik'. There are a number of useful analyses of the idea (developed, in fact, in the context of examining Aquinas' relation to it): Marion (1995), pp. 34–6; Boulnois (1995), pp. 86–90; Prouvost (1996), pp. 60–65.

13   These writers include Gustav Siewerth (*Das Schicksal der Metaphysik von Thomas zu Heidegger* [1959]), Bertrand Rioux (*L'être et la vérité chez Heidegger et saint Thomas d'Aquin* [1963]) and Johannes Lotz (*Martin Heidegger und Thomas Aquin: Mensch, Zeit, Sein* [1975]). For a detailed discussion of these and other such writers, see J. D. Caputo, *Heidegger and Aquinas. An Essay on Overcoming Metaphysics* (New York: Fordham University Press, 1982), pp. 211–45. Caputo is not convinced that any of them show Aquinas' metaphysics of *esse* to be free of onto-theology, although he thinks that there is a mystical element in Aquinas that allows him to escape the charge.

14   Gilson (1962) proposes this idea most directly, first published in 1948. A different exposition of Gilson's ideas is given in his English book, *Being and Some Philosophers* (Toronto: Pontifical Institute of Mediaeval Studies, 1952, 2nd edn).

15   See J. Derrida, *L'Écriture et la différence* (Paris: Seuil, 1967), p. 216, n. 2; G. Deleuze, *Différence et répétition* (Paris: Presses Universitaires de France, 1968), pp. 52–8. Both these passages are cited by Milbank in *TST*, p. 302.

16   '... si l'on prend "ontothéologie" au sens plus précis défini par Heidegger, l'ontothéologie commence avec Duns Scot ...'.

17   Contrast the scholarly scruple and detailed learning of writers such as Courtine and Boulnois, whom superficially Milbank may seem to resemble.

18   This formulation is a softening of Milbank's claim, in *WMS*, p. 44, that for Aquinas 'the domain of metaphysics is not simply subordinate to, but completely *evacuated* by theology'. The article of which this chapter of *TA* is an adapted reprint (Milbank, 1999) is a reply to a critique by Nicholas Lash ('Where does Holy Teaching Leave Philosophy? Questions on Milbank's Aquinas', *Modern Theology*, **15** (4), October 1999, pp. 433–44) where the comment about the 'evacuation' of metaphysics is singled out for special comment (p. 433).

CHAPTER 5

Duns Scotus and Suárez at the Origins of Modernity

Richard Cross

It is a commonplace of recent 'broad-brush' intellectual histories that Heidegger's onto-theology is a central component of modernity, and that, whatever these two things (onto-theology and modernity) are, they are bad. It is often hard to get any real impression from these sorts of narratives just what onto-theology is. But there is no shortage of arguments to show why – whatever it is – it is bad. This sort of situation should perhaps lead us to a healthy exercise of the hermeneutics of suspicion. For there seems to be a pervasive reluctance to question the validity of the whole onto-theological analysis. It has become, in certain theological circles, a sort of *positum* that forms the starting point of a theological enterprise, but is not itself open to interrogation. So questioning the whole story – and the place in it of Scotus and Suárez – is what I propose to do here. I shall largely limit myself to the contributions made by John Milbank, since these appear to have assumed normative status for those of his followers who write on the topic: it is possible to find just the same account of, for example, Scotus, in the various writers of Radical Orthodoxy.[1]

The crucial feature of onto-theology in Milbank's account is, as far as I can see, that it in some sense prioritizes *being* over God: it makes being 'a possible object of knowledge which is *unproblematically comprehensible* without reference to any non-material or absolute beings'.[2] Central in the story are both Scotus and Suárez. Scotus' innovation is his theory of the univocity of being, according to which *being* is somehow common to both God and creatures. Suárez's contribution is the anticipation of a thorough-going distinction between general and special metaphysics. General metaphysics is the study of being. Special metaphysics here is a branch of a broader discipline, and it is specifically natural theology. Natural theology, then, is subordinated to the general study of being, and God is somehow restricted to the horizon of human conceptuality.

The central problem seems to be that these onto-theological features of modern thought are held to entail that being is 'a conceptual idol' (*WMS*, p. 41). The analysis raises questions that can have, in principle, both philosophical and historical answers. Does onto-theology *entail* the sorts of positions that Milbank and others claim followed from it somehow? And was it, as a matter of historical fact, understood to do so, whether explicitly or implicitly? The latter of these questions is about the complex historical development of ideas, and my guess here is that this question does not admit of any simple or straightforward answer. Clearly, *something* happened between (say) Aquinas and Christian Wolff. But the right answer is that *many* conceptual innovations occurred in this period, and perhaps that not even all of these together were sufficient for Wolff's unadulterated rationalism. On the level of the implicit causal conditions for modern metaphysics, it is not likely to be plausible to answer that there was just one fundamental shift that explains the subsequent development. As a general rule, the processes of history are almost infinitely more complex than this.

One point is clear. What Milbank, following hints in Heidegger, finds objectionable about both ontology and natural theology, as practised in the modern period, is not what Kant finds objectionable about it. For Kant, the problem is a straightforwardly philosophical one: how to derive necessary truths from contingent facts. Kant holds that, without the synthetic *a priori*, it is not possible to give an account of the claims of metaphysics. And the synthetic *a priori* is bound up with Kant's whole transcendental project. The problem is that metaphysics – the science of being and necessary truths – can apparently tell us nothing about the empirical world; indeed in so far as it attempts to do so, it simply ends up with analyses that are in conflict with those of the empirical sciences – witness for example the Leibniz–Clarke correspondence, in which Leibniz appeared to show, by reasoning from necessary truths, that Newton's empirically based science had to be false: at the time, an obviously problematic conclusion. The synthetic *a priori* is supposed to allow for the noetic structure that experience itself exhibits. We accept that certain sorts of judgment – most notably those concerning mathematics and geometry – are non-logically necessary ('non-logically' since they do not derive merely from the contents of certain concepts). From this, we can accept as plausible the view that there are other judgments that are necessary in this way too: most notably, those concerning the existence of space and time – in other words, those which ground our empirical experience.[3]

Kant's objections to traditional natural theology – what Kant called 'onto-theology', with a sense very different from Heidegger's – are linked to these insights in a very straightforward way. Logically necessary truths simply derive from concepts, and tell us nothing about extramental reality. But all natural theology (all special metaphysics) presupposes the ontological argument for God's existence, since every argument for God's existence requires for its success that the object whose existence is allegedly demonstrated exists as a matter of logical necessity.[4] (I doubt that this claim is true, since the success of, for example, a cosmological argument does not require that the object whose existence is demonstrated exists logically necessarily – witness for example Richard Swinburne's enthusiastic acceptance of a cosmological argument and equally enthusiastic rejection of God's logical necessity.[5])

Heidegger is no Kant, and his conceptual grasp of the sorts of problems that modern metaphysics raises seems far less secure. Indeed, as I shall show in a moment, it rests at the point relevant to my discussion upon a seemingly straightforward philosophical mistake. And this mistake infects most of the accounts that follow his. But let me begin by trying to pinpoint some of the features of onto-theology, as Heidegger himself understands it. Heidegger is not always the most perspicuous of writers. But one recent commentator has helpfully summarized his position in four claims that together constitute onto-theology. First, that metaphysics is an autonomous discipline whose subject is being *qua* being. Second, in order for being to be known, there must be a concept of being: more precisely, a (conceptual) *representation* of being. Third, since everything is a being, metaphysics is the science of all that is. Fourth, metaphysics is also, *derivatively*, the science of God in so far as God is the highest of all beings.[6]

As I have already indicated, the conjunction of claims such as these is felt by Milbank and others to be objectionable on the grounds that the claims make being an idol, something placed over and above God and creatures. Heidegger himself drew at least this latter conclusion. Onto-theology identifies being as the ground of all that is, whether created or uncreated (Heidegger, 1982, p. 63). This in turn means for Heidegger that there is a sense in which everything so grounded *requires* being. As he rather graphically puts it, even 'the Gods need being' (Heidegger, 1989, p. 438).

Milbank happily accepts this analysis. He contrasts Aquinas' understanding of God with that which he takes to be characteristic of modernity by noting that God, for Aquinas, is

> a principle no longer conceived as itself a representable object or being, which would depend for its foundation upon what it is supposed to found, in line with the characteristic contradiction of onto-theology. (*WMS*, p. 41)

Onto-theology, then, involves asserting that God depends for his foundation on being; and this contradicts the evident truth that God, as the creator, is supposed too to found (or cause) being.

There is on the face of it an ambiguity here, depending on whether we understand 'being' to pick out a concept, *being*, or a thing, Being. To help see what is at stake in this distinction, we can make use of some of the things that Scotus (in particular) and Suárez have to say on the subject. For Scotus gives the basic account; Suárez provides some clarifications that allow us to see just where Aquinas may stand on the question at issue. When I have discussed Scotus' view, I will return to the assessment of Heidegger and his followers. At the end, I will briefly consider Suárez and suggest what we can learn from Suárez for an understanding of Aquinas' account.

Before I examine Scotus' view, I will very briefly lay out the contours of what I take to be Aquinas' theory. I shall not diverge far from the sort of account of Aquinas that Milbank appears to want to defend, even though it is controversial.[7] Aquinas holds that our words signify (features of) things. For example, in using a word to describe God, our words really signify the relevant divine perfection, and they do so by means of our concept representing the relevant perfection (*ST*, 1.13.1 [I/i, 63]). Likewise, if we use the same word to describe a creature, the word really signifies the relevant creaturely perfection – again, by means of our concept. And, Aquinas holds, the thing signified – the perfection – is the same in each case. But for any perfection, God has that perfection in a very different way from the way in which creatures have it. God has it *per essentiam* – necessarily, as a result of the sort of thing he is – whereas creatures have it *per participationem* – by participation, in so far as they derive from God, the first cause. So the word that we use to describe God and creatures signifies the perfection in very different ways in the two cases. In Aquinas' Latin, the word has the same *res significata* – the perfection – but different *modi significandi* (*ST*, 1.13.4 [I/i, 66]). This means that the word is used *analogically* in the two cases. Although it signifies the same perfection, the way in which the perfection is possessed means that the same perfection is nevertheless somehow very different in the two cases, and thus that the sense (*ratio*) (*ST*, 1.13.4 [I/i, 66]) of the word used to signify the perfection is very different in the two cases (*ST*, 1.13.5 [I/i, 67–8]). Finally, and importantly, for Aquinas the words we use to refer to God have their primary or proper sense precisely as referred to God. The sense of the term as ascribed to creatures is merely derivative of the proper sense (*ST*, 1.13.6 [I/i, 68–9]). Hence, for God to have a perfection *per essentiam*, and for creatures to have it *per participationem*, means that both causal and predicative relations are parallel: God is the cause of the perfection, and has the perfection as it most properly should be; creatures are caused, and have the perfection in a derivative sense (see Boulnois, 1995, p. 103). It is presumably this that Milbank has in mind when he holds that *being*, for Aquinas, cannot be properly understood without theology, since the application to God is in some sense prior to the application to creatures.

Aquinas' account – according to which a word used analogically can signify one and the same perfection, through one and the same concept, despite the fact that the sense (the *ratio*) of the word is different in the various cases, has a curious consequence, one that I will return to later when considering Suárez. Basically, it means that both the perfection and the concept representing it must have, as it were, a certain intrinsic flexibility or latitude. For Aquinas claims, in effect, that one and the same concept can have different senses, and that one and the same perfection can exist in various ways corresponding to these different senses. Scotus accepts a very different account of all this. For Scotus, a concept is a sense of a word, and there is no way in which one and the same concept can have different senses. Analogous concepts are, thus, composites of more than one concept, or of a concept and some extrinsic modifier. Scotus' reason for this, which I will discuss below, is basically that his claims about concepts are necessary for us to be able to think rationally at all. Scotus thus believes that there is a sense of *ens* – and other key concepts – which is *univocal* to God and creatures: one and the same concept is ascribed to God and creatures, and in just the same way (Scotus, *Ord*. 1.3.1.1 [Vatican, III, 1–48 = *PW*, 14–33]). In some ways, this involves a massive shift from Aquinas' view. For it immediately involves denying Aquinas' claim that the primary sense of any word that can be predicated of God and creatures is the sense that applies in the case of God. For Scotus, contrariwise, the concept applies properly – that is, without qualification – to neither God nor creatures (Scotus, *Ord.* 1.3.1.1–2, nn. 38–40 [Vatican, III, 25–7 = *PW*, 24–5] and Cross, 1999, p. 38). The concept as such is a *vicious abstraction*, an abstraction that does not correspond to any real extramental property of a thing.[8] Univocal concepts are *general* terms (Scotus, *Ord.* 1.3.1.1–2, n. 57 [Vatican, III, 39 = *PW*, 26]) and general terms signify either genera or things analogous to genera. And we can learn a lot about the theory of univocity if we consider the application to genera.

Consider, for example, the genus *animal* as related to two of its species, *dog* and *cat*. Dogs and cats are animals in precisely the same sense – just as God and creatures are beings in precisely the same sense. But these claims, of course, tell us nothing about the properties had by real objects, dogs, cats, God, creatures. *Animal* and *being* are just concepts; they do not pick out any real properties of things. What is true is that dogs and cats are irreducibly different kinds of animal; God and creatures are likewise irreducibly different kinds of being. And this claim, in itself, does not tell us how, or in what way, these various things (dogs and cats, God and creatures) are different.[9]

We can put the same point a different way. In Scotus' theory, to say that things 'are' in the same sense is to tell us nothing about the things under discussion, because nothing just 'is' at all. In reality, things 'are' in as many different ways as there are kinds of thing. There is no extramental property, *being*, shared by all beings, just as there is no extramental property, *being an animal*, shared by all animals. To say that a dog, or a cat, is an animal is just a way of saying that in virtue of instantiating respectively the extramental properties of *being a dog* or *being a cat*, they fall under the concept of *being an animal*; and it is likewise with the concept of *being*. When we claim that things 'are' in the same way, we are saying no more than that they fall under the same vicious abstraction. We are not saying anything at all about the way in which they 'are' in extramental reality. For Scotus, the claim that there is any *metaphysical* purchase in the contrast between divine and creaturely predications would be completely rejected.

Thus far, of course, I have not presented a *theory*: I have merely repeated Scotus' assertion that there are some vicious abstractions under whose extension God and creatures fall. But there is a theory in Scotus, and it is a *semantic* theory: a theory of meaning, about the necessary conditions for our being able to use certain words in certain contexts. Scotus holds that a necessary condition for our being able unequivocally to use the same word to refer to different things is that the significate of the word is, or includes, a univocal concept. The arguments are well known, and I will not repeat them here. The gist of them is that we cannot successfully use a word to refer to an object unless we have some idea of the sense of the term; and we can have no idea of the sense of a term unless the significate of the term is, or includes, a univocal concept.[10]

Does this semantic theory have any ontological consequences or presuppositions? I think that it does, and we can see what it is if we consider more closely the claim that *being* and the other transcendentals are merely vicious abstractions. If 'being' does not signify a real property of something, then the fact that all things, God and creatures, fall under the extension of the concept *being* is not the result of all things sharing some extramental property. In the case at hand, the sort of commonality that Scotus has in mind is reducible to *similarity*: similarity (in the relevant respect) is the explanatorily basic feature in virtue of which the univocal term 'being' can be predicated of everything there is.[11] There is no real commonality underlying this similarity. Scotus holds that the nature of the relation between God and creatures is sufficient to explain similarity in the absence of commonness. Scotus consistently distinguishes the relation of *imitation* or *representation* from the similarity of univocity (Scotus, *Ord.*, 1.3.1.1–2, n. 56 [Vatican, III, 38–9 = *PW*, 26]). Imitation is the similarity of the creatures to their exemplar cause, their being 'measured' by it. It is asymmetrical, and (in scholastic jargon) non-mutual (real only in the creature) (Scotus, *Ord.*, 1.3.2.un., n. 297 [Vatican, III, 180]). And the exemplar cause of creatures is nothing other than the divine essence: all creatures imitate, in certain respects, the divine essence (Scotus, *Ord.*, 1.8.1.3, n. 74 [Vatican, IV, 186–7]). This suggests that Scotus' account of the extramental basis for univocity is ultimately the asymmetrical relationship of imitation. Thus we can predicate certain concepts of God and creatures ultimately because creatures imitate God in certain ways.[12]

Ontologically, this is not far removed from Aquinas' account. Aquinas claims that for a creature to participate in the divine essence is merely for the creature to be made by God to imitate him in a certain respect (*ST*, 1.14.5 ad 3 [I/i, 80]). So both thinkers are happy to claim that there is a real extramental relationship of imitation here. For Aquinas, the likeness of analogy is just the likeness of imitation. For Scotus, the univocity theory presupposes imitation. The difference is that Scotus does not build the notion of imitation into his univocity theory, which remains in itself a merely semantic theory. Thus, Scotus' theory is wholly consistent with the view that creatures somehow participate in divine attributes, or are made in the image and likeness of God. The semantic theory is wholly consistent with Scotus' constantly reiterated belief that God contains all the perfections of creatures 'in an eminent way' (see for example Scotus, *Ord.*, 1.8.1.3, n. 116 [Vatican, IV, 207–8]). Neither does Scotus' semantic theory entail that there is anything about the creaturely attributes that is not caused. Nor does it entail that there is a realm of intelligibility somehow prior to God. The difference between Scotus and Aquinas on this point thus lies in the additional work that they want their theories of religious language to do. For Aquinas it is a way of talking about the asymmetrical representation relationship that exists between creatures and God; for Scotus, it is not, even though it entails (presupposes) this relationship.

This helps us to see precisely what Milbank's misunderstanding here is. Consider the following:

Being [sc. Scotus] could be either finite or infinite, and possessed in the same simple meaning of existence when applied to either. 'Exists', in the sentence 'God exists', has therefore the same fundamental meaning (at both a logical *and a metaphysical level*) as in the sentence, 'this woman exists'. (*TST*, pp. 302–3)

There could scarcely be less equivocal evidence of Milbank's profound failure to grasp that Scotus' univocity theory is no more than a *semantic* theory, a theory about how we can use certain words in certain contexts. As I noted above, Scotus does not think that anything just *is*, in whatever sense. The theory is not supposed to be one that – like Aquinas' analogy theory on Milbank's understanding – tells us something about the relationship between God and the world. On Milbank's understanding, Aquinas' claim is that if we are to be able to use certain words in certain theological contexts, then it must be the case that God and the world are related in a particular way. Scotus' theory is neutral about this relationship claim. Instead, he claims that, if we are to be able to use certain words in certain theological contexts, then it must be the case that there are certain *concepts* under whose extension God and creatures fall. The semantic theory does not in itself include any ontological commitments: in itself, it is just to do with the extension of certain concepts that are in themselves vicious abstractions, that do not correspond to any one extramental property. There are ontological consequences, as I have tried to show; and these ontological consequences are very similar indeed to some of the claims that Aquinas wants to make with his analogy theory, as Milbank understands him.

Given that there is an underlying similarity between the views of Aquinas and Scotus, why should Scotus want to distinguish so clearly the semantic theory from the ontological? Why, in other words, should he want to reject an analogy theory of the kind proposed by Aquinas, especially given that this rejection has the consequence of making *being* a vicious abstraction? As I suggested above, Scotus believes that his univocity theory is required for any rational thought. He raises the objection specifically in relation to the disciplines of metaphysics and (revealed) theology. As both Aquinas and Scotus understand the matter, metaphysics and theology are scientific. This means, minimally, that they make extensive use of *deductive* arguments.[13] Scotus' claim is that a deductive discipline requires terms whose significates are univocal, and can be known to be univocal: it requires, in other words, concepts that are the same in intension, or have the same sense. The reason is that deductive arguments require that any word that appears repeatedly in the premisses must have just the same sense in the various premisses. More technically, deductive arguments require unambiguous middle terms, and unambiguous terms are those whose significates are univocal, the same in intension and with the same sense (Scotus, *Ord.*, 1.3.1.1–2, n. 40 [Vatican, III, 27 = *PW*, 25]; 1.8.1.3, n. 67 [Vatican, IV, 183]). Furthermore, a syllogism is supposed to yield a conclusion that can be known to be as certain as the premisses – and this condition can be met only if the middle term is univocal. This argument is fatal for Aquinas, since he believes that both metaphysics and theology are scientific; he should thus believe that there are univocal terms to serve as the middle terms in syllogisms. At the very least, he should construct a semantic theory to show how validity is preserved in the absence of univocity.

It is important to grasp that Scotus understands his argument to apply as much to revealed theology as to natural theology, and that he believes himself to have Patristic warrant for the claim that revealed theology is a deductive discipline – he believes himself, in other words, to be operating fully within the context of the tradition. Scotus holds that the Church Fathers use deductive arguments (his example is from Augustine's Trinitarian theology, but the Greek Fathers too are full of rigorously deductive arguments in both natural and revealed theology) (Scotus, *Lectura*, 1.3.1.1–2, n. 113 [Vatican, XVI, 266–7]). The argument about univocity is thus fundamentally one from authority – the authority of the Fathers' own practice of theology – and it is that anyone whose theological praxis includes deductive arguments implicitly or explicitly accepts that there are univocal concepts. As Scotus puts it, 'Masters who write of God and of those things that are known of God, observe the univocity of being in the way in which they speak, even though they deny it with their words' (Scotus, 1639, 1.3.1, n. 7, XI, 43^b, noted in Swinburne, 1993, p. 76.)

It seems to me, then, that a closer examination of Scotus' main argument actually helps us clarify the nature of Milbank's project: the exclusion of all argument from systematic theology. This would certainly explain the curious, hermetic and allusive rhetoric that Milbank and his followers adopt as their chosen discourse. It would also explain the tendency to assert positions without arguing for them. But if we think – as Aquinas and Scotus would – that this would result in the radical impoverishment of orthodox systematic theology, then we will want to resist not only Milbank's conclusion, but also the rejection of Scotus' univocity theory, irrespective of any other supposed historical consequences of the theory.

Whatever we think of the motivations behind Scotus' univocity theory, being clear on the theory itself helps us to see precisely what is at stake in the ambiguity that I identified above in the critique of being and onto-theology deriving from Heidegger. For claiming that God falls under the extension of a concept – *being* – is very different from claiming that God somehow requires Being for his existence, as it were. In general, claiming that something falls under the extension of a concept does not entail that the reality of the concept is in any sense necessary for the existence of the thing that falls under it. That there is a concept *being* may well be necessary for the truth of the *statement* 'God is'. If the issue is the truth of a statement, then we need signifiers and signification, and Scotus' view is that the word 'being' will need to signify the concept *being* for statements about God's existence to be true. But we do not need any of this for what the statement asserts to be the case. The concept *being* is in no sense necessary for God to exist. If onto-theology is that being somehow grounds the existence of God, then Scotus' claims about the concept *being* do not amount to onto-theology. Conversely, if onto-theology is that God and creatures fall under the extension of the concept *being*, then Scotus' claims do amount to onto-theology, but onto-theology does not entail that there is any sense in which being grounds God – contrary to Heidegger's mistaken suggestion.

Perhaps, it will be objected, I have not paid sufficiently close attention to what Milbank actually says about the subject. For he is usually careful to note that it is the *concept* of being that modernity – taking its lead from Scotus – idolizes. So let us consider this criticism a little more closely. According to Milbank, following Marion closely, onto-theology entails both idolizing the concept *being* (*WMS*, p. 41) and idolizing *creatures*: '[I]t is not clear that he [Marion] also acknowledges Scotus' *idolatry towards creatures*' (*WMS*, p. 44). Just like the Heideggerian claim about the priority of being, these charges seems to rest on an almost simple-minded further philosophical mistake, or pair of related mistakes. For to claim that God falls under a concept that is shared with creatures does not itself entail idolatry in the sense of worshipping a creature. One's attitude to something that falls under the extension of a concept does not *eo ipso* entail that one has the same attitude to everything that falls under the extension of that concept – in this case, one's attitude to God does not entail that one adopt the same attitude towards creatures, even granted that God and creatures fall under the extension of one and the same concept. Neither does any of this entail that one have the same attitude to the concept itself. I may be fond of Rameses the cat without being fond of his malevolent brother Felix. Equally, I can be fond of Rameses but regard affection as a wholly inappropriate attitude to take to the concept *being a cat*. I can worship infinite being without thereby being constrained to worship finite being, or the concept of *being*.

Still, despite these sorts of claim in Milbank, perhaps the real concern is more complex than this. After all, Milbank sometimes talks as if the real issue is *epistemic*: that onto-theology makes theology somehow dependent on conceptually prior *knowledge* unproblematically derived from creatures:

> [F]or Aquinas the difference of *esse* from essence in the *ens commune* of creatures, and yet its real finite occurrence only in essence, is 'read' in *entirely* theological terms as the site of the internal fracture of creatures between their own nothingness and their alien actuality which is all received from God. This means that the domain of metaphysics is not simply subordinate to, but completely *evacuated* by theology, for metaphysics refers its subject matter – 'Being' – wholesale to the first principle, God, which is the subject of another, higher science, namely God's own, only accessible to us via revelation. This is *not* a matter of mere causal referral, but of the entire being of *ens commune* and its comprehensibility. (*WMS*, p. 44)

It is worth being clear that the sort of theology relevant to the issue here is not revealed theology – which no one takes to be in any sense a part of metaphysics – but natural theology, the enterprise of demonstrating God's existence and nature from the existence and nature of the universe.[14] So the claim should be that onto-theology makes *natural* theology somehow dependent on conceptually prior knowledge unproblematically derived from creatures. I agree that Heidegger's onto-theology, in so far as it posits a natural theology, does just this. But it is surely trivially true of *any* natural theology that it is somehow dependent on conceptually prior knowledge unproblematically derived from creatures. That is just what – by definition – natural theology is. Now, it may be that the whole project of natural theology will prove to be unsuccessful. But a natural theologian, such as Aquinas, is perfectly happy with the project as just outlined. Aquinas is explicit that his proofs for God's existence – good, valid, deductive proofs that yield *knowledge* – are *not* properly part of faith, but are merely preambles to the faith (*ST*, 1.2.2 c and ad 1 [I/i, 11–12]). And they yield knowledge, as Aquinas notes, in virtue of their being based on premises that are known – premises about entities in the world, conceptually prior for us, and unproblematically derived from creatures.[15] Note further that, for Aquinas and Scotus alike, God's existence falls under the science of metaphysics. Thus, they both accept that the subject of metaphysics includes created *ens* – being – as known without revelation, and they both accept that one of the goals of metaphysics is to arrive at a certain, admittedly restrictive, knowledge of God by natural reason, unaided by any divine revelation.[16] To this extent, metaphysics includes natural theology under its description. Note too that Aquinas and Scotus both accept that the practice of theology (the science whose subject is God as known through revelation) *presupposes* the results of metaphysics.[17]

Care should be taken here. To claim that a concept is unproblematically comprehensible – which is what I am claiming for Aquinas' concept of being as derived from creatures – does not mean that it is fully comprehensible. I doubt that anyone would claim that our claims about creatures are fully understood by us, still less our claims about God. As I have already indicted, Scotus is clear that neither of these sets of claims is fully comprehensible by us. And as I have already pointed out, Aquinas himself holds that the epistemological route is the reverse of the one Milbank proposes: it is our understanding of *ens commune*, and other simple, finite concepts, that enables us to infer God's existence and nature in natural theology. What all sides in the medieval debate agree on is that concepts such as being are sufficiently clearly comprehensible to ground natural theology. Where Scotus and Aquinas would differ is in the former's claim that grounding natural theology requires univocity.

It is admittedly true that we do not need a theory of *being* in order to have a natural theology. We do need something like the notion of a substance or a cause, or perhaps a process or state of affairs, and we might feel that these notions are best explicated in terms of being. But every natural theologian needs such concepts – the only question is whether or not such concepts are analogous, and Scotus' position is that they simply cannot be – as a matter of conceptual necessity; it is not possible both that the notion of being is analogous and that metaphysics and natural theology make use of deductive arguments. Scotus thinks he is merely making explicit conditions for natural theology that everyone has to accept. He claims that thinkers who claim explicitly not to accept them are mistaken, and that implicitly they do accept these conditions. If Scotus is right, then there is in a very real sense no natural theology that is not onto-theology (in Heidegger's sense). If Scotus is right, so much the worse for thinkers who deny this. But, as I have tried to show, onto-theology simply does not entail the sorts of harmful conclusion that Milbank and others suppose.

What about revealed theology? Could there be a revealed theology that does not presuppose any prior creaturely knowledge? That there should be seems to be implied in Milbank's critique – again apparently based on a fuller treatment of the same subject in Jean-Luc Marion. Marion seems to believe that any theology that makes human concepts a necessary condition for the human reception and comprehension of divine self-communication is idolatrous.[18] In Milbank's analysis, a theory of analogy of the kind accepted by Aquinas presumably allows there to be divine self-communication without the need for any prior human concepts on the grounds that the content of the divine revelation remains intrinsically unknown. But this is incompatible with the view that theology is a science, or that deductive argument is possible in theology. Indeed, a consequence of the rigidly apophatic view implied here is that what is received in revelation is no more than a set of linguistic rules. What motivates the idolatry claim? It seems to be that God's inability to communicate to humans other than through concepts of human fashioning somehow makes God less than absolutely God, and thus misidentifies God. But it does not seem to me that making God's revelation dependent in this way threatens divine supremacy. Consider an analogous case. Suppose that God is not the direct cause of all that there is – that, in other words, occasionalism is false – and that there are genuinely causal relations between creatures. In this case, God's being the primary cause of all there is is dependent upon genuine causal relations between creatures. But it would be implausible to argue that anyone who rejects occasionalism is *ipso facto* idolatrous – although if my interpretation of Marion is correct, it would seem by analogy to be a consequence of his position. If no aspect of God's relation to the world can rely on anything other than what God has created directly, then God cannot be the creator God accepted by orthodox Christians.

The place of Suárez in all this is rather interesting. For Suárez takes a position that is clearly related to the positions both of Aquinas and Scotus, though distinct from each of these positions. Like Scotus, he holds that there is a single concept of being that is, in itself, a vicious abstraction. Like Aquinas, he denies that any such concept could count as univocal, on the grounds that the concept, as exemplified in extramental reality, is exemplified in radically different ways by God and creatures.

A considered refutation of the sorts of reading of Suárez found in the Radical Orthodox theologians has already been offered elsewhere. Robert C. Miner deals with three charges made by Milbank and Pickstock against Suárez: that he invents the distinction between general and special metaphysics; that he 'separates philosophy from theology for the sake of affirming the autonomy of philosophy' (Miner, 2001, p. 26); and that he 'reconfigures metaphysics as a science of mere possibles, abstracted from creation' (ibid., p. 27). In response to these claims, Miner notes that the distinction between general and

special metaphysics is not made, in this form, until Wolff (ibid., p. 26); that
Suárez's prioritizing of philosophy over theology is more a 'pedagogical
propaedeutic than an epistemological foundation' (ibid., p. 27); and that
possible beings are as dependent on divine creative power as actual beings (ibid,
p. 28): the last of which, incidentally, is a claim true of Scotus too (see Cross,
2001, pp. 29–31). Here, I will focus rather on the question of the way in which
being is common to God and creatures according to Suárez. Again, I hope my
remarks will be sufficient to show that Suárez would not assert that Being is
some extramental object prior to God and creatures. Suárez does, however,
provide an interesting way of making sense of what he takes to be an *aporia* in
Aquinas' account.

According to Aquinas, a word such as 'being' signifies one and the same
perfection when predicated of different sorts of thing, but does so in a different
manner in each case. Suárez, in line with many of the Spanish or so-called
'Baroque' scholastics, understands this to mean that there is a concept of being
that can be predicated of (say) God and creatures, and is in this sense common
to God and creatures alike (Suárez, *Disp. metaph.*, 2.2, nn. 8–17, I, 377–87).
This concept is the subject of metaphysics, and thus, as for Scotus, the subject
of metaphysics is a concept whose extension includes God (ibid., 1.1, nn. 26–7,
I, 230). Likewise, as for Scotus, this concept is a vicious abstraction. Suárez
puts this by claiming that the common concept is 'confused' (Suárez, *Disp.
metaph.*, 2.6, n. 7, I, 446), which means that, while the definition and extension
of the concept are clear, the concept as such does not correspond to any single
extramental feature of the world – a feature that, for example, could be really
shared by all the objects that fall under the extension of the concept.[19] Suárez
denies that the confused concept of being is univocal, since univocity for Suárez
(as perhaps for Aquinas) requires that the objects to which the concept is
ascribed instantiate the concept *in the same way* (ibid., 28.1, n. 17, IV, 235).[20]
Roughly, to use Thomist language echoed though not explicitly used by Suárez,
univocity requires not only the same *res significata* but also the same *modus
significandi*. This latter criterion is never satisfied in the case of our talk about
God. So the concept *being* is ascribed to God only analogically (ibid., 28.1, nn.
16–17, IV, 233–5).

How does all this relate to Aquinas? It seems to me that Aquinas believes that
there is a concept – indeed, an extramental perfection – that has, as it were,
different ways of being instantiated or exemplified. Although Aquinas does not
put the point this way, it seems reasonably Thomist to claim that one and the
same extramental perfection has different *modes* in different things. Aquinas
puts the point by claiming that the same perfection exists in God 'in a more
eminent mode' than in creatures (*ST*, 1.13.3 c. [I/i, 66]). As I noted above,
Aquinas holds that one and the same concept can have different senses, and one
and the same perfection can include these different senses somehow. Suárez's
doctrine seems to be one way of attempting to spell this out in more detail.
Thus, Suárez holds that the concepts of being *proper* respectively to God and
creatures include all that the bare, *common*, concept of being does, but that these

former concepts are less 'confused' and more 'precise': by means of such proper concepts, some really existing thing is 'more expressly conceived as it is in itself' (Suárez, *Disp. metaph.*, 2.6, n. 7 [I, 446]).[21] For Suárez, specific differences – the properties that distinguish species within genera such as being – are 'grades' or degrees of a form, somehow intrinsic to it: in the case of the differences of being, somehow contained within the extension of being, and somehow containing being within their intension (ibid., 2.5, nn. 5–16 [I, 429–38]). As for Aquinas, being seems to include a certain flexibility or latitude in its possible senses. For Scotus, on the other hand, the modes of being – say finite and infinite – are intrinsic to it in the sense that being cannot be exemplified without one or other of them. But they are not intrinsic in any stronger sense. Being lacks the sort of internal latitude that Aquinas and Suárez posit. One simple concept, for Scotus, includes just one sense. Thus, Scotus denies that, for example, specific differences are included under the extension of being or, equivalently, that specific differences include being in their intension (Scotus, *Ord.*, 1.3.1.3, nn. 131–6 [Vatican, III, 81–5]).

Suárez presents his view as an interpretation of Aquinas. What he is trying to achieve, I think, is a defence of Aquinas' theory of analogy. But there are nevertheless significant differences. The development of the theory operates – unlike Aquinas' – at the purely semantic level. Thus, he is concerned with concepts as signified by the words we use, and his claim is that the basic sense of being is – as Scotus holds – a vicious abstraction proper to neither God nor creatures. Suárez would, I think, regard the incursion of a metaphysical claim into this theory – such as the Thomist claim that the significate of 'being' is a perfection that is found properly in God and derivatively in creatures – as simply confused, and as failing to address the semantic issue that any theory of analogy worthy of the name needs to address. Thus, Suárez reasons that analogy is impossible without a common concept. Like Scotus, he realizes that a bare appeal to participation solves no more problems than it raises – and certainly that it does not cast any light on the relevant semantic issue. His overall solution seems less satisfactory than Scotus'. But it is important to see that the problem he is grappling with is (as it should be) fundamentally semantic. To this extent, it is metaphysically neutral or harmless.

Conclusion

Overall, I have tried to argue that Milbank's worries about onto-theology do not really stand up to scrutiny, for the simple reason that he mistakenly understands a merely semantic claim to have certain ontological consequences that it manifestly does not have. A close reading of Scotus and Suárez can help diagnose these difficulties. Scotus shows that any understanding of theology – natural or revealed – that includes a robust sense of the possibility of using reasoned argument in the discussion of divine matters must needs accept something like Scotus' theory of religious language.

Catherine Pickstock has recently cited me in support of her reading of Scotus:

> Richard Cross ... upholds the doctrine of univocity and correlates this with the approach of analytic philosophy of religion. ... These correlations are indeed coherent, and explain the distance of radical orthodoxy from analytic philosophy of religion in its dominant modes. (Pickstock, 2001, p. 414)

But in so far as Aquinas makes it clear that both metaphysics and revealed theology – *sacra doctrina* – are scientific, he is committed to just the same analytic philosophy of religion as Scotus. Pickstock, it seems, agrees with me that Scotus' claims about religious language are necessary for analytic philosophy of religion. So she should ultimately agree too that Aquinas' position – practising *scientific* metaphysics and theology without a univocity theory of religious language – is just in the final analysis incoherent, and thus unsustainable. Aquinas denies onto-theology in the sense I have been discussing here: the lesson is that he ought not, lest his whole project collapse. And if Scotus is right, much the same could be said for significant parts of the Patristic tradition too.

Notes

1 Catherine Pickstock adds some curious misunderstandings and confusions of her own: see her *AW*, pp. 121–40. I have dealt with these at length in Cross (2001), § 4, and shall not repeat my analysis. Pickstock, presumably writing before the publication of my article and other essays in the same issue of *Antonianum*, suggests that 'while the treatment [of Scotus] is to some extent controversial, it is emphatically neither eccentric nor unscholarly', optimistically adding that 'the criticisms from certain quarters in relation to Duns Scotus ... are themselves presented in an unsubstantiated fashion, to such an extent that it is sometimes difficult to understand where precisely one is supposed to be at fault' (Pickstock, 2001, pp. 411 and 415). Cross (2001) makes it abundantly clear where and how the account of Scotus is not only eccentric and (so it seems to me) unscholarly, but profoundly at fault. The issue of *Antonianum* (**76** [2001], fasc. 1) in which Cross (2001) is printed is devoted to scholarly corrections to the accounts of Scotus found in Radical Orthodoxy. Pickstock's account of Scotus' epistemology is corrected in Noone (1999) – again a piece presumably unknown to her when she wrote Pickstock (2001). A large part of what follows is based closely on sections of Cross (2001).

2 *WMS*, p. 41 (Milbank's emphasis), referring to Courtine (1990), pp. 436–57, 521–38.

3 For an excellent and well-documented introduction to some of these issues, see Gardner (1999), esp. chs 2–4. The difficulty for the Kantian project in general is in showing that *every* non-idealistic form of metaphysics is inconsistent with the hypotheses of empirical science. We need metaphysics to deal with such central concepts (for us) as *person* and *identity*. (For example, if we are to speak of me as in any sense the same person over time – albeit one who has various social relations – then we need metaphysics: the notions of both sameness and personhood are unavoidably metaphysical in this sort of context. For an excellent discussion of this

point, see Harris, 1998.) Aristotle and Aquinas are clearly committed to a metaphysical project of this sort. Scotus, in so far as he recognizes that a necessary *semantic* condition for our practice of metaphysics is that there are univocal concepts of universal extension, makes a crucial contribution to the debate, one that is itself necessary, I should judge, for any wholly successful metaphysics.

4   See Gardner (1999), pp. 240–41.

5   For the cosmological argument, see Swinburne (1991), pp. 116–32; for the denial of God's logical necessity, see Swinburne (1993), pp. 241–92.

6   Boulnois (1995), pp. 86–7, summarizing Heidegger (1992), p. 19.

7   Contrast for example the purely logical understanding of the theory defended by McInerny (1961).

8   Scotus discusses this at length in *Ord.*, 1.8.1.3, nn. 137–50 (Vatican, IV, 221–7), where he tries to show how it can be the case that 'a concept can be common without any community (*convenientia*) in the thing or in reality': *Ord.*, 1.8.1.3, n. 82 (Vatican, IV, 190).

9   Note that the analogy to an Aristotelian genus is mine; in fact, Scotus thinks (mistakenly in my view) that an Aristotelian genus does have some extramental reality prior to the reality of the species that fall under its extension, even though nothing can be an instance of a genus without too being an instance of a species: see Scotus, *Ord.*, 1.8.1.3, n. 137 (Vatican, IV, 221–2).

10 See Cross (1999), pp. 35–7. Whether or not Scotus is right is a substantive philosophical and theological question – though oddly enough not one which is given any serious discussion in any of the writers I have mentioned thus far. Perhaps the most threatening objection to Scotus' view is that it is ultimately naïve about concepts, supposing for example that there is a system of concepts that can be clearly distinguished from each other, whose contents are clear and irreducibly simple. Still, it is hard to see that this is necessarily false. After all, it does not commit Scotus to the view that our words necessarily clearly signify such concepts. Indeed, he holds very often that our words signally fail to do this. Still, even if the best guide to the sense of a word is its use (its *extension*), this does not mean that the sense of a word is reducible to its extension. Scotus supposes that there are determinate concepts, and that these concepts exhibit logical relations to each other. How well or poorly we grasp these concepts – and thus how well or poorly we understand the words whose senses are these concepts – is a different matter. Scotus is not simple-minded about this: like Aquinas, he holds that we can speak more clearly than we can understand (see for example *Ord.*, 1.22.un., passim [Vatican, V, 339–47]; note that this limitation extends not only to God-talk but to *every* claim that we make about the created world); but that we need some sort of understanding – such that our descriptions must have some conceptual content – in order to speak at all, and not just remain silent.

11 For 'similitudo univocationis', see *Ord.*, 1.3.1.1–2, n. 56 (Vatican, III, 38–9 = *PW*, 26).

12 This suggestion will not ground Scotus' general theory of univocity. But it will allow him to claim a principled foundation for the theory as applied to our talk about God.

13 For metaphysics, see Aquinas (1995), 5.4, n. 4, p. 195; Scotus (1997–), 1.1, n. 30, III, p. 27; for (revealed) theology, see *ST*, 1.1.2, 1.1.8 (I/i, 3 and 7), and the useful discussion in Jenkins (1997), ch. 2; Scotus, *Ord.*, prol.5.un.1–2, *passim* (Vatican, I, 151–237).

14 Milbank clearly suggests, in the passage just cited, that the theology he has in mind is *revealed* theology. This is certainly a mistake. Aquinas does not think that we need revelation to understand that all creatures are dependent on God, as a glance at the careful structure of *Summa contra gentiles* will show. These sorts of claim fall indisputably, for Aquinas, under the proper domain of metaphysics.

15   One kind of demonstration is 'through an effect, and is said to be a demonstration of a fact. And this is through those things which are prior for us. For since some effect is more manifest to us than its cause, we proceed through the effect to knowledge of the cause': *ST*, 1.2.2 c (I/i, 11).

16   On the subject of metaphysics, see Aquinas (1959), 5.4, nn. 3–4, pp. 194–5; for the exclusion of God from *ens commune*, see *ST*, 1–2.66.5 ad 4 (I/ii, 292); Scotus (1639), prol.3.1 (text in *PW*, pp. 10–12). On the goal of metaphysics, see Aquinas (1959), 5.4, n. 3, p. 194; Aquinas claims that God is known in metaphysics 'as the cause of all things', and 'through his effects'; Scotus, 1639, prol.3.1 (text in *PW*, pp. 11–12). Boulnois claim that, for Aquinas, 'God remains outside metaphysics', on the grounds that metaphysics does not 'start with' God's existence (1995, p. 100) is disingenuous. Metaphysics does not include God as part of its subject matter – that is, as its starting point. But God is included in metaphysics as a goal of metaphysical enquiry.

17   On the presupposition of metaphysics, see *ST*, 1.2.2 ad 1 (I/i, 11–12); for Scotus see the comments on Antonie Vos, *Johannes Duns Scotus*, Kerkhistorische Monografieën (Leiden: J. J. Groen en Zoon, 1994), in Cross (1999), pp. 154–5, n. 6. On the subject of theology, see *ST*, 1.1.7 (I/i, 6), and Scotus, *Ord.*, prol.3.un.1–3, nn. 151, 167–8, 170–71 (Vatican, I, 102, 109–14).

18   Marion has in mind the concept of being, and more specifically he understands Heidegger to be claiming that, in the tradition of onto-theology, any human talk about God depends not on there being a thing, Being, on which God factually depends, but merely on there being a *concept* of being: see Marion (1991), pp. 49–52.

19   Scotus would put the same point slightly differently, claiming that such a common concept is 'imperfect and inadequate': see *Ord.*, 1.8.1.3, n. 138 (Vatican, IV, 222).

20   Compare *ST*, 1.13.5 (I/i, 67), where it is claimed that any word describing a perfection in God fails to be univocal on the grounds that 'it leaves the thing signified (*res significata*) as unknown, and as exceeding the signification of the name'; see too *ST*, 1.4.3 (I/i, 23).

21   Suárez of course holds, like Aquinas, that God is *ens per essentiam*, whereas a creature is *ens per participationem*: see Suárez, *Disp. metaph.*, 28.1, n. 13 (IV, 200), referring to Aquinas, *Summa contra gentiles*, 3.66, n. 2413 (III, 90).

CHAPTER 6

Milbank and Modern Secularity

Neil G. Robertson

As the subtitle to John Milbank's *Theology and Social Theory* suggests, his aim, and the aim of the Radical Orthodoxy movement as a whole, is to take us 'beyond secular reason'.[1] Milbank claims that modern secularity is problematic both in itself and in its relation to Christian theology. It is problematic in itself because it is ultimately a self-destroying nihilism, an inherently unstable and impossible standpoint that results in postmodernity, itself a celebration of being as nothing or pure flux. In Milbank's view, modern secularity has the exact structure of evil; it is a turn to an independent self that is in truth, in itself and for itself, nothing. Milbank proposes as a remedy to this inner dissolution of modern subjectivity a post-postmodernism that is also the recovery of pre-modernism – a standpoint beyond secular reason. Modernity is equally problematic, for Milbank, from the perspective of Christian theology. Modernity is founded on an ontology of violence and power, in contrast to the ontology of peace that belongs to Christian orthodoxy. The efforts of modern theologians to mediate or find a place for modern secularity is in Milbank's eyes to make a pact with the devil; any allowance for modern secularity necessarily compromises the integrity and primacy of Christian theology (*WMS*, pp. 219–32).

While Milbank wants to view modernity and theology as essentially distinct, he does not see modernity as grounded independently from theology. Efforts to claim for secularity an independence from theology, even when those efforts are theologically motivated, still play into the hands of secularity by giving it an irreducible integrity and completeness. Rather, secularity is to be understood – in contrast to its own self-understanding – as inherently religious and theological. In this claim, Milbank develops the standpoint of Karl Löwith which questions 'the legitimacy of the modern age' relative to its dependence on a theological horizon of significance (Löwith, 1949).

For Milbank the religious roots of modernity are threefold. First, it has a heretical origin in late-medieval theology, particularly in Duns Scotus and Suárez, which involved a univocity of being and a voluntaristic deity (this strain is exemplified by the thought of Descartes, Hobbes and Spinoza). Second, it arises from a resurgence of pagan fate, *fortuna*, and manipulation in the Renaissance, exemplified by the thought of Machiavelli. Third, it is tied to a theodical account of political economy that is simultaneously heretical (insofar as a secular providence is invoked) and pagan (insofar as it involves violent imposition, agonistics and a historicist sensibility). Milbank's argument is that these pagan–heretical roots to modern secularity both undermine modernity's claim to legitimacy, rationality and necessity (by showing modernity to be an imposed and contingently realized *mythos*) and explain the inherently nihilistic character of modernity – that it is rooted in violence and arbitrariness as the ontologically real. What modernity reacts against in both its heretical and pagan aspects is a conception of being as a graciously effected teleology of ethically constituted practices whose source and end is a Divine and Trinitarian enfolding creativity. Milbank is here consciously building on the analysis of Alisdair MacIntyre among others (see *TST*, p. 5; MacIntyre, 1981). For MacIntyre, what destroys both the possibility of ethical community and rational morality is the break with a practical teleology that characterizes modern moral theory and perverts modern social and political life. In turning to an inward grounding of morality, moderns render impossible a stable connection of 'is' to 'ought', of nature to reason, leaving as the only 'glue' to social life external force and manipulation, and so making plausible the Nietzschean and Foucauldian account of morality as will to power (Reno, 2000, pp. 37–44).[2] The nihilism of modernity suggests to MacIntyre and Milbank the need to turn away from the modern self and its secular world, toward a received and open community that is at once divinely given and humanly enacted. Milbank's vision is of a total community that is poetically/liturgically realized, giving aesthetic shape to the Divine donation of grace. An image of this community is Dante's *Paradiso* – a community of practices and virtues living in concord and complementarity – except that Milbank would seek to loosen the substantial logic and hierarchy of Dante's vision in the direction of a realm more of difference than of distinction and subordination. With this evacuation of medieval substantial logic, Milbank raises the possibility that this paradisal community can be realized here and now; it is not, as it is for Dante, a resolution beyond the oppositions, corruptions and violence of natural life.[3] Against Milbank's purely 'positive' conception of ethical life, the moderns insist on the necessity of inherently conflicting natural interests, which is the necessary conclusion once gracious community is refused – isolated individuals can only be united in and through conflict and self-interest. Modernity is, from this point of view, simply and directly evil – at one with Dante's *Inferno* – and should as such be rejected.

To readers of contemporary philosophy and political theory, the general outline of Milbank's critique of modernity is familiar. With Nietzsche, Heidegger, Karl Löwith, Leo Strauss and Étienne Gilson (to name but a few), Milbank shares the view that modernity is nihilistic, and that this nihilism reveals a suppressed, forgotten or overlooked principle that we can now recover through a return to an older tradition or standpoint refused by modernity, but nonetheless presupposed by it. For Heidegger or Nietzsche this return was to the pre-Socratics; for Löwith, it was to the Stoics; for Strauss, to Plato; and for Gilson, to Aquinas. Milbank's own return is somewhat more complex in that he seeks a return to a whole tradition from Augustine to Aquinas, but – in the spirit of Heidegger – as hermeneutically appropriated from a postmodern standpoint that brings to light a tradition now liberated from residual paganism, substantialism and so on. Indeed all of these returns are to a pre-modernity which makes available a non-metaphysical or phenomenologically derived teleology (Robertson, 1998, 1999). For Milbank, together with the whole phenomenological tradition, the ultimate polarity is between nihilism and meaning; the 'other' to modern nihilism is a being that 'gives' meaning and is thus (by an ontological difference) beyond all subjective appropriations and reductions. In general terms, Milbank's critique of modernity is not obviously distinguishable from that of Heidegger, Strauss or Gilson.

However, while there is a shared logic or shape in these various critiques of modernity, there are significant differences. These differences reside primarily in the characterization of the principle returned to (being, nature, God) and in the corresponding account of the modern refusal or forgetting (modern metaphysics, modern political thought, modern secularity). Where these theorists agree is in the notion that the principle forgotten or refused in modernity ontologically precedes and structures the shape of the modern rejection of it. This undermines modernity's claims to integrity and independence.[4] Modernity's essential dependence is demonstrated by the self-negation of its attempt to establish itself independently of this beginning. For Heidegger, the form of the principle is a Parmenidean principle, lost sight of in the metaphysics of the being of beings, which reaches its apotheosis in modernity as technological will, and which in turn calls forth a return to the thinking of being (Heidegger, 1977, pp. 3–35, 53–112). For Strauss, this Heideggerian account is misplaced: modernity is a political phenomenon that induces nihilism by breaking with a teleologically informed nature. For Strauss, the failure of modern political philosophy – begun in Machiavelli – is made manifest in the total occlusion of the political in Heideggerian historicism, which failure then points us back to a Platonic conception of an abiding nature (Strauss, 1950, pp. 29–36; idem., 1959, pp. 9–54; idem., 1991, p. 212). For Milbank these accounts are still secular; they assume a finite immanence, and thus remain open to a postmodern deconstruction that exposes their latent nihilism or not-yet-beyond-modernity character. Modernity needs to be seen as primarily a refusal, not of being or nature, but of participatory transcendence – in short, of Christian theology. Milbank is happy to acknowledge that modernity is, as Heidegger maintains, metaphysical, or that it is, as Strauss argues, a lowering of political horizons, but more fundamental for Milbank, modernity is secular. Modernity, for Milbank, is most basically not an effort to establish a metaphysics forgetful of being or a political philosophy essentially independent of nature (it is these too); rather, the project of modernity is primarily to establish a human realm independent of Divine grace.

The different principle which Milbank puts forward – Christian and theological – together with his partial absorption of postmodernity produces a distinctive conception of meaningful life. It is not Heideggerian thinking or Straussian political philosophy, but rather liturgical *poiêsis*. Beyond these differences of approach, however, there is also an important difference of content; Heidegger and Strauss are what Peter Levine has usefully identified as Nietzschean anti-humanists, where Milbank is what Levine describes as a Wittgensteinian humanist (Levine, 1995). That is, Milbank is postmodern to this extent: he does not think there is a rise beyond historical life to an authentic grasp of being or nature beyond all the closed horizons of inauthentic humanity. Rather, Milbank builds on MacIntyre's and Charles Taylor's integration of Wittgensteinian historicism within a Heideggerian phenomenology so that there can be no encounter with the principle which is not already within language games: the principle is only knowable as enacted within a liturgical community (Taylor, 1995, pp. 61–78). For Milbank, modernity separates us, not only from the principle (the Christian God) but also from other human beings. In liturgical *praxis* alone do humanity, the world, and God come together as a meaningful, positive whole, free of dualism and opposition.

There are many questions that could be asked about the tensions and ambiguities of Milbank's position as a whole: is it postmodern or anti-postmodern? Is it humanist or anti-humanist? Is it this-worldly or other-worldly? Is it pre-modern or postmodern? Is it about presence or absence? Milbank says that his standpoint is beyond all such contraries and so is not one-sided. One thing is clear, however: he is determinedly opposed to modern secularity.[5] I want to raise some concerns relative to Milbank's account of modernity. I will argue, in opposition to Milbank, that (1) modernity has its own principle (modern self-consciousness) and integrity, and (2) rather than being heretical and pagan, modernity is a correction of the heretical and pagan tendencies of medieval, late medieval and Renaissance thought and culture.[6] While I concur with Milbank that modernity is 'theological' in its origins, I argue that, in fact, it reflects Augustinian and Chalcedonian orthodoxy. I argue for the integrity of the early modern standpoint largely in its own terms. This is not to deny that there is not a subsequent history that brings to light the limitations of the early modern nor a need to correct the self-understanding of the early moderns – especially their sense of themselves as initiating a simple break with the past and beginning anew. However, the beginning point for any reassessment of modernity must be with its self-understanding and sense of its own integrity; it is this that Milbank fails to do. My further claim is that once modernity is seen in its own terms, any simple reduction of it to nihilism as its necessary result and inner truth can no longer stand. From the beginning modernity is both a nihilism or negativity together with an inner self-overcoming of this negativity: Descartes will produce a science of the world from the nothingness of our natural efforts to know it; Hobbes will produce an ordered social life from the nothingness of our given desires and inclinations. Certainly the relation of the two sides – the negative and the positive – deepens and develops through the whole history of the classical modern period, but the fuller claim of the modern is that the deeper the power of the negative, nihilistic side, the more complete the recovery is in the positive, meaningful side.

My argument follows Milbank's account of modernity. First, I suggest that Milbank does not sufficiently distinguish the modern from the pre-modern, and in particular that he conflates the late medieval and Renaissance with the modern proper. Second, while the modern does, at least initially, break from a communitarian ethics – whether ancient or medieval – this break establishes a more stable and peaceful grounding of the political and ethical. Third, once we recognize the proper principle of modernity, Milbank's own critique of modern political economy, as heretical theodicy and agonistics which functions through an ontology of violence and power, will be revealed as misplaced. The early modern political economists provide a secular or self-enacted education which moves citizens towards a concrete spirituality reflective of Christian orthodoxy. By contrast, Milbank's apparently Christian politics and ethics are not in fact comprehensive of the difference between good and evil, but rather a Gnostic flight from evil. What makes Milbank's account of modernity compelling is that it reads back into the modern period, nineteenth- and twentieth-century 'results'. Nineteenth- and twentieth-century secularisms – liberal, Marxist and fascist – collapse the modern principle into opposing moments through a reductionist naturalism. It is to this that Milbank rightly opposes his theological recovery – but then claims to find these positions in classical modernity itself and so fails to discover the deep spirituality of the modern.

Milbank suggests in a number of places that modern thought did not begin, as traditionally conceived, with Descartes and Hobbes, but rather with figures such as Duns Scotus, Ockham, Suárez, Pierre d'Ailly, Jean Gerson and Machiavelli, who are normally thought to be late medieval or Renaissance thinkers. By turning our attention to these earlier figures, Milbank is able to claim that modernity is (a) theological in its roots and not therefore a self-grounded secularity and thus (b) 'pre-established' by a pre-modern hermeneutical shift, and so (c) inherently caught up in the confusions of the collapse of late medieval theology and Renaissance politics. Milbank's claim is that, epistemologically, modernity is founded on the univocity of being initiated by Duns Scotus and reiterated in the metaphysics of Francis Suárez. (For an effective critique of the claims of both Milbank and MacIntyre, see Miner, 2001.) This account of being stands in contrast to the Thomistic account that being is analogical and belongs properly only to God and in a secondary sense to creatures. It is Scotus' account of the univocity of being that reduces being to the being of beings and so ushers in metaphysics and secularity (*WMS*, pp. 41–50). Descartes is then simply continuing in a radicalized form these initial perversions of theology (see Milbank, 2001a, pp. 388–9, n. 44). Similarly, Hobbes is understood to be building on a late medieval shift from the Augustinian–Thomistic God, understood as the Trinitarian source of a teleologically structured creation, to God understood as unified, arbitrary will. The human image of this new theology is the pure, exclusive holder of *dominium* (as in D'Ailly and Gerson). Finally, for Milbank, what Machiavelli brings to light, alongside these heretical reconfigurings, is a resurgence and radicalizing of paganism; the world is portrayed as fate, violence and *fortuna* in contrast to Christian providence. Indeed, Milbank wants to argue that modernity is not simply a reinterpretation of Christianity, but is, rather, a violence against

Christianity. Modernity is not only ontologically premised on violence, its coming-to-be is an act of violence imposed upon an existing historical life (*TST*, p. 37).

Relative to Milbank's claims that modernity begins in the late medieval and Renaissance return to nature, and the violence and conflict endemic to that return, I argue that, by contrast, modernity – the modernity of Descartes and Hobbes – must be seen as arising out of a clear perception of the violence and instability of the late medieval and Renaissance world, and so, as a corrective, builds on the failure and despair of that culture. Milbank tends to elide the distinctions between late medieval/Renaissance and modern secularities and so loses sight of what is distinctive in modern secularity. To establish this distinctiveness in the short span of this chapter I will need to make some broad assertions about the pre-modern.

The Problematic of Late-Medieval/Renaissance Secularity

In both late medieval/Renaissance secularity and modern secularity there is a return to nature. In the former, this return is in tendency confused, unstable and violent; in the latter, it is in tendency orderly, stable and pacific. In the late Middle Ages and Renaissance, the return must be seen against an assumed background of given realities – the hierarchies of medieval culture generally. This background renders the return to nature ambiguous, and so for the late Middles Ages and Renaissance the distinction between sin and secularity is unclear. An image for this may be found in Petrarch's vexed attachment to his beloved Laura: is it his own free activity or a distraction from higher ends (Petrarch, 1985, pp. 11–19; idem., 1989)? The possibility of an independent secularity that is not sin lies in a more radical stepping back or 'disengagement', to use Charles Taylor's term, than that achieved in late medieval and Renaissance culture, so that in the modern the human is altogether beyond the hierarchy of finite teleology expounded by Aquinas and poetically figured by Dante (Taylor, 1989, pp. 143–58). There are then two 'stepping backs': the incomplete one of late medieval/Renaissance thought and the complete one of modernity.

It is important to see, however, that the source of both of these disengagements lies in medieval theology. Already in Aquinas and Dante there is a tension between the relation of the human to the hierarchy insofar as it graciously raises him to the vision of God, and the relation of the human to the hierarchy from the attained standpoint of that vision. From the latter perspective the hierarchy, from one side, does nothing to obstruct the relation of the human soul to its end in God; from the other side, relative to this absolute end, the hierarchy is found inadequate.[7] It is this insight that is the beginning point for Scotus and late medieval theology generally. In Scotus' assertion of both the unknowability of God and the univocity of being there is, as Milbank brings out, a certain stepping back of the human and the Divine from the hierarchical procession and return. An extreme statement of this is, of course, Ockham's assertion that God could have saved humanity in the form of an ass. Another example of this new standpoint is the portrayal of creation in Pico della Mirandola's *Oration on the Dignity of Man*. Pico describes the peculiar place of the human in creation, a place he suggests is not properly recognized by earlier writers:

> He lastly considered creating man. But there was nothing in the archetypes from which He could mold a new sprout, nor anything in His storehouses which He could bestow a heritage upon a new son, nor was there an empty judiciary seat where this contemplator of the universe could sit. ... Finally the best of workmen decided that that to which nothing of its very own could be given should be, in composite fashion, whatsoever had belonged individually to each and every thing. Therefore He took up man, a work of indeterminate form; and plac[ed] him at the midpoint of the world ...
> (Mirandola, 1965, p. 4)

Here is an image of the general character of late medieval/Renaissance culture. The image can take one of a variety of directions, not simply that followed by Pico: towards a more external and nominalist relation to nature, towards a mystical relation to God, towards a univocity of being, towards a divine voluntarism, towards a juridical appropriation of the world. All these positions become available when the human has been separated from and made indeterminate relative to the created order. However, what I want to bring out is the instability in this new human dignity. The problem is that, for Pico, while the human is beyond the hierarchy and free, the only content for this indeterminate being is found in returning to the hierarchy: becoming an angel or a beast. The difficulty is that no single place in the hierarchy is adequate to the human. This disjunction between freedom and content is the source of an unstable, and indeed insatiable, relation of the human to the world. We find this instability in Machiavelli's depiction of the restlessness of humans or in Marlowe's Dr Faustus' dissatisfaction with the 'orthodoxy' of the received sciences (Machiavelli, 1970, p. 200; *Doctor Faustus*, Act I, lines 1–64). If Milbank were describing only late medieval/Renaissance culture, he would be right in seeing in it both paganism and heresy, as a new kind of indeterminate humanity faces and would take hold of a given hierarchy or being that lies before it. For Pico, filled with the confidence arising from medieval culture that the created order is 'for us', there is the ambition to become an angel, and more than an angel, and at the same time to acquire a total and inward knowledge of the cosmos. However, the instability of Renaissance secularity quickly makes itself felt. The pursuit of knowledge collapses into scepticism so that, at the end of this period, Montaigne is left with 'Que sais-je?' as his motto.

Equally unstable is late medieval and Renaissance practical life. The Renaissance confidence in finding a common life dedicated to virtue and civic concord all in relation to a common good readily collapsed into the world of *raison d'état* and a belief that only Machiavellian *virtù* could realize public order and peace. As Machiavelli argues, if we can be both angels and beasts, it is foolish to assume we will be angels (*The Prince*, XV). The release of Renaissance confidence in man's freedom in the world where we discover in the finitude of a given nature the conflict and competition inherent in that freedom leads to a destructiveness that Machiavelli sees is only controllable through the same fraud and violence, but used by a public authority and exercised with *virtù*. But Montaigne, who has witnessed in the Wars of Religion the incapacity of even a Machiavellian *virtù* or *raison d'état* to bring civil peace, recognizes a *naïveté* and false assumption at work in Renaissance secularity. Machiavelli had assumed that a Prince of sufficient *virtù* and ruthlessness could mould the warring interests of the city into a public life. Here a confusion endemic to the late medieval/Renaissance form of secularity may be seen: was the Prince a public figure, subordinating his ends to the city, protecting property and women, arming the citizenry? Or was the city subordinated to the Prince's pursuit of glory, merely an instrument of his ambitions? Here is the instability of the Prince and his ambiguous relation to his populace: are they subordinated to his public authority, or are various among them endlessly seeking to wrest from him his private possession of the state? This instability, which can appear to Machiavelli to be liveable, becomes unliveable in the face of religious dissension. Montaigne brings out this collapse of Renaissance ambition:

> Among the likes of us there are two things which ever appeared to me to chime particularly well together – supercelestial opinions: subterranean morals ... They want to be beside themselves, want to escape their humanity. That *is* madness: instead of changing their Form into angels; they change into beasts; they crash down instead of winding high. (Montaigne, 1987, pp. 1267–8)

For Montaigne, the Renaissance belief – even of Machiavelli – that human ambition, whether for God or glory, could possess its object in the world is found vain and self-destructive. The late medieval/Renaissance world assumed a being or reality over against an indeterminate humanity which could attain content only in that being or reality. The course of the Renaissance was to dissolve the belief that there was such a being or reality, so that we are left with nothing. Here Marlowe's *Dr Faustus* can be seen to portray this result: Faustus, having freed himself from the hierarchical order of the sciences for a knowledge and activity adequate to his dignity, is destroyed at the conclusion of the play in the obliteration of finite temporality. It is the nihilistic conclusion to late medieval/Renaissance secular culture that Milbank fails to bring to light. Yet, without it we cannot understand the specific character of modern secularity. Both Descartes and Hobbes build upon and build into their positions the failure of pre-modern secular forms.

Descartes and Modern Philosophy

The form this correction takes in Descartes is through his radical doubt at the beginning of the *Meditations*. Here, late medieval and Renaissance scepticism is radicalized and all given or assumed being is dissolved as insufficient to provide a starting point for knowledge. The givenness of nature which remains as a residual pagan element in late medieval and Renaissance culture is here retracted. For Descartes, thought will proceed only on a self-certainty – itself grounded on the perfection of God. From this inner self-relation, thought can enter into and come to know a nature that is present for thought. Here Descartes can know from within himself what is believed through medieval theology – that through an inner and complete relation to God, humanity can enter into and know nature without relapse into a loss of self or confusion of ends. The inner self-consciousness that defines the specifically modern allows for a human knowing of all things within God, as Malebranche will later come to put it. There is not in this modern standpoint the opposition of late medieval/ Renaissance culture, of a vanishing human knowing or freedom to an equally unstable and uncertain world, whose result is scepticism, violence and nihilism. Rather, Descartes is assured through his purely inward relation to God that what he knows certainly is also true. From this point of view, nature is a totality of causes that are open to human knowing – and thus the realm of fate and *fortuna* is altogether banished (see *Meditations*, V and VI). Put to one side as inadequate is a Neoplatonic ascent of knowing to a unified standpoint beyond the division of knower and known. For Descartes, rather, the demand of certainty is to start straightway with a self-complete standpoint which then enters into the relation of knower to known, subject to object. The distinction of the natural and the supernatural, nature and grace, is overcome, at least relative to the objects proper to enlightened human subjectivity.

The consequence of Descartes' radical inwardness is that nature acquires a much more radical 'otherness' and independence. Nature cannot be known as an organic cosmos, constituted through an interlocking teleological order. Nature has become a mechanism, in which motion in the older Aristotelian sense does not occur at all: all motion is external and indifferent to place. Here occurs an evacuation of natural teleology which parallels the evacuation of ethical teleology which Milbank laments in Hobbes and modern social and political thought generally. It is tempting to read this development as an atheism that makes nature indifferent to an order of participation, and so makes it subject to technological will (Milbank, 2001a, p. 337). Indeed, though he does emphasize theological aspects of this new relation to nature, Milbank does not see it as distinguishable from a Nietzschean willing. Milbank sees the modern relation to nature as ultimately Fichtean and this, in turn, as essentially Nietzschean and postmodern (*TST*, pp. 155, 294–6; *WMS*, p. 40). Milbank reads back into Descartes this later development. For Descartes and the early moderns generally, up to the turn to 'critique' in the 1750s and later, the 'externalization' of nature as *res extensa* or mechanism does not – or does not simply – mean that nature is reducible to technological will or subjective appropriation. Seeing nature as *res extensa* brings to nature as a whole an objectivity and substantiality which is grounded in its divine foundation. What for Descartes makes nature both knowable to us and divinely secured in its objectivity is the 'idea' – binding on human rationality, nature and God.[8] As Descartes brings out in the Fifth Meditation, the whole essence of an idea (in that it is not nothing) is that it is not a construct of will, but a reality binding on thought. It is the objectivity of ideas, together with their clarity and distinctness, that allows self-consciousness to know nature in its absolute truth. This is what distinguishes modern science from the wilfulness of pre-modern claims to knowing where the distinction between the imaginary construction of the object and its independent being cannot be adequately secured. As Descartes and Hobbes argue, the Aristotelian account of motion is still anthropomorphic, a construct of imagination and not a necessary idea of thought: to grasp the principle of inertia requires a de-situating or de-contextualizing of both scientist and nature (Hobbes, 1990, p. 15). The very independence and externality of Cartesian nature is found not only in its mechanization – where the parts seem to fall away from an organic whole – but equally in a more complete unity of whole and part than could be attained in pre-modern science (see Johnston, 1991). Here there can be no play of *fortuna* or fate or a prime matter resistant to form; rather, nature is known as inwardly derived and belonging to the self. That is to say only with the moderns is nature *known* as created; its independence has been negated, and its being is seen to lie directly and radically in the divine creative power (*Meditations*, III). As Milbank notes in relation to modern social and political thought (and this is equally true of Descartes), God is understood to be present to his creation more directly than for the medievals (*TST*, p. 38). It is this immediate relation of God and the created order together with the radical unity of that order that gives rise to the centrality of theodicy in Descartes' *Meditations* and early modern thought generally (*Meditations*, IV; on the role of theodicy in Descartes, see Janowski, 2000). What is necessary to see in the deeply unified account of nature in modernity is that not only is there a release of nature into its own activity, but also there is a total unity to this activity – precisely because all is caused in a total mechanical set of relations, the rationality of the whole is present in each of the parts and not although, but because those parts are so indifferent to this rationality (*Discourse on Method*, V). This is the end of a finite teleology but the presence of a total or substantial teleology (Milbank, 2001a, pp. 335–8). This sense of nature is at work in the whole early modern period, and is evidenced by the confidence in that period that nature, in its very 'atheism' or independence from God, displays the divine at every point.

In Descartes, then, there are two totalities – the totality of *res cogitans* where every individual thought or idea belongs to a totality of thought (as Spinoza later brought out especially) and the totality of *res extensa* where every movement of matter belongs to a total movement. It is crucial to see in Descartes the unity of these opposed substances in God and for self-consciousness. Descartes is not in the end a dualist, but is rather seeking a more complete unity of self and world, soul and body than is available on an Aristotelian or generally pre-modern account (see *Meditations*, VI; Andrews,

2001). How this is to be accomplished remains under-developed in Descartes, but the principle that there is the unity in opposition – for us as well as for God – underlies the modern period as a whole. The modern confidence is that only through a radical alienation from nature can we be at home in nature, with a stability unknowable by ancient or medieval lights. Indeed, one of the signs that Milbank himself is not free of modernity is that although he would correct the medieval relation to embodiedness, this is only possible from the standpoint of the modern return to nature. What Milbank misses in his portrayal of Descartes as appropriating subjectivity is the inner self-completeness of the Cartesian self-consciousness that frees it from the instability in knowing and desiring that belongs to the pre-modern self, and the reconciliation to nature and body precisely in their recognized objectivity so that nature is no longer an external other to be dominated or a sheer nothingness to be wilfully reconstructed.

But does this objectivity of nature, and reconciliation with it, not make legitimate the evil and indifference of the world? Milbank wants to assert that the early moderns so built evil, self-interest and indifference into the world that theirs is an ontology of power and violence. Milbank claims that assertions of theodicy merely mask the violence of modernity in an ideological way (*TST*, pp. 37–40). Against this, Milbank posits a 'Christian' ontology of peace where there is positive difference, but not the opposition of good and evil as inherent – for Milbank, evil is a contingent element arising from refusal of the given good. But is Milbank's ontology, in fact, Christian? Does it conceive of evil in a way adequate to orthodox Christianity? It certainly falls short of an Augustinian account, in which God creates foreknowing the evil of the devil in order that he can turn this evil to good (*civ.* 11.17). For Augustine, while evil is not a Manichean reality, the doctrine of original sin and God's predestinal creation requires that evil be seen for us fallen creatures as more than contingent. That is to say the demand of orthodox Christianity is not simply a Gnostic escape from evil by a re-imagining of ontology, but rather the appropriation and conversion of evil as belonging to the Divine Providence. It is this Augustinian and orthodox conception of the relation of good and evil that is built into the modern conception of theodicy. Milbank appears to want simply to suppress or evade evil (in his terms simply evacuate secularity and modern self-consciousness) rather than appropriate and overcome it. As such, his 'ontology of peace' is naïve; it can preach peace, but can never make it actual. Rather, insofar as moderns build into their positions the total self-destructiveness of medieval and Renaissance culture, theirs is an ontology of peace.

Are the claims of a modern ontology built on self-consciousness in fact secure? Fundamental to Milbank's critique of Descartes, and deeply tied to his claim that modern secularity is a self-destroying form of *theology*, is his acceptance of Heidegger's claim that modernity, especially in the form articulated in Descartes' philosophy, is 'onto-theological' (see Heidegger, 1969, pp. 42–74; Marion, 1999; Milbank, 2001a, pp. 344–55). Onto-theology, as this thought was developed in Heidegger, and as it is used by Milbank and others, is the characterization of Western (for Heidegger) or modern (for Milbank) metaphysics as a radical reduction of being and beings to representational thought and above all as 'cause', so that, at its fullest expression (Descartes' expression), God as *causa sui* becomes the absolute causality of all causes (Heidegger, 1969, pp. 71–2). All beings, even the highest, have thereby been reduced to a representational logic (onto-theologic). The further development of onto-theology is to its own self-undoing: onto-theology shows itself in 'technology', through this reduction of all beings to representation, to be nothing but the purest nihilistic willing: Nietzsche is the inner truth of Descartes.

At first sight, Descartes does seem to be the clearest case of an onto-theologist who through his method and radical doubt turns all beings into representation and so available to technology. But underlying Milbank's claim that Descartes is 'reducing' beings to representation (by 'refusing' the standpoint of substantial forms and reciprocity) are two assumptions: (1) that there is a world of 'beings' there in their own 'being' that are being so reduced, and 2) that the thinking that is conceiving the world through ideas is a finite, subjective thinking imposing itself upon the pre-given world of 'beings'. While these assumptions do belong, in some manner, to the neo-Kantian schools in which Heidegger was educated (see Rose, 1981, chapter I), and from which he broke with the assistance of Husserl's phenomenology, they are assumptions that do not belong to Descartes or the early moderns generally. In fact, Descartes' doubt at the beginning of the *Meditations* achieves a break with 'intentional' late medieval/Renaissance theories of representation, which, due to the unstable relation, inherent in those theories, of subjective representation and objective reality were subject to sceptical dissolution. Descartes' beginning in self-certainty – and not representational truth – is precisely for the sake of grounding, and so transforming, representation in a standpoint beyond representation's purely finite and subjective character. Indeed, Descartes' first proof for the existence of God is explicitly prior to the grounding of clarity and distinctness as criteria of truthful 'representation'.[9] The whole point of the *Meditations* is to move the reader from certainty to truth (see Andrews, 2000, p. 5). In this movement, the grounding of thinking in the divine actuality is the crucial turning point. Here 'ideas' (precisely *not* representations derived from external things) that belong to finite thinking can be thought, on the basis of the certainty of the divine substance, as forming a total science in their interconnection. These 'ideas' are, in their truth, of divine origin and so not imposed upon 'beings' by a subjective, finite, merely human thinking, but rather are a necessity and reality that is the truth of both human thinking and 'beings'. Descartes' science is not in principle, then, a reduction of beings to subjective representation (something he accuses pre-modern theories of doing), but rather an objective account of what actually is, grounded in the divine as infinite and undeceiving source of both what is and what thinks. Indeed, Descartes is perfectly clear that his science is limited to what can be *known* by finite thinking (and so not reductionist) and that what *is* may exceed that thinking in unknowable ways, but that nonetheless what is known within the limited sphere of finite mind is true both for thought and for beings (Descartes, 1984, I, p. 248; III, p. 34).

In fact, it belongs to Milbank's standpoint that he cannot take seriously Descartes own account of his position. In order to explain Descartes' turn to inner self-certainty to ground a science of nature, Milbank resorts to the same old canard that Nietzsche and Heidegger used relative to Socrates and Plato: that in the face of the 'flux' of beings, the thinker retreats in 'fear' to the safe citadel of stable rationality which is then imposed on the flux (Milbank, 2001a, pp. 337, 359). All of this is not only *ad hominem* psychologizing, but begs the crucial question: are there 'beings' in the phenomenological–ontological sense that Milbank assumes and which must be grasped as such, or, rather, does the world only disclose itself in its truth through a self-certain thinking grounded in the divine actuality? This may be a naïvely ahistorical way of putting the question, but it should at least be obvious that (a) it would be completely opposed to Descartes' deepest intentions and the whole point of his argument to impose a reductionist (and therefore falsifying) *mathesis* upon beings and (b) the assumption that beings 'are', prior to their being extensional 'ideas', is precisely what Descartes' own argument challenges. This is not the place to engage in a full consideration of the contemporary phenomenology and ontology that serves as the background to Milbank's critique of Descartes; it is enough to see that so long as this phenomenology and ontology are simply assumed, an undistorted interpretation of Descartes is necessarily foreclosed and an understanding of modern philosophy, according to its own principles, pre-empted.

Hobbes and Modern Political Thought

What Descartes and his modern progeny accomplished in epistemology and ontology, Hobbes and others accomplished in social and political thought. Hobbes approaches social and political life through its negation in the state of nature. Here the logic of late medieval and Renaissance political life is left to its logical conclusion – total war and despair, where, as Hobbes famously states, 'The life of man, [is] solitary, poore, nasty, brutish and short' (Hobbes, 1990, p. 89). Hobbes argues that it is only in our recognizing the futility and instability of all natural ends and desires – including both late medieval rights of *dominium* and the Machiavellian pursuit of glory – that there can be the possibility of constituting a state. This insight allows Hobbesian individuals, and moderns generally, to will directly a sovereign power to bear the person of the state, and thus take up a standpoint beyond all particular ends so as to be able to order them from a standpoint prior to those ends. (For Hobbes as the first to articulate the concept of the state as beyond private possession, see Skinner, 1989, pp. 90–131.) As Hobbes puts it, the first law of nature and basis of the modern state is 'That every man, ought to endeavour Peace ...' (Hobbes, 1990, p. 92). Hobbes establishes in his political thought a distinction of the universal public will of the sovereign (the law) and the particular wills and interests of the citizens (the silence of the law). For Milbank, this represents Hobbes' liberalism, formalism constraining arbitrariness. This is to miss the way Hobbes, like Descartes in relation to his 'dualism', unites the two sides. Certainly in Hobbes the private and public are to be separated to avoid a Machiavellian confusion and instability, but he argues that in this very distinction the two sides connect and unite. This unity is present in the sovereign who knows his subjects' activity belongs to him – as Hobbes had depicted in the famous frontispiece to *Leviathan*. This unity is also known in the subjects, who are both authors (by covenant) of the sovereign's laws, and agents of their own private and civil lives occurring within that authorization (Hobbes, 1990, XVII, especially p. 120 and XXI). As Milbank notes, Hobbes is able to compare the constitution of the modern state to God's creation of the world (Milbank, 1990, pp. 9–11). But beyond this allegory, in *Leviathan* Hobbes grounds the state upon the divine foundation of the total causal structure of the world. From this point of view, the state is the result of power – but crucially of absolute power, where nothing stands outside of the total causal order. Violence is only the arbitrary resistance to this order: power and rationality are completely united. It is this inner connection between inert, indifferent matter and a rational totality, socially realized in the unity of private and public ends, that is to become the basis of the language of theodicy and providence in eighteenth-century discussions of political economy. What occurs between the strongly absolutist monarchy of Hobbes and the *laissez-faire* political economists of the eighteenth-century is an inner education, a 'civilizing', so that the individual could inwardly – and not only through an external constraint – sustain the unity of private and public. It is this inner discipline that allows the confidence that citizens can actively participate in and even resist their governments without relapse into the anarchy of late medieval/Renaissance culture. In Foucauldian fashion, Milbank criticizes this new inner discipline, and yet at the same time, in his confidence that he can correct ancient and medieval patterns of social hierarchy and domination, he shows his continuing reliance on these modern accomplishments.

This Hobbesian radical foundation of the modern state in the total negation of given ends and practices seems to have as a consequence the dissolution of the ethical whole that structured ancient and medieval society and allowed there to be a sense of place and meaning for individuals. Milbank is perfectly right to suggest that Hobbes, Spinoza and later political economists such as James Stewart not only do not uphold the skein of given practices, but, insofar as these practices are subversive of the modern state or the general movement of social life, they oppose them. I do not propose to whitewash the violence and abstractness with which the early modern state and political economy reduced pre-modern institutions and forms. However, what is problematic in Milbank's account is that he equates this violence and levelling with Machiavellianism – that it is the work of a manipulative will. The modern answer to the use of state power against subversive practices is that the evil does not reside so much in the state exercising its objective reality, a reality subjectively and inwardly affirmed by its citizens. Rather, evil resides in those citizens who hold to their private ends to the point of undermining the state. That is, they seek to return modernity back to the state of nature that is late medieval and Renaissance culture. Those who hold to private practices are the true Machiavellians. This answer may be too abstract and self-serving, but it has the merit of clarifying the distinction between modern and pre-modern accounts of power. There is nothing that is in principle manipulative in the modern for it is the claim of the modern that, as both Descartes and Hobbes make clear, it operates through a rationality open to all, so that all punishment and use of force is, in principle, self-punishment.

But even if one wants to allow to modernity a historical reality, its overcoming of medieval and Renaissance secularity in a new inward secularity, is it not still a deeply unchristian development to build social and political life on self-interest and a diremption of the individual from the ethical community? Here one needs to be clear about the crucial double-sidedness of modern secularity: it is a return to nature and bodily existence from out of the medieval elevation above these, but it carries into its return the alienation from nature achieved in medieval spirituality. From this point of view, the self-love and agonistics of modern life are both real and unreal – and moderns know this two-sidedness. Finite aims and ambitions both are the place of individual happiness, freedom, self-expression and duty, and also are known as vain and empty. Modernity, on the one side, disciplines us in the face of an objectivity, whether of nature or the larger movement of society and the market and the law. Equally, on the other side, it releases us to the indulgence in and fulfilment of private satisfactions and enjoyments and gives space for the free development of practices and civil society more generally. Further, moderns know the inner connection of these two sides. It is crucial that, because of the inward freedom of the modern in the face of the total destruction of natural ends at the source of modernity, the greed, competition and pursuit of self-interest which are released in modern social and political life both have been already inwardly negated, and are effectually sustained in that negation through the presence of the absolute state and the general movement of society and economy. This means that, far from blackening the soul with sin, modern competition and agonistics are the process of liberation from sin. That is to say, modern life, rather than evading evil, inwardly dissolves its power (see Goethe's *Faust*). While Hobbes saw this purgation as belonging to the state of nature primarily, the course of modernity into the eighteenth century made this purgation the continuous work of social and economic life. Competition and desire are known not as private sins, but as the whole movement of society and the state within us and as such already overcome and contained, and in the process towards such an overcoming.[10]

Conclusion

Rather than modernity being, as Milbank contends, an ontology that legitimates violence and power, it is the very inward self-overcoming of such a standpoint. As such moderns are able to know the inner unity of themselves as both natural and rational – politically this is a knowledge of the inner connection between private ends and the political good – and the divine substance as the unity of these moments. Here is imaged secularly the unity of natures in one person of Chalcedonian orthodoxy. The very concept of the secular establishes the notion of an independent, self-determining, even atheistical humanity that is yet inwardly related and only possible on the basis of a God present at every point. In short, rather than being a resurgent paganism and heretical Christianity that Milbank sees, modernity is an expression of orthodoxy and the route towards an adequation of the human to the divine such as to complete the medieval desire to understand *cur deus homo*.

Notes

1   My thanks for their comments and criticisms on earlier versions of this chapter to Wayne Hankey, Ken Kierans, Simon Kow, Angus Johnston, Ian Stewart and Christopher Snook.

2   See MacIntyre (1981), pp. 109–20. Consider here also the use of Foucault in Milbank's account of modernity, for example *TST*, pp. 36, 43, 260, and Chapter 10 generally.

3   Here consider the difference between Dante's portrayal of the Earthly Paradise and the Heavenly Paradise in the *Divine Comedy*; also the role of the Emperor in Dante's political thought in *De Monarchia*. On Milbank and Radical Orthodoxy's determination to overcome the medieval failure to adequately celebrate 'our finitude – as language, as erotic, and aesthetically delighting bodies' (*RO*, p. 4); and their attempt to attribute such a reconciliation to mediated grace alone requires eliding the distinction of natural/supernatural, earth/heaven, this life/the next, see *TST*, pp. 81, 167.

4   The governing logic of this approach is brought out in Heidegger (1962), I.5, pp. 89 ff., 'Assertion as a Derivative Mode of Interpretation'.

5   In this chapter I will use the terms modernity and modern secularity interchangeably. It is important to say that Milbank is not opposed to modernity understood more broadly, but only to the dominant secular modernity; indeed he sketches what he refers to as an alternative modernity in 'Baroque modernity', which includes Nicholas of Cusa, Pallavicino, Vico, Herder, Hamann and Jacobi.

6   The modernity referred to in the chapter is the classical modernity from Descartes to Kant. However, for the sake of space, only the early or pre-critical forms of modernity will be considered here.

7   Compare Aquinas, *ST*, 1.12.8, 1.62.9, 1.106.1, 1–2.38, 2–2.2.3. On the transition from Aquinas to Scotus and Ockham see Doull (2003), pp. 219–49, 239–40. Consider here the conclusion of Dante's *Divine Comedy* 'Paradiso', Canto 33. On this, see Johnston (1991), p. 63.

8   The binding of the ideas upon God is conditional in Descartes upon the prior creation of the ideas. In subsequent rationalists this condition is retracted in the critique of the doctrine of the creation of eternal truths, especially in Malebranche,

Spinoza and Leibniz. See Marion (1998), pp. 280–83. However, this doctrine can be seen to reappear in the form of the distinction between the phenomenal and the noumenal in Kant.

9   Andrews (1998) corrects the view that Descartes' argument is circular (requiring God to ground clarity and distinctness as the criteria of truth and yet needing clarity and distinctness to prove God's existence).

10   See Hirschman (1977). Goethe's *The Apprenticeship of Wilhelm Meister* argues that to condemn the self-interest, commercialism and individualism of modernity from a religious or aesthetic high ground is to turn the whole against its parts. The end of education or apprenticeship is to bring unified ends and divided means together as one totality.

CHAPTER 7

Radical Orthodoxy and Apocalyptic Difference: Cambridge Platonism, and Milbank's Romantic Christian Cabbala

Douglas Hedley

Radical Orthodoxy claims to represent an 'alternative vatic, "Platonic" tradition within British culture' (*WMS*, p. 2) in the tradition of Ralph Cudworth, and John Milbank suggests that Cudworth prefigures Balthasar in trying to restore a 'sacral cosmology' (*RO*, p. 19). Indeed, Milbank appeals to Cudworth and Henry More as having 'diagnosed' and 'resisted' the modern subject (Milbank, 2001a, p. 336). The inheritance of the Cambridge Platonists in Radical Orthodoxy is explicit and emphatic. It is perplexing, however, for the post-liberal John Milbank to claim the lineage of these Cambridge men. Why does Milbank, whose central position is that *only* theology gives a true account of the real, who attempts to rid theology of any 'false humility', seek to link himself with a quintessentially *liberal* school like the Cambridge 'men of latitude' (Milbank, 1990, p. 1)? This essay explains why the famed 'comprehension' or tolerance of the Cambridge Platonists is quite incompatible with the *jusqu'au boutisme* of Radical Orthodoxy, with its urgent appeal to challenge a world which is 'soulless, aggressive, nonchalant and nihilistic' (*RO*, p. 1).[1]

I suggest, however, that there is a genuinely *Platonic* tradition vastly more akin to Milbank's own temperament. This is a strand of trenchant and uncompromising critique of liberalism, 'rationality' and the 'secular' which is a much more obvious candidate for the roots of that apocalyptic élan of Radical Orthodoxy than those moderate 'heirs of Erasmus', the Cambridge Platonists: the Platonic Catholic counter-revolutionary thought of Joseph de Maistre (1753–1821) whose visceral hatred of Protestantism and Enlightenment and whose denunciations of the satanic nature of the secular is startlingly close to Radical Orthodox theology. The temper of *Radical Orthodoxy* is – as the name suggests – a revolutionary conservatism, very much like the Catholic Neoplatonic strand of thought which emerges in the wake of the French Revolution, and which is an obvious precursor of the staunchly Anglo-Catholic Radical Orthodoxy in both its Catholicism and its Platonism.[2] Here we find a political theology which is expressly aimed at the process of secularization and the Enlightenment critique of religion, since Catholics like de Maistre saw the cataclysm of the French Revolution as a challenge to the validity of the concept of salvation. The French Revolution constituted a decisive rupture with any notion of providence in historical progression.

But these principles are utterly opposed to the latitude of the Cambridge Platonists. These were men of moderation in a period of political turbulence: the Civil War and the Restoration. Moderate Royalists, their capacity to have close relations with Cromwell and Parliament and (in the case of Cudworth) retain their positions after the Restoration was regarded as pusillanimous by many. One might designate them as cautious liberals. Perhaps their faith in divine goodness and providence generated a basically optimistic temper which cohered with their Whig politics. The idea of the 'candle of the Lord' which was the basis of Whichcote's, Cudworth's and More's faith in human rationality is in opposition to de Maistre's eloquent and unrelenting critique of that secular reason which he saw as ushering in and responsible for the cruelty and destruction of the revolutionary Terror. The providential God of the Cambridge Platonists – omniscient, omnipotent and good – is *prima facie* unlike the God of de Maistre – that *deus absconditus* of the Catholic restauration, who eludes the rational intellect and whose providential will is inscrutable. The response to revolution, war and dictatorship was diametrically opposed. The Cambridge Platonists reacted to the English Civil War with a conviction of the need for tolerance and 'latitude', but they were equally mistrusted by Puritans and High Churchmen. As Beiser notes: 'In demanding that religion rise to the challenge of the new philosophy and science, the Cambridge Platonists brought religion itself into the modern era' (Beiser, 1996, p. 139). By way of contrast, de Maistre responded to the horrors of his day with a brilliant and eloquent theological critique of the modern secular epoch.

Cudworth's insistence upon the cultivation of human autonomy and agency through the natural course of events, and the discovery of natural laws, under the general guidance of providence and prescience contrasts with the stark oppositions of Milbank or de Maistre: secular or Christian, secular philosophy or Christian theology, *praxis* or *theoria*, and so on. Of course, the sturdy refusal to accommodate the modern world, the fear of the domestication of religion into morality, the resisting of secular norms – these characteristic tenets of Radical Orthodoxy have a good Barthian–Kierkegaardian provenance. The rhetoric of confrontation in Radical Orthodoxy is characteristic of much theology since Karl Barth. Theological liberalism, especially of the Protestant variety, has seemed a lost cause since Barth's *The Epistle to the Romans* in 1918 (*Römerbrief*). The Cambridge Platonists are clear precursors of modern theological liberalism. Indeed, the temper of Milbank's work is deeply indebted to the German antihumanistic pathos of *Entscheidung* (decision) of the 1920s and 1930s, especially as mediated by the French avant-garde in the 1960s. And de Maistre's legacy was felt keenly in both periods.

By contrast, the Cambridge Platonists inspired Ernst Cassirer to write a homage to liberal values in his seminal work *The Platonic Renaissance in England*. Cassirer wrote this 1932 work on the Cambridge Platonists in order to emphasize a tradition of 'liberal humanitarian ideals of individuals within society possessing inalienable rights' during the traumatic period prior to

Hitler's seizure of power (Lipton, 1978, p. 159). The Cambridge Platonists represented a rich humanistic and liberal tradition, the value of which appeared particularly pressing to a Jewish German intellectual in the inter-war period. That book was an attempt to show, quite correctly, that the spirit of Kant was akin to and dependent upon other European traditions – at a time when Heidegger was insisting upon the incommensurability of the Germanic and Greek with the decadent Western cultures of Britain, France and America (Heidegger, 1960, pp. 14–15).[3] Ernst Cassirer writes:

> The Cambridge School is merely one stage of this journey, and the thinkers of this school play only a modest role in this great intellectual process of development. But it is their undisputed achievement that they did not let the torch they bore go out; and that, in spite of all the opposition of contemporary philosophy and all attacks of theological dogmatism, they preserved a nucleus of genuine ancient philosophical tradition, and passed it uncontaminated to the centuries to come. (Cassirer, 1953, pp. 201–2)

Cassirer saw the Cambridge Platonists as light in such dark days as a testimony to the humanistic principle of the veneration of a common European culture and intellectual canon – and the value of continuity of esteem. Amidst the intellectual frenzy of the *Katastrophenjahre* of the inter-war period, and the popularity of prophets of occidental gloom such as Spengler, Cassirer could find 'a nucleus of genuine ancient philosophical tradition' in these Cambridge divines. But can Radical Orthodoxy really follow these Cambridge 'heirs' of Erasmus? Some detailed reflection reveals that Radical Orthodoxy has far more affinity with the position of de Maistre than the Cambridge Platonists.

Orthodoxy

Let us first consider how 'Orthodox' were the Cambridge Platonists. The appellation 'Cambridge Platonists' is a creation of nineteenth-century historiography. The Platonists were 'latitudinarians' for their contemporaries, a word which expressed some contempt. A conservative orthodox Protestant divine and contemporary critic of the Cambridge Platonists like Antony Tuckney, the great Puritan Master of Emmanuel College, remarked that the term 'Orthodox' was 'stomached' while these men were more interested in their liberalizing 'moral divinity'. This is far in spirit from the vaunted post-secular hegemony of theology proposed by Radical *Orthodoxy* and its robust refusal to accommodate the modern world. Indeed, Tuckney's critique of Whichcote is much like that of Barth's critique of Harnack. The nineteenth-century Scot John Tulloch waxes eloquent about the liberalism of Whichcote:

> Traditionalism, whether of dogma or institution, affects him little. He moves in an ideal and open atmosphere, unfamiliar to the school-theologian. ... Man's knowledge does not lie in incommunicable spheres – the   secular and the spiritual; but in

different planes of elevation, the lower tending towards the higher, and the higher sending down its light to the lower levels of intellectual aspiration. (Tulloch, 1966, p. 113)

Westcott, in his excellent essay on Whichcote notes that 'he has an imperfect conception of the corporate character of the Church ... little or no sense of the historic growth of the Church. His teaching on the Sacraments is vague and infrequent' (Westcott, 1891, pp. 393–4).

Even a resolutely High Church contemporary theologian like Jeremy Taylor in his *Liberty of Prophesying* shares the liberal position of the Cambridge Platonists that is opposed to dogmatic orthodoxy: the life of a Christian is essentially spiritual – the acknowledgement of and faith in Christ as saviour (Taylor, 1822). Outward liturgy, worship and ecclesial order are matters indifferent compared with the interior spirit of Christ: what Cudworth calls the '*inward Reformation of* the heart' (Cudworth, 1647, p. 82). Certainly true religion has little to do with ritual performance: 'as if Religion were nothing else, but a *Dancing* up and down' (ibid., pp. 56ff.). John Smith, too, is resolute in his critique of any mere '*Formal* and Ritual way of Religion' which derives from '*baseness* and *Servility* of Mind'. This is particularly striking in the wake of the Laudian decrees of the 1630s (Smith, 1660, p. 51). Superstitious forms of religion are the subject of severe critique by the Cambridge Platonists, and Protestants in the seventeenth century were inclined to see Roman Catholicism – and *a fortiori* ritualism within the Church of England – as a paradigm of superstition and a breeding ground for the 'brat of Atheism' (ibid.).

Cudworth's views on the Eucharist are set out in his learned essay *A Discourse concerning the True Notion of the Lord's Supper*. The main target is the Roman Catholic view of the Lord's Supper as a sacrifice. Cudworth argues that the Eucharist is properly understood as a feast of '*Amity and Friendship*, betweene God and men' (p. 70) which recalls Christ's own sacrifice. Cudworth's analysis of the 'Grand Errour of the Papists, *concerning the Lords Supper being a Sacrifice*' (p. 2) presents the starkest imaginable contrast to Catherine Pickstock's rhapsodic encomium of the medieval Roman rite of the Mass as the consummation of Platonism and assertion that 'the event of transubstantiation in the Eucharist is the condition of possibility for all human meaning' (*AW*, p. xv).

Simon Patrick, in his *Brief account of the new sect of Latitude-men* observed of the Cambridge men:

As for the Rites and Ceremonies of Divine worship, they do highly approve of that vertuous mediocrity which our Church observes between the meretricious gaudiness of the Church of *Rome*, and the squalid sluttery of Fanatick conventicles. (Patrick, 1662, p. 7)

Many of the most distinguished Platonists in the Church of England, like the Caroline divine Thomas Jackson (1579–1640) or the Non-Juror William Law (1686–1761) were High Churchmen. Hence it is especially puzzling why

Radical Orthodoxy should wish to trace their lineage to thinkers with so little expressed interest in 'poesis' in the Radically Orthodox sense of liturgy within the ecclesial community. More strikingly, the Cambridge Platonists seem to represent all that Radical Orthodoxy finds abominable in Modernity – the 'modern type', as Westcott puts it (Westcott, 1891). The proper idea of the Church, for Whichcote, is not ritual but moral, its ideal contemplative *theoria* rather than liturgical practice.

Religion

The liberalism of the Cambridge Platonists was deeply reflected in their views on religion (Pailin, 1984). Harrison notes: 'That the limits of human knowledge necessarily issue in pluralism of belief was an axiom of the Renaissance Platonists which found wide acceptance amongst their heirs at Cambridge' (Harrison, 1990, p. 59). Cudworth argues that the more intelligent of the ancient pagans 'notwithstanding the multiplicity of Gods worshipped by them, did generally acknowledge One Supreme, Omnipotent and Only Unmade Deity' (Cudworth, 1678, p. 265).

With regard to Judaism and Islam, Henry More and Cudworth are surprisingly tolerant – especially compared with contemporaries. John Smith certainly shows a detailed knowledge of the thought of Maimonides in his chapter on 'Prophecy' in his *Select Discourses*, and Cudworth was part of the committee which organized the re-entry of the Jews into England, and met Menasseh ben Israel. On Islam, Henry More can claim that the Prophet did not 'utterly pervert and deprave the Mystery of the Gospel' and consequently Islam was a providential force in the world – attacking 'heathenish Idolaters ... *disobedient* and *Hypocrital Christians*' and indeed the '*external Dominion of the Devil in the World*' (More, 1708, p. 115). More, like Cudworth, believes that rather than 'reproaching all other Religions, in damning the very best and most conscientious *Turks, Jews and Pagans* to the Pit of Hell', Christians should employ the common reason of mankind to refute errors (ibid., p. 343). He emphasized the agreement between religions on the basis of natural reason. Moreover he extolled the virtues of pagans in contrast to the poor morality of many Christians.

This latitudinarianism is the opposite of Milbank's resolutely Barthian call for the 'end' of dialogue with other religions, 'mutual suspicion' and the 'work of conversion' (Milbank, 1990). Julius Lipner, among others, has chastised Milbank for his dogmatic and eurocentric position, linked to a breezy dismissal of other religions. With regard to Hinduism, Lipner criticizes Milbank's excessive dependence upon Nirad Chaudhuri's book *Hinduism*. Lipner observes wittily: 'It is a bit like relying on a book about Christianity by Bertrand Russell to learn about the Christian faith' (Lipner, 1994, pp. 262–3). But such is a post-liberal theology that relishes the refusal of 'false humility' and rejects dialogue.

Historiography

The Nietzschean-cum-Heideggerian historiography of Radical Orthodoxy is a crucial element in their theological position. Cudworth's view of Descartes as reviving the ancient Mosaical atomic philosophy is clearly utterly incompatible with the view of Descartes in Radical Orthodoxy as the villain who inaugurates the subjective *cogito* of 'modernity'. Yet this reflects a deeper contrast between the men of latitude and the post-liberal Radical Orthodoxy. Milbank's philosophical historiography depends upon a decisive 'fall' in the thirteenth century. Here we have a rather Heideggerian view of the history of ideas whereby the evil figure of Duns Scotus inaugurates modernity by breaking down the doctrine of analogy and introducing a tendency to speak of reality as if it were merely a set of discrete facts. From the Pandora's Box of the subtle Scotus, Enlightenment philosophy developed natural laws, the nation state, capitalism and sundry other ills which constitute modernity.

Cudworth's historiography depends upon the opposite conception of *nihil novi sub sole*. Spinoza and Hobbes are repetitions of ancient materialism and atheism. Thus the relationship to Cartesianism reveals a very big difference between the Cambridge Platonists and Radical Orthodoxy. The Cambridge Platonists introduced Descartes' thought into Cambridge. The shift from a Latin scholastic curriculum to modern Anglophone philosophy via Cartesianism and Newtonianism was swifter at Cambridge than at Oxford because of the Cambridge Platonists (Gascoigne, 1989). Although the Platonists influenced scientists such as Newton, John Ray and Nehemiah Grew, they were also inheritors of the Erasmian tradition. As good humanists, the Platonists believed in discovering perennial universal truths in ancient texts.

Descartes is central to Radical Orthodoxy's narrative of emergent 'modernity'. 'Descartes follows in the tradition of Duns Scotus, for whom a being is that which is univocal and therefore graspable ... .' (*AW*, p. 62). Cambridge theologians of the seventeenth century were distinguished by their interest and enthusiasm for modern science. Whereas Radical Orthodoxy chastises Descartes for his 'total demystification of matter' (*RO*, p. 82), Cudworth exclaims:

> we can never sufficiently applaud that ancient atomical philosophy, so successfully revived of late by Cartesius, in that it shows distinctly what matter is, and what it can amount unto, namely nothing else but what may be produced from mere magnitude, figure, site, local motion and rest. (Cudworth, 1996, p. 151)

Henry More also embraces enthusiastically much in Cartesian physics. More declares:

> we both setting out from the same Lists, though taking several ways, the one travelling in the lower Road of Democritism, *amidst the thick dust of Atoms and flying particles of* Matter; *the other tracing it o'er the high and aiery Hills of Platonism, in that more thin and subtil Region of* Immateriality, meet together

notwithstanding at last (and certainly not without a Providence) *at the same Gaol*, namely at the Entrance of the holy Bible ... (More, 1712, p. xii)

There is much in More's philosophical poems which expands this view of harmony between Descartes and the Platonic project.

The Cambridge Platonists were deeply critical of Descartes on particular issues, and Henry More becomes evidently increasingly disenchanted with Descartes. However, the criticisms of the Cambridge men were often combined with much admiration and they clearly preferred Descartes to the 'asinine feast of sow-thistles and brambles' – the Protestant Scholasticism which still formed the staple fare of Cambridge philosophy teaching in this period. Indeed the diatribes against the wordiness of the schoolmen forms the basis of another huge gulf between the Cambridge Platonists and Radical Orthodoxy.

Linguistic Reality

Theology, Milbank insists, must abandon all quasi-scholastic attempts to relate faith to a universal base of reason. The overcoming of modernity is not a simple return to the premodern since the medieval age was 'unable to overcome entirely the ontology of substance in the direction of a view which sees reality as constituted by signs and their endless ramifications' (*WMS*, p. 85). Whichcote can hardly be clearer in his rejection of this when he writes that 'Christian religion is not Mystical, Symbolical, Aenigmatical, Emblematical, but unclothed, unbodied, intellectual, rational, spiritual' (Whichcote, 1930, p. 99).

Yet as ever, the Nietzschean Milbank is fascinated by his own genealogy. This linguistic turn is not a secular phenomenon but a 'delayed achievement' (*WMS*, p. 97) of Christian theology: '*Factum* for Vico is *Verbum* in God, and so the made, cultural object is promoted to the status of a divine transcendental (in the scholastic sense), and this is equivalent to saying that God in his creation *ad intra* in the Logos "incorporates" within himself the creation *ad extra*, including human history' (*WMS*, p. 80). For Cusanus, Vico and Hamann 'man as an *original* creator participates in some measure in creation *ex nihilo*'. These theologians are precursors of a theological linguistic turn. Hence the 'post modern embracing of a radical linguisticality' and the evacuation of a metaphysics of substance is not a problem for Christian theology but 'has always been secretly promoted by it' (*WMS*, p. 85). Unlike Henry More, for whom God is defined in his *Enchiridion Metaphysicum* as 'First Substance', Radical Orthodoxy can reject any metaphysics of substance and embrace the idea that for theology there is no certain knowledge, but merely a network of meanings governed by language itself: Christian theology is an exercise in 'unlimited semiosis'. Here Milbank just presupposes that either language is founded upon logocentric correspondence or is in a state of inescapable flux: this alternative opens up the 'aporias which either point to a nihilist abyss, or can only be resolved by the supremely poetic figure of Jesus, the incarnate Logos ... a linguistic and poetic reality' (*WMS*, p. 3). But one might simply reject the initial dilemma. Perhaps we can escape language, after all – it was the insistence of the humanists that translation and interpretation was an enlarging of one's horizons.

Perhaps, *contra* Milbank, language is merely one aspect of our cognitive apparatus. This seems to be the view of Cudworth, who claims that 'Words and syllables which are but dead things, cannot possibly convey the living notions of heavenly truths to us' (Cudworth, 1647, p. 5). The goal of thought for him is the inexpressible and hence supra-linguistic state of union with the Divine. Pierre Hadot, thinking of Plato's *Phaedrus*, has spoken of the 'ontological value of the spoken word'; this living and animated discourse was not principally intended to transmit information, but to produce a certain psychic effect in the reader or listener. Thus the 'propositional element' was not the most important element of ancient philosophical teaching, and Hadot has frequently cited Victor Goldschmitt's formula that ancient philosophical discourse was intended to 'form more than to inform' (Hadot, 1995, p. 19). But this *formation* within the Platonic school meant a strict ascetic discipline. 'If thou beest it, thou seest it, as Plotinus speaks ...' (More, 1660, p. 407).

The Cambridge Platonists were interested in the relation between language and an intuitive knowledge which transcends articulation: a knowledge which is a 'spiritual sensation' but which expresses itself best in the good life: a divine life rather than science. Radical Orthodoxy could not accept this position because it conflicts with the postmodern/neo-Heideggerian dogma that language is the 'house of being', that is, that we can never escape it. John Smith disagrees fundamentally (and I think correctly) with the notion that knowledge is necessarily linguistic: We have not 'attained to' the '*right knowledge* of truth', when ... by logical analysis, we have merely explicated the 'dependencies and coherencies' of the '*outward shell* of *words and phrases*' with one another ... (Smith, 1660, p. 8).

John Smith thinks that true religion transcends mere concepts::

> all that Knowledge which is separated from an inward aquaintance with Vertue and Goodness, is of a far different nature from that which ariseth out of a true *living sense* of them, which is the *best discerner* thereof, and by which alone we know the true Perfection, Sweetness, Energy, and Loveliness of them, ... which can no more be known by a naked Demonstration, then [*sic*] Colours can be perceived of a blinde man by any Definition or Description which he can hear of them. (Smith, 1660, p. 15)

Such is 'divine life' rather than a 'divine science' – the former is to be understood more by a '*Spiritual Sensation*, then by any *Verbal description*' (Smith, 1660, p. 1).

Furthermore, Cudworth diagnoses the confusions and delusions of Enthusiasm as rooted in the conviction that 'Religion and the Spirit is founded in nothing else but a Faculty of Rhetoricating and extemporizing with Zeal and

Fervency, which they take to be nothing less then Divine Inspiration' (Cudworth, 1664, pp. 63–4). Milbank presupposes the Nietzschean standpoint of a materialistic relativism which, like Protagoras, exposes 'truth' as a fiction, and the linguistic deconstruction of metaphysics. Milbank's account of the 'linguistic construction of the human world' (*WMS*, p. 2), the mediating role of 'fictional constructs' and, indeed, of the 'real *itself* as linguistic' (*WMS*, p. 3) is Nietzschean rather than Christian. Milbank's view needs to be close to Derrida's anti-foundationalism. However, this appropriation of the poststructuralist view of language presupposes a strongly apophatic theology. The postmodern denial of certainty is buttressed (as it were) by the radically unknowable God of Christian theology. Here Radical Orthodoxy and the Cambridge Platonists are on a collision course. Not only do the Cambridge Platonists think that intuitive knowledge transcends articulation, but – notwithstanding their Platonism – they have surprisingly little sympathy for the apophatic tradition in theology.

Apophatic Theology and the Priority of the 'External'

Wayne Hankey in a series of trenchant articles has demonstrated the strong later Neoplatonic component in the thought of Radical Orthodoxy. Hankey notes the role of Pseudo-Dionysius as the mediator of the Iamblichean–Procline tradition to Aquinas; 'for Thomas, Dionysius ... gave Christian authority for the turn to the sensible in the ascent to God'. Indeed John Milbank agrees with Hankey's diagnosis that the theology of Radical Orthodoxy is rooted in 'the Dionysian legacy of theurgic neoplatonism' (Milbank, 1999, p. 485). Hankey asks 'How do we come to a self that cannot know itself by a turn *interiore* but rather ascends only through its turn to the empirically perceived other?' (Hankey, 2001, p. 82). Commenting on recent scholarship, Hankey notes the link between the soteriology of Iamblichus and the prominence of the external:

> The return of the Iamblichean–Procline totally descended soul towards the One demands that what is above be accessible to the alienated individual and operate graciously towards it. Grace, not an effort to lift the soul towards its higher intellectual life, predominates: 'the soul's access to the divine must come "from without" (*exothen*) which was one rationale for the practice of rituals given *exothen*, from the gods'. With Iamblichus and his successors, the saving ascent is not possible in virtue of a division of the self and a move *interiore*. Rather a move to the external is possible and necessary ...' (Hankey, 2001, p. 83).

Milbank insists upon the reliability of the senses and the importance of the recognition of God as visible in the world. The fault of modernity was its shift of the human gaze inward rather than outward. Radical Orthodoxy can celebrate the sensible and the sensual. The 'true self' is 'precisely that which is most radically "exteriorised", or turned from itself towards the "external"'. This preference for the 'external' or for the Dionysian legacy is not shared by Cudworth. He admires Socrates who knew that 'knowledge was not to be poured into the soul like liquor, but rather to be invited and gently drawn forth from it ...' (Cudworth, 1996, p. 78) and Cudworth claims that it is evident that 'there are some ideas of the mind which were not stamped or imprinted upon it from the sensible objects without, and therefore must needs arise from the innate vigour and activity of the mind itself...' (ibid., p. 83). Moreover, the obsession with the outward and the sensible is for Cudworth a 'Sottish Conceit' conducive to atheism (Cudworth, 1678, p. 731), and he refers to the strongly apophatic theology of later Neoplatonic provenance as 'a certain kind of Mysterious Atheism' (ibid., p. 585). Henry More explicitly prefers the 'divine' or 'deep Plotin' to the post-Iamblichean Neoplatonic tradition. The preference of the Cambridge Platonists for Plotinus over against the 'Junior Platonists' of the Iamblichean–Procline tradition and the 'dismal apprehensions' within the *via negativa* of the Areopagite is quite clear (Smith, 1660, p. 129). Inge observes that 'Smith was well read in mystical theology, and was aware how much his ideal differed from that of Dionysian Mysticism' (Inge, p. 290).

Count Joseph de Maistre is a good example of a Catholic Platonist who draws on many of the aspects of the Platonic tradition which Milbank himself requires but cannot find in the Cambridge Platonists. De Maistre is often seen as an anachronism: an ultramontane Roman Catholic Savoyard critic of the French Revolution. Isaiah Berlin has proposed the opposite in insisting that de Maistre was 'ultra modern' (Berlin, 1990, pp. 91–174). In a fascinating essay 'Joseph de Maistre and the Origins of Fascism', Berlin sees de Maistre's vision of the human autonomous will weakened by sin and requiring, by default, strict obedience to the divine representative, as prefiguring fascism. While Berlin's assessment of de Maistre as a proto-fascist is almost certainly false, Berlin was correct to see the considerable impact of de Maistre on twentieth-century critiques of liberalism.

The political theology of de Maistre was fuelled by a powerful Neoplatonic element derived from the great French expert on Jacob Boehme, Louis Claude de Saint Martin, a representative of conservative freemasonry which endeavoured to harmonize with Catholicism. Especially important was the work of the messianic figure Martinez de Pasqually, 'Traité de réintegration' – a treatise concerned with creation and redemption and showing a clear Christian Neoplatonic provenance (Berlin, 1990, pp. 103–4). Joseph de Maistre knows that the philosophy of Saint Martin is a mixture of Platonism, Origenism and Hermetic ideas on a Christian foundation and it has strong affinities with German Idealist–Romantic thought (de Maistre, *Soirées de Saint-Pétersbourg*, 1884–86, vol. 5, p. 249).

The analysis of secularity follows from this analysis of the terrifyingly destructive reality of secularism and liberalism – despite its claim to liberate, it is but a 'déstruction violente de l'espèce humaine'. In the wake of the Revolution, Christianity and secular philosophy are at war: 'c'est le combat du christianisme et du philosophisme. La lice est ouverte, les deux ennemies sont aux prises, et l'univers regarde' (de Maistre, *Considérations*, 1884–86, vol. 1, p. 50). The radical opposition of Christendom and the secular in Milbank is profoundly reminiscent of de Maistre's invective against the Satanic French Revolution. So too is the millenarian air – the logic of secularism is 'imploding', Radical Orthodoxy announces. Milbank wishes to perform his task of redeeming estrangement in which the word of God is made 'strange' and shocks.

Another point of contact between de Maistre and Milbank is that they both reject the idea of *neutral* rationality. Rationality is parasitic upon decision in faith. Here we find analogies with Kierkegaard's refusal to domesticate religion in terms of human morality or rationality in writings such as *Fear and Trembling*. Radical Orthodoxy engages in no dialogues and defers to no experts because it does not recognize a neutral territory 'outside' the theological.

Finally, for both Milbank and de Maistre it is the Mass that offers a path to the *deus absconditus* – it is the sole model for a participatory, saved, community. In *Theology and Social Theory*, one can find a most illuminating discussion of de Maistre's concept of sacrifice. Milbank, in contrast to his breezy skirting of the English Platonists, can write with real expertise, insight and sympathy about de Maistre (*TST*, pp. 66ff.). This should not surprise us. Many of the French avant-garde reflect the legacy of de Maistre in their interests and obsessions. Girard's thoughts on the scapegoat is the most obvious instance. But one might consider the peculiarly French fascination with violence, sacrifice and sovereignty evident in Bataille, Blanchot and Foucault, with its evident affinities with the deep pessimism of de Maistre.[4]

Yet this makes Milbank's critique of de Maistre all the more puzzling. In part it is just legerdemain. Consider the following claim. It is misleading, Milbank insists, to call de Maistre 'Counter-Enlightenment'. He is rather "hyper-" or "post-"Enlightenment, which even anticipates elements in the thought of Nietzsche. De Maistre at least (who had Masonic connections) can scarcely be considered as orthodox Catholic ...' (*TST*, p. 55). Yet I am not sure that pious defender of papal infallibility, de Maistre, would have deferred lightly to Milbank's preference for such orthodox 'Catholics' as Hamann, Herder and Jacobi, or even the good Bishop Berkeley!

Religion, Ethics and Autonomy

Ethics is another point of stark contrast between Cambridge Platonism and Radical Orthodoxy. Radical Orthodoxy bears the clear influence of Karl Barth on this, as on many other issues. For the early Karl Barth the absolute difference of God means the impossibility of any real link between ethics and the Kingdom of God. In his later work he integrates ethics *within* dogmatics. Cudworth, as one of the founders of liberal theology, takes a very different position. 'Christ was Vitae Magister not Scholae: and he is the best Christian, whose heart beats with the truest pulse towards heaven; not he whose head spinneth out the finest cobwebs' (Cudworth, 1647, pp. 13–14). Ethics is not subordinated to doctrine as in Barth. Rather, the true Christian is not he who 'believes all the vulgar Articles of the Christian faith, … [and] plainly denyeth Christ in his life'. This was no liberal platitude when preached to the victorious House of Commons with a strong Calvinistic component. And Cudworth is clearly assuming that there are moral norms exterior to any particular Christian community.

In an essay entitled 'Can Morality Be Christian?' Milbank starts with characteristic brio by insisting in Barthian manner that morality cannot be Christian: 'Christian morality is a thing so strange that it must be declared immoral or amoral according to all other human norms and codes of morality' (*WMS*, p. 219). Cudworth would have been frankly horrified by such antinomianism, as would Whichcote, who says 'We must be men before we can be Christians' (Whichcote, 1930, p. 110).

Wayne Hankey has argued persuasively about the centrality of autonomy for Milbank. But again it is very puzzling why Milbank feels that Cudworth is an ally in the trenchant critique of autonomy. Cudworth is much more obviously a precursor of Kant. It was Arthur Lovejoy who first argued that Cudworth anticipated Kant, and, moreover, that the Cambridge men of latitude and William James both embody the Kantian principle of 'primacy of practical reason' (Lovejoy, 1903, p. 266). Cudworth, while Master of Clare College, preached to Parliament:

> I do not here urge, the *dead Law of outward Works*, which indeed if it be alone, subjects us to a *State of Bondage*; but the *inward Law* of the Gospel, the *Law of the Spirit of Life*, than which nothing can be more free and ingenuous: for it doth not act us by Principles without us [*sic*], but is an inward *Self-Moving* Principle, living in our Hearts. I do not urge the Law written upon *Tables of Stone* without us (though there is still a good use of that too) but the Law of Holinesse written within, upon the *Fleshly Tables of our hearts* … . The Law that I speak of, it is *a Law of Love*, which is the most powerfull Law in the World; and yet it freeth us in a manner from all Law without us, because it maketh us become a *Law unto our selves*. … Love is at once a Freedome from all Law, a State of purest Liberty, and yet a Law too, of the most constraining and indispensable Necessity. (Cudworth, 1647, pp. 73ff.)

Cudworth's contrast between the outward law and the interior law by which we become a 'law unto ourselves' is extraordinarily close to Kantian autonomy as opposed to heteronomy. Cudworth argues for *a priori* ethical insight into binding principles regardless of any external force, be that community or even God's command. This is not anti-theistic because of the Platonic conviction that the soul is akin to the Divine, and in following its true nature the soul cannot be in opposition to God. As Smith strikingly formulates: 'the *Internal & God-like frame of Spirit* which is necessary for a true conjunction and union of the Souls of men with God' (Smith, 1660, p. 311). Henry More uses just this premise to argue that ethical principles can be proved rationally. Cassirer was right when he observed that the Cambridge Platonists form two independent movements tending toward the same end; they are two important stages on the way leading from Luther to Kant, from the concept of freedom of the Reformation to from the concept of freedom of idealism, from the principle of justification by faith to the principle of the autonomy of will and of the practical reason. (Cassirer, 1953, p. 81)

Moreover, Frederick Beiser's work on the Cambridge Platonists starts with an observation concerning the postmodern disillusionment with 'the Enlightenment faith in reason' evinced by Radical Orthodoxy. His exploration of the Cambridge Platonists is part of an attempt to show that the 'Enlightenment faith in reason was not a lazy dogma but a hard won conclusion' (Beiser, 1996, p. ix). In the context of the English Civil War the moderation and rationality of the Cambridge Platonists was the very opposite of lazy or complacent.

Conservative Revolutionaries: Milbank, de Maistre and the Critique of Liberalism

Milbank sees himself as a Christian Socialist. It may seem perverse to associate his thought with a reactionary like de Maistre, and it may appear more attractive to ally Radical Orthodoxy with thinkers untainted by fascism. However, as Coleridge was keen to observe, 'extremes meet'. The critique of liberalism in de Maistre exerted an influence upon German Romanticism. Figures like von Genz, August Wilhelm Schlegel, Friedrich Schlegel, Novalis, von Baader and Schelling all agreed with de Maistre's apocalyptic vision of the horror of the Revolution as the revelation of the grim reality of secular utopia.

De Maistre's apocalyptic vision finds its clearest analogy in the twentieth century in the thought of Carl Schmitt (Zaganiaris, 2001, pp. 147–67). Schmitt in his *Politische Theologie* of 1922 saw Marxist atheism as the final conclusion of the secularization of modernity. This process of replacing God with man was envisaged by Schmitt as rooted in the ideas of national sovereignty and the liberal state. Schmitt counters the optimistic anthropology of modernity with a pessimistic account derived from de Maistre and Hobbes. The basis for this emphasis upon a powerful state was a reliance upon the doctrine of original sin of the Catholic reactionaries such as de Maistre or de Bonald, as well as the pessimism of Hobbes, the *bête noire* of the Cambridge Platonists. The concept of the state presupposes politics, which for Schmitt is based upon the opposition of friend and foe. It is the sovereign who possesses the right to determine the foe. The problem with liberalism was its failure to consider the significance of the friend/foe relation as constitutive for politics. The foe becomes rather the partner in a futile and infinite conversation that can only result in compromise rather than struggle: reason cannot be the basis of any state but brute decision. It was precisely a visceral opposition to such a view of politics that fuelled the polemics of the Cambridge Platonists against Hobbes.

But the German left in the inter-war years shared much of Schmitt's Hobbesianism. Walter Benjamin, in particular, was aware that his thought shared in its critique of liberalism much in common with the right-wing Carl Schmitt. The early Frankfurt School shared the view of the Romantic right that the Enlightenment was a form of oppression, and both late capitalism and state socialism are viewed as expressions of instrumental reason. Reason, as *universal* 'Begriff' under which any *particular* individual is subordinated, becomes an expression of the will to power. We might consider the extreme pessimism of Horkheimer and Adorno concerning a total society and its commodity culture. Adorno's longing for the 'Nicht-Identisch' is related to the claim that Enlightenment is totalitarian; it is the unrelenting demand for system and unity which enslaves us all (Adorno, 1979, p. 7). Milbank agrees with this diagnosis of 'late capitalism' as in essence totalitarian. And a French writer of the avant-garde like the early Foucault in *Surveiller et Punir (Discipline and Punish)* presents the work of a liberal reformer like Bentham as part of the oppressive dimension of supposed emancipation. Here we see the radical rejection of humanism in Milbank:

> Importantly, the *nouveaux philosophes* at times try to resist the temptation, apparent in Foucault, to creep back into humanism. We may hanker after the liberal subject as a bulwark against fascism, but fascism will always be able to announce, truly, the illusory universality of this subject. (*TST*, p. 319)

Fascism was correct on Milbank's account in exposing the 'illusory universality' of the liberal subject. He continues that for the *nouveaux philosophes*

> it is not, as for Hobbes or Foucault, that the essence of all politics is power, but rather, as for de Maistre, de Bonald and Carl Schmitt, that all politics invents power by proclaiming a religion which channels the mythical power of a fictive God or gods ('fictive' does not here necessarily mean 'untrue'). If power after all dominates, then this is not because of its material reality, but because of the arbitrariness of all its material inventions. The perfect form of politics, as of religion, argues Bernard Henri-Lévi, in the wake of Carl Schmitt and the Catholic positivist tradition, is monotheism, because this posits a single, absolute source of power. (Ibid.)

Milbank is absolutely candid about his own sympathies when he writes: 'There is much in this line of thought that is of great value, and which the rest of this book will seek to pursue' (*TST*, p. 320). Finally, I think one should consider the importance of Karl Barth as a part of the decisionistic climate of the 1930s and *a fortiori* anti-liberal tradition influencing Milbank. The mood of decision did not just influence epistemology and politics, but also theology. Barth, writing about the biblical first commandment, insists that it is a *commandment*:

> We can understand the first commandment when we understand it in the biblical context and we understand the theological axiom really as that which presents itself

as a commandment. It is essentially not just a Divine communication about Himself – about his uniqueness or perhaps that there are no gods besides him. It is not simply a revelation of Divine truth. Rather it is a commandment directed to those sole objects of his word in Israel. God does not describe himself as Lord, he behaves as such in so far as he demands, rules and forbids: 'You shall have no other gods besides me!' One should not abstract from this divine behaviour, from this real Lordship of God. The theological axiom is a Divine statement ... it primarily and decisively means: obedience or disobedience. The Divine truth, which is expressed through the commandment, is there by virtue of a Divine decision and one or another in a human responsive decision. (Barth, 1982, p. 131, own trans.)

The authoritarian and anti-liberal nature of Barth's thought is unmistakable. The divine imperative is based upon an external sanction – the inscrutable divine decision. The original obligation of man to God is based on will not nature. This passage was composed in 1933 and it resounds with the language of *decision*.

Milbank's postmodern scepticism of Nietzschean provenance is linked to the recovery of theology's counter-narrative: 'The end of modernity ... means the end of a single system of truth based on universal reason, which tells us what reality is like. ... [T]he point is not to "represent" ... externality, but just to join in its occurrence, not to know, but to intervene, originate' (Milbank, 1991, pp. 225–6). The '*nouveaux philosophes*' are conscious 'that one can only oppose Nietzsche and his followers by invoking a counter-mythology and a counter-ontology, not by trying to reinstate a humanism founded upon "universal reason", nor by seeking a level of narrated "reality" beneath the play of *simulacra*' (*TST*, p. 320).

Cudworth provides a striking articulation of the opposing liberal position. He objects

that *Religion* is no *Figment of Politicians* ... As the *Religion* of an *Oath*, is a *Necessary Vinculum* of *Civil Society*; so *Obligation in Conscience*, respecting the Deity as its Original, and as the Punisher of the Violation thereof, is the very Foundation of all *Civil Sovereinty*. For *Pacts* and *Covenants* (into which some would resolve all *Civil Power*) without this *Obligation in Conscience*, are nothing but meer *Words* and *Breath*: and the *Laws* and *Commands* of *Civil Sovereigns*, do not make *Obligation*, but presuppose it, as a thing in Order of Nature *Before* them, and without which they would be *Invalid*. (Cudworth, 1678, p. 697)

In other words, 'obligation' is a matter of *nature*, not convention. Cudworth is resolutely essentialist. And one can see, of course, why a Platonist would be inclined to argue thus. It is not poetic counter-narration that is required here, but the recognition that obligation properly understood is categorical, not hypothetical: its binding nature is *intrinsic*. Milbank's poststructural subversion of a single system of truth based on universal reason points via Schmitt and de Maistre back to Vico (Berlin, 1990, p. 141). The loss of certainty is compensated by the appeal to participation in the unknowable God. But Cudworth fulminates against such a move to deny human autonomy and knowledge in the name of divine dependence:

It is a fond imagination for any to suppose that it is derogatory to the glory of God to bestow or import any such gift upon his creatures as knowledge is, which hath an intrinsical evidence within itself ... . Wherefore since it cannot be denied but every clear apprehension is an entity, and the essence of truth is nothing but clear intelligibility ... it cannot be denied but that men are oftentimes deceived and think they clearly comprehend what they do not. But it does not follow from hence, because men sometimes think they clearly comprehend what they do not, that therefore they can never be certain that they do not clearly comprehend any thing. ... I shall conclude this discourse with that of Origen against Celsus, 'Science and knowledge is the only firm thing in the world', without a participation of which communicated to them from God, all creatures would be mere *ludibria* [playthings] and vanity'. (Cudworth, 1996, p. 142)

Whereas Radical Orthodoxy is opposed to 'a single system of truth based on universal reason, which tells us what reality is like', the doctrine of participation is construed by Cudworth to mean that the human mind has access to the eternal and immutable essences as they exist in the divine mind. Here we have yet another striking opposition between the essentialism of the Cambridge Platonists and the instrumentalism of Radical Orthodoxy.

Conclusion

Radical Orthodoxy's claim to have roots in the Cambridge Platonists, those men who praise the 'indestructible basis of reason and the essential elements of our higher humanity' (Tulloch, 1874, II, p. 14) is *prima vista* puzzling. And indeed when we examine the major tenets of Radical Orthodoxy we find not just that they are incompatible with those of those seventeenth-century men of Latitude, but in opposition. First, the Latitudinarians are an instance of a thoroughly Christian and clerical aspect of the Enlightenment: these men of Latitude were no counter-cultural prophets like Hamann, de Maistre or Blake, but powerful university professors and heads of colleges who helped forge the 'Enlightenment' or 'Modernity'. Second, they do not fit Milbank's narrative because, as Cassirer rightly claims, the Cambridge Platonists insist upon the idea of fixed universal rationality and that 'Science and knowledge is the only firm thing in the world'. With their characteristic sobriety and latitude, the Cambridge Platonists are simply the most unlikely candidates imaginable for Milbank's polemical and apocalyptic narrative.

I have suggested that Platonism of this modern *magus*, John Milbank, is grounded in the fertile soil of Catholic reaction to the French Revolution. De Maistre had a radicalized and apocalyptic view of the Enlightenment in the wake of the French Revolution and the Terror which is very close to Milbank's own Romantic Christian Cabbala. Milbank is, of course, a great admirer of the Counter-Enlightenment, especially Hamann. The brilliant and polemical Catholic Platonic theorist de Maistre shared much of his mystical Christian Platonism with Hamann. But it was via the influence of de Maistre's genius (and Hamann) upon German Romanticism that many twentieth-century intellectuals, from Schmitt and Heidegger, to Benjamin and Adorno, inherited the bleak view of Enlightenment as a wolf in sheep's clothing. Radical Orthodoxy requires the apocalyptic vision of de Maistre and his pupils for its historiography. At this point, we confront a deep paradox within Radical Orthodoxy: its critique of 'modernity' is itself radically modern.

Notes

1   On the general question of Radical Orthodoxy and political liberalism, see C. Insole (2004), pp. 15–157, and my own review of Radical Orthodoxy in the *Journal of Theological Studies* (2000), **51** (1), pp. 405–8.
2   I am deeply indebted to the work of Wilhelm Schmidt Biggemann and his book *'Die Politische Theologie der Gegenaufklärung. Saint-Martin, De Maistre, Kleuker Baader'*, Berlin: Akademie Verlag, 2004. My thanks to David Leech and Brian Hebblethwaite for reading a draft of this chapter and for helpful suggestions.
3   See the absurdities about 'Die Bodenlosig des Abendländischen Denkens' beginning with Cicero's translations from the Greek into Latin as described in James Vigus and David Grumett, Heidegger's *Der Ursprung des Kunstwerkes* (Stuttgart: Philipp Reclaim, 1960), pp. 14–15.
4   Cf. Owen Bradley, *A Modern Maistre: the Social and Political Thought of Joseph de Maistre* (Lincoln, NE and London, University of Nebraska Press, 1999).

CHAPTER 8

Theology, Social Theory and Dialectic: A Consideration of Milbank's Hegel

David Peddle

John Milbank's *Theology and Social Theory* is a vigorous attempt to release theology from its self-inflicted bondage to the anti-theological reason characteristic of modern social theory. Milbank wishes to show that theology does not require sociological diagnosis of social problems and moreover that there is not a significant sociological 'reading' of religion and Christianity of which theology must take account (*TST*, p. 3).[1]

Milbank relies on an archaeological approach through which he deconstructs the objectivity and neutrality of the social sciences by indicating their origin both in a new cultural practice which they help to sustain and as a heretical expression of Christianity (ibid.). Thus the social sciences cannot claim a 'scientific' relation to the secular nor an unbiased access to the religious. On his view, 'scientific social theories are themselves theologies or anti-theologies in disguise' (ibid.). Milbank's point in excavating the site of modernity is to uncover the questionable theological roots of sociology – and of modern thought in general. By disentangling contemporary theology from its 'dependence' on these theological-cum-sociological presuppositions, he wishes to retrieve a richer ecclesial tradition – one simultaneously pre-modern and post-modern, a theology aware of itself as culturally constructed (p. 6).

While Milbank finds anticipations of his own deconstruction in Hegel, he nevertheless argues that Hegelianism remains under the dominion of scientific politics and political economy, subscribing in its fundamental thought to a violent pagan theology (p. 4). Over and against this Hegelian view, he upholds what he calls a Christian vision of ontological peace (p. 434). He states: 'no claim is made to "represent" an objective social reality; instead the social knowledge advocated is but the continuation of ecclesial practice, the imagination in action of a peaceful, reconciled social order' (p. 6).

In this essay I give an account of Milbank's archaeology of Hegelian thought in terms of his view of the two sources of modernity as expressed in the thought of Hobbes and Machiavelli, and the synthesis of this dyad in modern political economy. Then I describe his detailed arguments against Hegel and suggest a reading of Hegel's thought which poses a challenge to Milbank's interpretation while at the same time supporting his sense of the limitation of Hegel's conception of punishment.

Milbank's Account of Modernity

On Milbank's view, modernity is characterized by both the nominalist voluntarism of Hobbes and the historical humanism of Machiavelli. In Hobbesian thought he finds a political realism which recognizes that liberal civil society can be sustained only if grounded in a single undisputed power (p. 13). This marks the invention of the secular as what Milbank calls a 'space of "pure power"' (p. 12). He thus illuminates the connection between modern absolutism and modern liberalism (p. 13) – a connection often masked by a too-easy distinction of Hobbesian conservatism and Lockean liberalism. Secured in an individualist notion of will, Hobbesian liberalism cannot adequately conceptualize social processes, what Milbank calls 'collective making' (ibid.). In consequence, on the Hobbesian account, social cohesion can be obtained only through the external unities of sovereign dominion and economic contract. For Milbank, this construction borrows heavily from late medieval Christian theology with its distinction between God's *potentia ordinata* and *potentia absoluta* as expressed both in covenant theology and in the sense of God as an irresistible power (pp. 14–15).

Milbank develops further his sense of the importance of theological themes in this new science of politics in relation to biblical interpretation. He writes: 'the surviving presence of the authoritative text of the scriptures within this new space of sovereign power could not be denied' (p. 17). This presence survived in a biblical hermeneutic which merged the liberalism and absolutism of Hobbes's basic position. He states: '[B]oth Hobbes's *Leviathan* and Spinoza's *Tractatus Theologico-Politicus* comprise a political science and a Biblical hermeneutics bound together in one volume' (ibid.). Hobbes, on this account, upholds a positivist conception of revelation, under which the stable and meaningful communication of revelation requires mediation by the dictates of the sovereign: 'It was necessary for the new single power to lay claim to the right to interpret the Bible'(ibid.).

On Milbank's view, then, the voluntarist language of sovereignty and the continued authoritative presence of the Bible in early modern political thought thwarts the glib narrative of 'secularization' which reads the origins of the modern as a mere borrowing from medieval forms. He sees modern secularity as having fundamentally theological presuppositions. He writes: 'I am suggesting that *only* the theological model permits one to construct the *mythos* of the sovereign power, or sovereign person, so that it is not a case of "essentially" secular and pragmatic realities being temporarily described in antique theological guise' (p. 28).

However, as noted above, this is but one stream of modernity. On Milbank's account, whereas a nominalist voluntarism and positivist hermeneutics forge on the Hobbesian landscape a central place for Christianity (or an interpretation thereof), Machiavelli's secular space was constructed by a non-Christian *virtù*. He states: 'If the Hobbesian field of power seems to be constructed by a perverse theology, then the Machiavellian field of power is constructed by a partial rejection of Christianity and appeal to an alternate mythos' (p. 21). What Milbank finds objectionable in Machiavellianism is its pagan sense of human power as a form of virtue (p. 22).

We thus have before us what Milbank sees as the two presuppositions of modernity, the natural rights tradition and the humanist tradition. He finds in modern political economy a synthesis of these presuppositions through a development of the voluntarist account of social harmony. He argues, however, that whereas Hobbesian voluntarism required an a-historical contract theory, 'political economy on the other hand took a much more realist and historical view of human collaboration because it was concerned with the problem of an unintended harmonious effect' (p. 31). Also, political economy continues the Machiavellian stream of modernity in a political–economic surrogate for political virtue and a deepened reflection on the general interest (p. 32). In the thought of Adam Smith, for example, the Machiavellian civic hero is transformed into *homo mercans* and his desire for glory becomes a quest for public repute (p. 33).

Another Machiavellian aspect of political economy emerges most clearly in the work of James Stewart, which imagines a political authority based on economic dependency (p. 35). Not only does Stewart encourage an exclusivist disciplinary economy but, as Milbank contends, for Stewart, the bounds of the marketplace 'are initially marked out and constantly redrawn by arbitrary political violence' (p. 36). Milbank judges this celebration of the *libido dominandi* not heretical but pagan.

Nevertheless, in the conception of providence which emerges in political economy and which resolves and conceals the division and violence of its pagan moment, Milbank finds a heretical 'theodicy' (p. 32). Whereas the pagan Machiavellianism of Stewart secures the market system through violent appropriation, the heretical theodicist version of political economy incorporates a notion of divine *telos*. Milbank writes: 'the "hidden hand" of the market place is somewhat more than a metaphor, because God–Nature has replaced self-interest and the "trucking disposition" in individuals in such a way that their operation will result in overall harmony' (p. 40). Here the acts of militaristic violence characteristic of Stewart's account and vivid realism in regard to capitalism give way to mystification and a falsely peaceful development (p. 42).

Milbank's Critique of Hegel

Milbank argues that Hegel's religious and political thought remains within the problematic parameters of modernity. In this section I will sketch basic elements of his critique of Hegel. He states: '[The] main charge that will be brought against Hegel is that dialectics is just a new variant of modern politics and political economy' (p. 147). Further: 'Hegel's logic is simply another political economy and so inevitably another theodicy ...' (p. 148). At the heart of this criticism, then, is the sense that Hegel's philosophy replicates the pagan and heretical presuppositions of modern secularity.

Milbank develops his critique by focusing on what he considers to be Hegel's three great errors: (1) his retention of the Cartesian subject (p. 154); (2) his invention of the myth of negation (p. 155); (3) his misconstrual of infinitude (p. 157). Milbank portrays these errors as very much intertwined. He argues that Hegel, like Descartes, maintains that 'spirit is able to constitute a polar opposite to the objective sphere' (p. 155). On Hegel's transformation of this standpoint the opposition between the spiritual and the material that results becomes 'real contradiction', contradiction which itself exists. Nevertheless, for Milbank, Hegel's Cartesian bias is so pervasive that 'the resolution [of this contradiction] is a "return" to self and an immediate, automatic restoration of negated self-identity' (ibid.).

According to Milbank, Hegel's foundational emphasis on identity has the consequence that all difference implies contradiction or negation. Further, he argues: 'Because negation has the initiative, negation must always be "determinate negation" which means that denial of itself leads to a new positive upshot' (ibid.). Milbank denies the necessity of this further positive stage. He writes: 'There are no "inevitable" resolutions of historical tensions and conflicts' (ibid.).

Milbank's third criticism asserts that Hegel, in a fusion of these errors, misconceives the infinite because he defines it in relation to the finite, that is, as 'opposition sublated by identity', with the result that he fundamentally misinterprets the Christian doctrine of creation (pp. 157–8). On this account, Hegel's great errors lead him to conceive the creative activity of God as divine negation and self-estrangement – as a fall for both God and humanity. From this basic concept, Milbank argues, follow the two most objectionable components of the Hegelian view: (1) that there is a relatively unrealized (indeterminate) moment of divine reality; and (2) that evil is thus necessary to the development of human self-consciousness and freedom and to the divine love which reconciles humanity to God (p. 188).

Correlative to this criticism of Hegel's conception of divine self-estrangement and the necessity of evil is a further criticism of Hegel's conception of *Aufhebung*, conventionally translated as sublation. Milbank argues that Hegel's concept of sublation, a comprehension which both negates and preserves, leaves outside the return of the absolute to itself a realm of finitude that remains arbitrary and contingent. He states: 'Whereas Christianity subscribes to a total but unknowable providence, Hegel denies a complete providence yet claims a full knowledge of providence in the limited extent of its workings' (p. 159). What permits this 'metaphysical hubris', on Milbank's view, is Hegel's failure to recognize 'that the most surprising contingency, the sheerest givenness, occurs at the macro level, not the micro level' (p. 158).

The upshot of this criticism is that Hegel fails to unify the infinite and the finite because on the Hegelian account there is always a 'husk' of finitude that remains outside the divine reconciliation. As a result of this metaphysical structure, Hegel's thought is continuous with modern paganism allowing a realm of chaos uninformed by the divine idea – 'totally outside the reality of divine providence and divine goodness' (p. 159). Here Milbank has in mind a comparison with what he calls the Machiavellian 'field of power' (p. 21).

Milbank is also keen to illuminate what he sees to be the distortion of political life that results from Hegel's errors. He writes: 'Hegel subordinates the contingencies of human making/speaking to the supposedly logical articulation of subjectivity which is secretly in command throughout' (p. 157). This subordination, on Milbank's view, has the same structure as the Hegelian conception of Providence – it implies a realm of indifference, a realm necessary to but unredeemed by the state. For Milbank, this realm is the locus of the practice of capitalism and the administration of discipline, what Hegel calls civil society.

According to Milbank, Hegel follows Hobbes in portraying the origins of civil law and society in individual self-seeking (p. 170). What is then required is that this self-seeking and lawfulness be more deeply unified in the state. For Milbank, this unity occurs via the third stage of civil society, that is, police and corporation. He contends that this stage is intended as a transition from Hegel's conception of morality to ethical life. He portrays Hegel's account of this transition in terms of a twofold intrusion of the state into civil society.

First, the real state appears in civil society in the division of labour. On Milbank's account the division of labour and its 'secret coordination of blind passion' shows the invisible hand theodicy which is central to Hegel's view (p. 169). But for Milbank the division of labour is in no way an appearance (or as he puts it representational articulation) of the state. By contrast with the supposed self-consciousness and reason of the state, the realm of civil society is a realm of unredeemed passion. Civil society itself can never be ethically redeemed. On this portrayal, then, Hegel's division of labour is in no way ethical but 'part of a merely natural expansion of wealth' (ibid.). Second, on Milbank's account, ethical life intrudes at the level of corporation – in which through shared interest and sympathy members are protected and standards of production arise. But for Milbank the unification remains at the level of morality in the form of Enlightenment sympathy and benevolence. There is no structural transformation of society because 'corporation and state do not enter into the question of what should be made and how, nor into the determination of fair prices' (p. 170).

On Milbank's account the division of labour occurs at the level of the 'understanding' (*Verstand*). And what he means by this is a level of conceptualization characterized by a certain division, for example, between subjectivity and objectivity, finite and infinite. As a result of this conceptualization, he asserts, there will be limits to employee–employer sympathy as to a common corporate interest. What this entails is that the 'intermediary function' of the corporation collapses and cannot provide a local content for civic participation in the light of the capitalist economy (ibid.).

Finally, Milbank argues that Hegel's pagan emphasis on power and passion within the rubric of political economy renders his concept of punishment less than Christian. He states:

> [W]hile, at a certain level, one can transcend law, there cannot, for Hegel, be a society without law, a society where processes of forgiveness, contrition and expiation form of themselves a self-sustaining cultural process. Yet to deny this is at least a *possibility*, is to deny that there can be complete salvation within the physical bodily order. And this denial belongs intrinsically with Hegel's metaphysics, which posits a sphere of indifference, a realm which self-expression must enter, yet whose sheerly contingent elements can never be sublated by the Idea. (p. 167)

Thus conceived there would be no true community or reconciliation in Hegel's ethical and political theory. Milbank writes: '[Hegel's] political theory begins with the self seeking individual and concludes with the quasi-subject of the state organism. The "ideality" of the state, for Hegel, is ultimately the state's own power, cohesion and freedom' (p. 170).

Questioning Milbank's Divisions

On Milbank's account, then, Hegel by virtue of a foundational Cartesianism replicates the ontological and practical violence of modernity and is thus not able adequately to deconstruct the dialectic of secularity. Although his account is provocative and insightful, there is reason to interrogate its portrayal of Hegel's religious and political vision. In this section I wish to challenge Milbank's claims that Hegel conceives a division within the divine between its indeterminate and determinate moments and that Hegel conceives *Sittlichkeit* in such a way as to generate a division between civil society and the state. Also, by contrast with Milbank, I locate Hegel's philosophy of history within the Augustinian tradition. However, while critical of a number of Milbank's basic claims, I end by supporting his sense of the limits of Hegel's conception of punishment.

The Idea of God in and for Himself

There are occasions on which Hegel might be taken, as on Milbank's argument, to uphold a distinction between an indeterminate and a determinate trinity. Consider the *Science of Logic*:

> [L]ogic is to be understood as the system of pure reason, as the realm of pure thought. This realm is truth as it is without veil in its absolute nature. It can therefore be said that this content is the exposition of God as he is in his eternal essence before the creation of nature and a finite mind. (Hegel, 1969, p. 50)

But consider the *Encyclopaedia Logic* where he responds to his contemporary, Franz von Baader. Von Baader, in his 'comments upon some anti-religious philosophical doctrines of our time' (1824), criticizes Hegel's view as having a false conception of matter 'in that it affirms regarding the transcendent essence of this world – which contains corruption within it – that it is immediately and eternally emergent and emerging from God, as the eternal outgoing ([self]-emptying) of God which conditions his eternal re-entry into himself [as spirit]'. Hegel replies: '[I] do not see how to avoid admitting that this proposition is implied in the determination that God is the creator of the world' (Hegel, 1991, pp. 15–16). On Hegel's account, creation is God's eternal activity.

A clearer sense of Hegel's view on this question of indeterminate and determinate divine moments is to be found in his *Lectures on the Philosophy of Religion:* 'In accord with the first element then, we consider God in his eternal idea, as he is in and for himself, prior to or apart from the creation of the world so to speak.' However, he severely qualifies this statement: 'But God is the creator of the world; in so far as he is not the creator, he is grasped inadequately. His creative role is not an actus that happened once; [rather,] what takes place in the idea is an eternal moment, an eternal determination of the idea' (Hegel, 1988, p. 417). For further evidence, see *The Philosophy of Nature*:

> [E]ternity is not before or after time, not before the creation of the world, nor when it perishes; rather is eternity the absolute present, the now, without before and after. The world is created, is now being created, and has eternally been created; this presents itself in the preservation of the world. Creating is the activity of the absolute idea; the idea of nature, like the Idea as such, is eternal. (Hegel, 1970, § 247).

Thus Hegel does not conceive the Trinity as divided in the manner suggested by Milbank. When he speaks of 'God before creation' he is using the language of religious representation (*Vorstellung*). But it is not his intention that we simply remain within the insight that such language provides – as is characteristic of his thought, he employs representation only to show how it might be given more rational form. The weight of Hegel's argument is towards unifying the notion of creation and created in light of the conceptual logic of the Trinity.

Thus creation is not to be considered self-estrangement and fall in quite the way Milbank implies – it is not a loss of a prior unity; it does not step outside the divine unity but is an expression of God's own otherness. This is not to be conceived as mere difference but as self-difference, a difference which is integral to the divine self-hood, it does not await reconciliation but is reconciled in its difference.

Further, because there is not an immanent Trinity whose immediate unity lies beyond its determinate negation, there is not in evil that which is simply opposed to God. Consider the following statement from *The Philosophy of Nature*:

> [I]t is put forward as a further superiority of nature that throughout all the contingency of its manifold existence it remains obedient to eternal laws. But surely this is also true of the realm of self-consciousness, a fact which finds recognition in

the belief that human affairs are governed by providence ... but if the contingency of spirit, the free will (Willkür) does evil, this is still infinitely superior to the regular motions of the celestial bodies, or to the innocence of plant life; for what thus errs is still spirit. (Hegel, 1970, p. 18)

Human evil, then, on Hegel's view more fully expresses spirit than does nature. Moreover 'evil' is seen on the Hegelian view as necessary. He states: '[W]e must give up the superficial notion that original sin has its ground only in a contingent action of the first human pair. It is part of the concept of spirit that man is by nature evil; and we must not imagine that it could be otherwise' (Hegel, 1991, § 24).

For Hegel, the doctrine of original sin indicates that humans cannot remain in an immediate relation to nature, that we are beyond our natural being and that we make it an object of our self-conscious awareness. This division between ourselves and nature entails that we draw our purposes from no external source but from our own subjectivity. He writes: 'Inasmuch as [man] takes those purposes to their ultimate limits, knows only himself, and wills in his particularity without reference to the universal, be is evil, and his evil is his subjectivity' (ibid.).

On Hegel's view, this inward self-certainty is the ground of morality and has contradictory expression in conscience and wickedness. So far as the human will is given a content from its own inwardness, it lacks the objectivity of social customs, laws and institutions. For Hegel it is precisely this immediate goodness which cannot be distinguished from wickedness. Morality thus collapses into its own negativity, the annihilation of its own objectivity, but as such it becomes a negative proof that its objectivity lies elsewhere, that the self does not immediately determine the good (Hegel, 1973, § 511). Hegel states:

> The result, the truth of this semblance is, on its negative side, the absolute nullity of this volition which would fain hold its own against the good, and of the good, which could only be abstract. On the affirmative side, in the concept, this semblance thus collapsing is the same single universality of the will, what is the good. (Hegel, 1973, § 512)

That these sides cannot be sustained in their independence is for Hegel the transition to *Sittlichkeit* or ethical life. Thus, just as there is not a radical division between the divine unity and its created otherness, neither is there a Cartesian subjectivity which is in principle distinct from yet falls into evil. Hegel is quite clear that modern subjectivity is in itself no less evil than good.

Nature and evil thus conceived are not merely estrangements but rather expressions of spirit in which there is at once otherness and self-relation. God's return to self is not something that occurs 'after' such negations but is present 'already' within them. As such, these moments have a positive content – and in no way represent 'husks of finitude' which are not comprehended in the divine reconciliation. Hegel's ontology of creation and evil is thus not to be confined to Milbank's portrayal, which too eagerly paints it within the confines of the modern.

The Ethics of Civil Society

It is of interest, then, to examine Milbank's archaeology of Hegel's political thought. His claim that for Hegel civil society begins with individual self-seeking is not tenable (see Doull, 1973 and Peddle, 2000). It must be kept in mind that civil society is, for Hegel, an ethical realm and that *Sittlichkeit* secures both the moral aspirations and the self-interests of individuals, both equality and competition, for example. Civil society is not even to be considered simply a realm of individuals but as composed also of associations. While from one vantage point these associations remain abstract because of the self-subsistence of society's members, these 'self-subsistent' individuals have been educated to a common ethical order through their family life and religious education. Hegel writes:

> In respect of his relation to the family, the child's education has the positive aim of instilling ethical principles into him in the form of an immediate feeling for which differences are not yet explicit so that thus equipped with the foundation of an ethical life his heart may live its early years in love, trust, and obedience. (Hegel, 1967, § 175)

But 'love, trust and obedience' are clearly inadequate expressions of the relation of modern and post-modern citizens to the state. The *Bildung* or ethical education which occurs in the family is incomplete precisely because the family only partially educates individuals to the rational independence required by membership in the various associations characteristic of civil society. And so far as such an education occurs within the family, its result is a rational independence which leads individuals beyond family life. On Hegel's account, children develop and leave their natural family in order to make lives for themselves, and ethical life in its immediate union of universal and particular ends is thus sundered into a situation where the individual defines himself in contradistinction to the universal. This consciousness of one's distinction from the universal is crucial to the rationality and freedom of the state. It is in this realm, in relation to one's family and to the civil associations of which one is a member, that one can reflect critically on the state and its practices. Hegel wishes to secure a realm of difference internal to the state, in the divisions of class and association, which will allow individuals to be in a mediated relation to the government and the state proper. In this realm it is possible for individuals to have divided allegiances and in times of conflict to find their freedom more fully embodied in one of the particular institutions of the state, in family or corporation, than in the state proper. Likewise, it is possible to have recourse to the state against the injustice of one's particular associations.

For Hegel, then, while humans are political animals, the institutions of modernity maintain within them the space for independent critical reflection on the state. This is a nuanced account of the social being of individuals showing how private and public life are fundamentally entwined in their differences and how both emerge from an ethical institutional life. The dividedness of civil society is thus clearly ethical, promoting as it does a concrete, lived and institutional reflection of the workings of the state. Moreover, the content of these reflections is *in principle* not based on self-seeking alone but on a genuinely universal interest. Individuals work to provide for their families and to support the various other institutions of which they are a part.

Civil society, then, is primarily a realm of ethical education where the individual gains a deeper appreciation of the unity of private and public in the self and in the social order. For Hegel, while one is ethical at all points of one's institutional odyssey, in civil society one begins to conceive the union of individual and community not simply in subjective or private terms but also in objective public terms.

That civil society is a deepening of the individual's consciousness of an ethical order already grasped and not merely a realm of self-seeking and/or its correction may be seen in relation to Hegel's conception of the system of needs. On this account, human desires are for the most part produced through social interaction; likewise the objects of desire are produced by society and the value of these objects by human labour (Hegel, 1967, § 196). For Hegel the very multiplication of needs brings out the universality of desire and our mutual interdependence and equality (Hegel, 1967, § 190–93). Hegel's concept of civil society does not presuppose atomistic self-seeking individuals who can never be concretely reconciled in the state. By contrast, on his view, the members of civil society show in their rational independence an awareness of their interdependence with other citizens and a desire to promote not only their own interest but also that of others

Fundamental to Hegel's conception of civil society is that it is an ethical realm in which the satisfaction of individual desires occurs only in relation to other individuals and that this relation institutionally expressed is the objective enactment of freedom. It is therefore misguided to portray civil society as a realm of self-seeking and unredeemed passion. In fact, the whole conception of ethical life is animated in large measure by his sense of the redemption of passion. In relation to ethical institutions, individuals are freed *from* the moral division between a heterogeneity of needs and a homogeneous moral law *into* an inner universality which finds objective actuality in social institutions. Civil society demonstrates the universality of civic life by drawing individuals beyond their subjective isolation into an objective discipline – one becomes known not simply as a person but as carpenter, technician, civil servant, businessperson, or farmer.

Civil society and its division of labour is a definite form of self-conscious ethical life. Through the system of needs and the division of labour, one learns what Hegel calls rectitude, that is, knowledge of the attitudes and actions appropriate to one's labour or profession. However, the ethical identity accomplished in one's class and in the workplace is incomplete. Individuals transcend their class being: they may move between classes, being upwardly or downwardly mobile. Also individuals from different classes come into contact with each other. And as the system of need engenders an independence of class it becomes necessary to know the customs of many different classes if one is to work in civil society. The class system is clearly a prefiguration of the ethical fulfilment found in the state. It gives rise to a universality which its institutions cannot sustain on their own accord. The classes, Hegel argues, are superseded by and undergo modification through the working of civil law, the administration of justice, the process of education and religious instruction (Hegel, 1967, § 203).

Nevertheless, there is in civil society an ethical instability, and this is nowhere more apparent then in Hegel's portrayal of the corporation. For Hegel, the ethical unity present in the corporation has the limitation that it comes into opposition with other ethical unities, be they families or other corporations. The competitive and divisive interests of the economic sphere thus generate a realm of ethical conflict. Milbank captures something of this instability in his sense that 'the intermediary function of corporation collapses' (p. 170). But it is not clear that the instability of corporate life undermines Hegel's account of the state in the way that Milbank suggests. First, Milbank's reading of the logic and status of the transition from civil society to the state is misleading. He contends that the 'transition' from corporation to state is the stage at which 'one is supposed to cross the boundary between *Moralität* and *Sittlichkeit*' (p. 168). As argued above, however, civil society is already, in principle, beyond the level of *Moralität*. Determinate duties and rights are attached to one's roles in economic and family life – in institutions in which 'the absolute "ought" is no less an "is" ' (Hegel, 1973, § 514).

Civil society is an enactment, an instantiation of ethical life, according to Hegel, not something that is to be made ethical in some 'later' reconciliation in the state. His argument is rather that civil society is itself, in principle, animated and informed by the state, that civil society is one way in which the state gives expression to its ethical life. Further, Hegel would agree that the corporation conceived in distinction from the state cannot secure civic participation, nor, for that matter, can religion, family, or the legal system. But this is precisely the argument – that the ethical orders of family and civil society, which ever threaten to dissolve into the self-interest of kinship, individuals, classes and corporations, are stabilized and liberated to their universal dimension by being situated in relation to the institutions of the state. While particular businesses, classes, guilds, social clubs, families and corporations come and go, the state's interest in the welfare and civic education of its citizens remains.

For example, on Hegel's view, government agencies and regulatory bodies must ensure that individuals are not excluded from the common goods of society. Government will therefore be responsible for maintaining common capital and utilities (Hegel, 1967, § 235), for controlling quality and fixing prices of essential goods and services (ibid., § 236), and for removing even accidental obstacles to the rights of the individual and the public (ibid., § 230). Further, he recognizes that government must protect the welfare of citizens from the contingencies of the market. In an established civil society, poverty, in fact, is no longer to be considered a contingency. Rather, on Hegel's view it is a wrong done to one class by another. He contends further that how poverty is to be abolished is one of the most disturbing questions of the modern economy and state (ibid., § 244A). Moreover, he states:

> It has often been said that the end of the state is the happiness of the citizens. That is perfectly true. If all is not well with them, if their subjective aims are not satisfied, if they do not find that the state as such is the means to their satisfaction, then the footing of the state itself is insecure. (Ibid., § 265A)

From later standpoints it appears that Hegel inadequately comprehends the principle of equality as witnessed in his acceptance of class alienation and primogeniture, for example. This criticism has some validity and marks in Hegel's thought a certain abstraction relative to the concrete freedom and equality presupposed in the centuries after him. It is misleading, however, to conclude, as Milbank does, following Manfred Riedel, that Hegel was thus attached to pre-modern social structures. Rather, he found in the principles of the Prussian Enlightenment a less violent transformation of political institutions than present in the French Revolution, which resolved into a reign of terror (cf. Riedel, 1984; for the Prussian Enlightenment cf. Behren, 1985 and Doull, 2000). It is only on the view that civil society is an end in itself or on the assumption that classes are static forms imposed on social life and not themselves expressions of modern freedom that his depiction is found radically flawed. It is closer to the Hegelian argument to see historical–political forms both as stable and as containing within the logic of freedom – which is their very substance – the seeds of their own rational revision.

The corporation, then, is a partial expression of ethical life but it is *ethical* and no transition is required to make it so. Hegel writes:

> The state, as spirit, sunders itself into the particular determination of its concept, of its mode of being ... The laws regulating family and civil society are the institutions of the rational order which glimmers in them. But the ground and final truth of these institutions is spirit, their universal end and known objective. (Hegel, 1967, 263A)

Providence, Evil and Punishment

Milbank thus misinterprets Hegel's concept of civil society as he does his concept of creation. Because he does not adequately attend to the nature of determinate negation in each, he likewise fails in his interpretation of sublation in each realm. This misinterpretation of Hegel's concept of determinate negation and sublation is replicated in Milbank's general sense of his concept of providence. It is insufficient to portray Hegel's view as one of 'a necessarily self-estranged and self-returning God who leaves behind him the scattered husks of the merely material and indifferent' (p. 160). Throughout the Hegelian system, there is quite the contrary intention at all points. In his *Lectures on the Philosophy of Religion*, for example, he states:

> 'God himself is dead' it says in a Lutheran hymn, expressing an awareness that the human, the fragile, the weak, the negative are themselves a moment of the divine, that they are within God himself, that finitude, negativity, otherness are not outside of God and do not, as otherness, hinder unity with God. Otherness, the negative is known to be a moment of the divine nature itself. This involves the highest idea of spirit. (Hegel, 1988, p. 468)

Or consider Hegel's praise of *The Divine Comedy* in his *Lectures on Fine Art*:

> Here in the face of the absolute grandeur of the ultimate end and aim of all things, everything individual and particular in human interests and aims vanishes, and yet there stands there, completely epically, everything otherwise most fleeting and transient in the living world, fathomed objectively in its inmost being, judged in its worth or worthlessness by the supreme Concept, by God. (Ibid., p. 1103)

However, beyond his criticism of Hegel for leaving a realm outside providence, what Milbank finds theologically troubling is 'the embracing of a necessary passage through conflict and alienation, on the way from unfree nature to mature freedom' (p. 244). He distinguishes Hegel's concept of history from the Augustinian view of providence and argues that the concept of a resolution through necessary conflict entails that an unchristian violence permeate Hegel's concept of ethical life, in particular his concept of punishment. He writes that, by contrast with the Hegelian view, 'Augustine ... puts peaceful reconciliation in no dialectical relationship with conflict' (p. 389). But this seems an incomplete account of Augustine's view. Consider, for example, *City of God*. Augustine states:

> God, as he is the supremely good creator of good natures, so is He of evil wills the most just Ruler; so that, while they make an evil use of good natures, He makes a good use of even evil wills. Accordingly, He caused the devil (good by God's creation, wicked by his own will) to be cast down from his high position and to become the mockery of His angels – that is, He caused his temptations to benefit those whom he wishes to injure by them. ... [W]hile God in His goodness created him good, He yet had already foreseen and arranged how he would make use of him when he became wicked. (Augustine, 1950, 11.17)

And further:

> For God would never have created any, I do not say angel, but even man, whose future wickedness he foreknew, unless he had equally known to what uses in behalf of the good He could turn him, thus embellishing the course of the ages, as it were an exquisite poem set off with antitheses. (Ibid., 11.18)

While Augustine does not explicitly identify evil with the 'self-estrangement' of absolute spirit, he does include it within the economy of providence. Milbank's interpretation fails to uncover the Augustinian roots of Hegel's thought and presents only a partial picture of Augustine's view. The standpoint of theodicy represents an important moment of Augustinian thought and brings history into view without the theoretical division between what should have happened and what did happen. This standpoint captures the insight that there is no excuse for even the possibility of evil unless it is necessary, unless it unavoidably belongs to God's self-consciously wilful creatures and their free return to the divine principle which animates their ethical life.

Though Milbank's account of Hegel's concept of reconciliation is problematic, it nevertheless gestures towards a significant tension in Hegel's thought, a tension, one might say, between his non-moralistic account of evil and his moralistic account of punishment, specifically his acceptance of capital punishment. As noted above, Hegel argues that evil is a necessary aspect of the human spirit, that properly construed, humans are 'by nature evil'. In his *Lectures on the Philosophy of Religion* he states:

> The person who violates a commandment is evil, but only in this particular case; he stands in opposition to this particular commandment. In the Parsee religion [Zoroastrianism], we saw that good and evil, light and darkness, stand in universal antithesis to each other. There, however, the antithesis is external to human beings, and they themselves are outside it. This abstract antithesis is not present within them. It is required therefore that humanity should comprehend this abstract antithesis within itself. It is not that one has transgressed this or that commandment, but rather that one is intrinsically evil – universally evil, purely and simply evil in one's innermost being. (Hegel, 1988, pp. 446–7)

The reconciliation of the subject's inner division, the reconciliation of the natural and the rational will, is not something brought about through any activity on the part of the human subject but is already implicitly accomplished. Hegel writes: 'Put more precisely, the antithesis arises eternally and just as eternally sublates itself; there is at the same time eternal reconciliation' (ibid., p. 453). In the face of this eternal and implicit reconciliation of the division within the finite human subject, and the demand that this become explicit (p. 452), it is somewhat jarring that Hegel also supports capital punishment, which would seem the antithesis of forgiveness and reconciliation. When it comes to capital punishment, the dialectic which moves systematically through Hegel's thought is stalled.[2]

Let us sketch Hegel's argument for capital punishment. For Hegel, in the case of murder capital punishment is both the right of the state and demanded by the logic of the criminal's own act. Milbank is right here to place Hegel's argument in the trajectory of Rousseau and Kant (p. 168). Hegel contends that punishment is the objective expression of the criminal's own will. From a liberal standpoint, it is argued against this view that the individual may not in fact agree to give up his right to life in such a fashion. But over and against

Beccaria, for example, Hegel properly distinguishes the state from a mere collection of individuals as in contract doctrine. He says:

> [T]he state is not a contract at all nor is its fundamental essence the unconditional protection and guarantee of the life and property of the public as individuals. On the contrary, it is that higher entity which even lays claim to this very life and property and demands its sacrifice'. (Hegel, 1967, § 100)

Also Hegel argues that 'punishment is regarded as containing the criminal's right and hence by being punished he is being honoured as a rational being. He does not receive this due of honour unless the concept and measure of his punishment are derived from his own act' (ibid., § 101). And he concludes that in the case of murder capital punishment is necessary: '[S]ince life is the full compass of a man's existence, the punishment here cannot simply consist in a "value" for none is great enough, but can consist only in taking away a second life' (ibid.).

But there is some question as to what is given in the criminal's act and whether Hegel has adequately captured its logic and its measure. The individual is held responsible for his action only if it is the product of his self-conscious freedom, and in an act of murder the criminal's will has turned against the universality of its own rational freedom and its objective embodiment in the state, thus making itself into a law beyond the law. But does nullifying this breach of ethical universality require the death of the particular person who has infringed the law? I agree with Hegel that the state has the right to make this judgment but disagree that the acceptance of capital punishment is the right decision.

To accept capital punishment is to deny the fundamental Hegelian insight into the nature of evil – that it belongs necessarily to the concept of the human will. Capital punishment treats the murderer as if he were absolutely anathema, beyond redemption, radically other and outside the reality of civilized humanity. As such it is a return to a pre-ethical, to a moralistic standpoint which treats evil as radically distinct from conscience and the moral law. Hegel sees in the state an institutional standpoint beyond such legalism and moralism, as evidenced in his conception of the sovereign's right to pardon which 'is empowered to actualize mind's power of making undone what has been done and wiping out a crime by forgiving and forgetting it' (Hegel, 1967, § 282). Further he writes:

> This annulment of punishment may take place through religion, since something done may by spirit be made undone in spirit. But the power to accomplish this on earth resides in the king's majesty alone and must belong solely to his self-determined decision. (Ibid.)

Such a limited account, appropriate to the nation state of the nineteenth century, is inadequate both from the standpoint of the post-nation state and from the underlying movement in Hegel's own thought.

While Milbank is right to point out the limit of Hegel's account, it is not that Hegel's justification of capital punishment follows necessarily from his account of the divine principle, but rather that it is at variance with it. On a Hegelian view, the response to Milbank lies not in the eschewal of dialectic but in its deepened development.

Notes

1   References in this chapter are to *Theology and Social Theory* (*TST*), unless otherwise specified.
2   Capital punishment does not belong with any necessity to the Hegelian concept of the state and, in fact, runs against the general tenor of his thought. The antithesis between punishment and reconciliation establishes what, on Hegel's own view, is an improper division between the spirit of religion and that of the state (cf. Hegel, 1973, § 551). Also consider, for example, his praise of Pinel's humanitarianism (*Philosophy of Mind*, 1973, § 408).

CHAPTER 9

Better Well Hanged Than Ill Wed?
Kierkegaard and Radical Orthodoxy

Steven Shakespeare

In the collection of essays entitled *Radical Orthodoxy*, Søren Kierkegaard is lined up as one of the 'great Christian critics of the Enlightenment' (*RO*, p. 3).[1] It is asserted that these critics 'in different ways saw that what secularity had most ruined and actually denied were the very things it apparently celebrated: embodied life, self-expression, sexuality, aesthetic experience, human political community' (ibid.). In light of this, Kierkegaard and others claimed that only a transcendence which interrupted the self-contained realm of enlightened reason could really secure these worldly values. To assert the independence of the world and the secular realm ultimately rendered it unprotected against the violence of nihilism. Only as created, as gift, could the world discover its worth.

Kierkegaard appears only once more by name in this volume. He is referred to as the reviver of a 'radical pietist vision' in opposition to Kant (*RO*, p. 22). Continuing the work of Hamann, Jacobi and others, Kierkegaard attacks the Kantian assertion of the autonomy of reason and philosophy, which is offered in the name of making room for faith.

John Milbank's *Theology and Social Theory* also pays homage to the Dane in its opening pages, again as part of an eclectic collection of thinkers who 'construe human making as an opening to transcendence' and thus continue a tradition of 'counter-modernity' (*TST*, p. 4).

These references are undoubtedly marginal, and on their own would hardly warrant an investigation of Kierkegaard's significance for Radical Orthodoxy. However, in Milbank's own article 'The Sublime in Kierkegaard', we find a very different estimation. Here, Kierkegaard is lauded as 'the real inaugurator of the second phase of critique' of the sublime (Milbank, 1998, p. 131). The first phase, it is claimed, was instigated by Kant, for whom the sublime was the indeterminate reality, which fell outside the purview of theoretical reason. In the second phase 'sublimity is perceived to contaminate even what is deceptively taken for finitude' (ibid.). In other words, Kierkegaard begins to suggest that our own mundane reality, our temporal existence, is not a closed, self-contained world whose limits we can securely draw. Rather, it is itself indeterminable. It is constituted by its relationship to an otherness that cannot be captured by the fixed categories and schemas of Kantian rational thought.

Milbank goes on to suggest that Nietzsche and Heidegger, and poststructuralist writing in general, are parasitic upon Kierkegaard's initiative.

Moreover, he is the originator of 'a series of philosophic categories of a new kind' (Milbank, 1998, p. 132), which attempt to evoke the paradoxical structure of the world. Milbank lists these quasi-categories as 'repetition', the 'moment', '*inter-esse*' and 'anxiety'. He later refers to the 'paradox' and the 'absurd' in a similar vein.

It is, however, *repetition* which seems to occupy a privileged position in this semantic pantheon. Kierkegaard is further lauded as 'the instigator of the subversive, anti-metaphysical use of this *topos*' (ibid.) leaving Heidegger, Derrida, Deleuze and Lacan trailing in his wake.

Kierkegaard thus appears to be more than just one exemplar of a pietistical tradition. He is the inaugurator and instigator of a new way of doing philosophical theology, whose vocabulary sets the agenda for contemporary poststructuralism. The point here is not so much whether Milbank is right in this (though the history of ideas is full of unacknowledged debts to Kierkegaard), but whether it provides us with a way into understanding and critiquing Radical Orthodoxy better.[2] Armed with these enormous claims for Kierkegaard's importance, we can seek out and evaluate the impact he has had in the key works of the movement as a whole. And the elusive concept of repetition will provide our guiding thread.

Once More from the Top

Repetition does indeed seem to be a key idea for Radical Orthodoxy. In *Theology and Social Theory*, Milbank uses this Kierkegaardian idiom in his exposition of the work of Maurice Blondel. He is discussing the idea that the full meaning of what we do always escapes us, and that 'the search for more adequate action is simultaneously an attempt to *repeat* precisely, but in different circumstances, and so not *identically* the things that we have performed in the past' (*TST*, p. 211). This is further explained, with reference to Kierkegaard and others, as the rejection of the idea that 'action expresses a prior "original" in thought, or that action is measured by a Platonic, theoretical standard' (p. 213).

Leaving aside Blondel, what is important here is the claim that transcendence is not something that lies outside or merely accompanies our mundane actions, but rather constitutes them from the outset. Our actions, or their meanings, transcend our control. And this becomes a possible way of understanding the action of God in the world, one which is used to great effect in Milbank's Christology. Christ is both the divine origin of meaning and the inheritor of all human meanings. He is both given, and yet also poetically received and re-born, even eucharistically re-crucified, in our faithful response (or lack of it) (see Milbank, 1997b, pp. 123–44). Repetition is thus the mode of God's own incarnate action. God gives himself in Christ once and for all, but in a way that must ever be appropriated anew. And each new appropriation will be unique.

The identity of Christ, and therefore the identity of us all, arises out of this history of repetition. Milbank defines this as 'the constitution of an identity *only* through its reoccurrence' (Milbank, 1998, p. 132). There is no eternal human form, or eternal realm of meanings, to which we seek to return, or towards which we strive. Meaning flows out of the divine gift in creation and incarnation, but has to be lived, appropriated and made historically. What is given is not a static essence of truth, but dynamic participation in the life of God.

The connection with Kierkegaard's work comes out most clearly in the following passage:

> as Kierkegaard best understood, Christianity exceeds Platonism (or at least as the latter is commonly understood). It is not founded upon the vision of a transcendent original which we must imitate. Instead it makes its affirmations about the real, and about 'meaning', through the constant repetition of a historically emergent practice which has no real point of origination, but only acquires identity and stability *through* this repetition. And what is repeated is not an insight, not an idea (which is properly imitated), but a formal becoming, a structured transformation. The narrative and metanarrative forms of the gospel are therefore indispensable, not because they record and point us to a vision which is still available in its eternal 'presence', but rather because they enshrine and constitute the event of a transformation which is to be non-identically repeated, and therefore still made to happen. (Milbank, 1998, pp. 152–3)

It is worth quoting this at length, because it touches on some of the key characteristics of Radical Orthodoxy. First, it is anti-foundationalist. There is no neutral, atemporal foundation for truth or absolute starting point for rational thinking. As a corollary, it is defiantly opposed to the idea that there can be any secular reason, or secular starting point for theology, which does not conceal a violent, arbitrary nihilism behind its reasonable façade. Second, it is ecclesial. Meaning emerges through repetition, through a historical practice, which is also the creative, saving work of God. As the context and other writings make clear, this practice is located within the Church, and specifically focused in the action of the eucharistic offering. Third, Radical Orthodoxy is exclusivist. The rules for performing the saving repetition are given exclusively and definitively in the narrative and metanarrative resources of the Christian gospel, as received and handed on by the Church.

With these points in mind, it is worth exploring the dynamic of Kierkegaard's writings further, in order to see whether his communication – and the concept of repetition within it – really does support a Radical Orthodox theology.

Indirections

Kierkegaard is certainly one of the most innovative and influential figures in the philosophical and theological canon. The influence may be underplayed, though it can be seen at work in figures as diverse as Heidegger, Barth, Lukacs, Sartre and Derrida. The innovation is more obvious.

It has been traditional in Kierkegaard scholarship to divide his authorship into two phases. Up to 1846, he mainly writes in the 'teasingly, "masked" mode' to which Milbank refers in his essay (Milbank, 1998, p. 131). The works are largely pseudonymous, adapting the conceits of romantic novels, essays and aphorisms. After this period, Kierkegaard embarks on a more explicitly direct religious authorship.

This division is somewhat artificial, however. Kierkegaard's early 'aesthetic' works were always accompanied by religious discourses published in his own name. And his later writings also made use of pseudonyms at times. More significant than this, however, is the sense in which there is something essentially indirect, poetical and teasing about *all* of Kierkegaard's texts. This partly has to do with the need he perceived to communicate with an age that was so archly reflective and self-conscious that decisive religious categories had to be introduced to it in disguise. But it is principally the result of a general conviction that direct communication about Christian truth was impossible, or at most an ideal limit case, which could not be realized by anyone other than an apostle. In other words, Kierkegaard's indirect communication was not just a tactic adopted to suit the modern age, but his version of an unavoidable facet of Christian witnessing.

This is perhaps most famously expounded in the *Concluding Unscientific Postscript*, a work written in the name of one Johannes Climacus. The title is itself a topical satire on the idealist philosophy of the time. The book presents itself as an addendum, a surplus, which does not fit into the system of world-historical 'science'. The irony is compounded when we realize that this 'postscript' is far larger than the book it purports to expand, the *Philosophical Fragments*.

These issues of form and genre are not accidental. Both *Fragments* and *Postscript* examine the conflict between systems of knowledge which remain within immanence, and the faith which is open to the transcendent. Idealist philosophy is indicted for attempting to generate an all-consuming narrative of the world and an all-seeing perspective on truth from within the resources of reason alone. Climacus claims that this involves a sleight of hand. The categories of logic are illegitimately warped to try to capture the flux of existence; and the systematic philosopher assumes a vantage point which is actually impossible for any existing human being to occupy. The philosopher aspires to a view from nowhere, a God's-eye view from which all reality can be assigned its place in the system.

It is against this background that Christian truth is brought into play. Climacus writes that 'The systematic idea is subject–object, the unity of thinking and being; existence, on the other hand, is precisely the separation ... existence does space and has spaced subject from object, thought from being' (Kierkegaard, 1992b, p. 123). The temporality and finitude of existence mean that we cannot occupy the eternal vantage point of the system. Satirizing the idealist philosopher, Climacus says that 'Alas, while the speculating, honorable Herr Professor is explaining all existence, he has in sheer absentmindedness forgotten what he himself is called, namely, that he is a human being, a human being pure and simple, and not a fantastical three-eighths of a paragraph' (Kierkegaard, 1992b, p. 145).

This is the basis for the *Postscript*'s stress on subjectivity and the individual. Subjectivity is the sticking point for the system. It represents the irreducible particularity and passion that must shape our appropriation of truth in existence:

> Christianity therefore protests against all objectivity; it wants the subject to be infinitely concerned about himself. What it asks about is the subjectivity; the truth of Christianity, if it is at all, is only in this; objectively, it is not at all. (ibid., p. 130)

Religious truth cannot be reduced to an objective abstract doctrine, or metaphysical assertion. Christianity accentuates this by insisting that the eternal truth comes into being in time in a particular historical individual, and thus as a paradox. Therefore, 'Christianity is not a doctrine but an existence-communication' (ibid., p. 570). In context, this is clearly directed against the idea that Christianity is a metaphysical doctrine conformable to a particular operation of the understanding, a truth which can be derived by deduction or induction from self-evident principles or empirical facts.

Whether or not we accept that Kierkegaard was being fair to the idealists, we can see that his target was a certain myth which reason was telling about itself: that it could be a self-standing foundation for thinking the truth of existence, that existence itself was rational, and that wholeness lay in uniting thought and being in harmony. Climacus' gesture in the *Postscript* is to deny this form of closure by a reading of existence as inherently ruptured or wounded. The subjective thinker, he argues, 'is cognizant of the negativity of the infinite in existence; he always keeps open the wound of negativity, which at times is a saving factor (the others let the wound close and become positive – deceived); in his communication he expresses the same thing' (Kierkegaard, 1992b, p. 85).

Wounded communication must be indirect, as we can see from one of his later, more explicitly Christian, works. *Practice in Christianity*, published in 1850 under the name Anti-Climacus under Kierkegaard's 'editorship', might appear to be a revocation of Climacus' inadequate position (Climacus makes no claim to be a Christian himself). However, here too we discover that communication about the paradox of the eternal appearing in time is never straightforward:

> Reduplicated in the teacher through his existing in what he teaches, the communication is in manifold ways a self-differentiating art. And now when the teacher, who is inseparable from and more essential than the teaching, is a paradox, then all direct communication is impossible. (Kierkegaard, 1991, p. 123)

Anti-Climacus later bluntly remarks that

> Spirit is the denial of direct immediacy. If Christ is the true God, then he also must be unrecognizable, attired in unrecognizability, which is the denial of all straightforwardness. Direct recognizability is specifically characteristic of the idol. (Ibid., p. 136)

What matters here is the form of Christian life and witnessing, the passion of paradoxical faith and the imitation of Christ. Self-contained reason has to be broken open to receive this gift.

All of this might seem highly compatible with a Radically Orthodox perspective, which also attacks the myth of a purely secular, self-founded rationality, and unmasks the arbitrary and often violent gestures hidden behind the façade of all-seeing reason. Kierkegaard would have agreed that the key characteristic of modernity was its reflective self-consciousness, whose confident attempts to systematize all truth concealed a fear that doubt would corrode everything.

However, Kierkegaard also recognized that there was no going around this reflection and doubt. Dialectical questioning had relativized authorities which had previously provided an underpinning for Christian claims: Bible, Church and tradition. The *Postscript* spends some time demonstrating that critical reason had left appeals to these authorities trembling, and yet that this has actually done Christianity a service:

> Whether it is a word, a sentence, a book, a man, a society, whatever it is, as soon as it is supposed to be a boundary, so that the boundary itself is not dialectical, it is superstition and narrow-mindedness. In a human being there is always a desire, at once comfortable and concerned, to have something really firm and fixed that can exclude the dialectical, but this is cowardliness and fraudulence toward the divine. Even the most certain of all, a revelation, eo ipso becomes dialectical when I am to appropriate it; even the most fixed of all, an infinite negative resolution, which is the individuality's infinite form of God being within him, promptly becomes dialectical. (Kierkegaard, 1992b, p. 35n)

No longer should people confuse the truth of Christianity with a theory about the Bible or the Church.

It could be argued that Climacus' target here is the same as that of Radical Orthodoxy: arbitrary attempts to assert some kind of external authority in the name of the Bible or church magisterium which are a desperate reaction to modernity's separation of faith from reason. However, Climacus is more subtle than that. He specifically refers to the contemporary movement initiated by the Danish church reformer Grundtvig, in which the authority and authenticity of the Church was vested in a living tradition of oral truth, credal and sacramental, rather than simply in biblical texts or ecclesiastical pronouncements. No such ecclesiology can guarantee the essential continuity of tradition and the harmony of orthodox faith against the inquiries of dialectical reason (Kierkegaard, 1992b, pp. 34–45).

This sits very uneasily with the huge ecclesiological claims made by Radical

Orthodox writers. Hanby asserts that the human mind 'can only be an image of God, only manifest God in creation, insofar as it doxologically participates in God's charity through the historic ecclesia' (*RO*, p. 115). Bauerschmidt quotes Gregory of Nyssa's words that 'he who sees the Church looks directly at Christ' (*RO*, p. 212). Milbank unapologetically writes that 'a gigantic claim to be able to read, criticize, say what is going on in other human societies, is absolutely integral to the Christian Church, which itself claims to exhibit the exemplary form of human community' (*TST*, p. 388).

The problem lies with identifying this 'Church'. Which Church is it, in which period of history? Or is it a hidden, invisible Church? Neither would appear compatible with these same writers' stress on the Church as continuous, visible, eucharistic community. But as soon as we try to identify the Church that corresponds to these ecclesiological ideals, brute facts and dialectical reasoning make an annoying appearance.[3] For the Church to operate as Milbank and others wish it to operate – as a social space which can define what true human living is – a boundary must be drawn around it. It must be clear where the Church is, and how it is separate from compromised secular practices. For Climacus, however, the erection of any such boundary is suspect. He claims that Grundtvig has a deep need 'for something firm with which the dialectical can be held at bay. But such a need is simply a need for a superstitious fixed point ... every boundary that wants to exclude the dialectical is eo ipso superstitious' (Kierkegaard, 1992b, p. 44).

Of course, Radical Orthodox writers are far from naïve about the Church as it is and has been, and examples of their criticisms of church deficiencies could be multiplied. But this leaves unanswered Climacus' question as to whether the 'true' Church could ever be located and defined. And without such a Church, what status do Radical Orthodoxy's readings of the Christian narratives have?

I suggested that three key characteristics of Radical Orthodoxy are that it is anti-foundationalist, ecclesial and exclusivist. With respect to the first of these, it does appear to find an ally in Kierkegaard's critique of metaphysics. It begins to look doubtful, however, whether that alliance can be stretched to cover the latter two aspects as well. And if this is the case, perhaps we need to look again at what Kierkegaard's 'anti-foundationalism' actually involves.

These questions return us to the concept of repetition. As suggested earlier, Radical Orthodoxy's reception of this idea gives it an ecclesial, and implicitly exclusivist, dimension. Christian truth is narrated, performed and sacramentally repeated by and in the Church, and *only* there. But is this really what repetition meant for Kierkegaard?

Repeating Kierkegaard?

Catherine Pickstock's *After Writing* is perhaps the most audacious attempt to critique secular philosophy by deriving all truth and virtue from the ecclesially located practice of the Eucharist (and specifically the Latin Mass). In discussing

the real presence of Christ in the Eucharist, Pickstock echoes a familiar theme
when she writes

> I would argue, with Kierkegaard, that the original is established in time, that the
> temporal world *discloses* the origin, and that it is continuous with its forward moving
> repetition, since the eternal 'original' also exists in supplementing itself in an infinity
> without bounds. (*AW*, pp. 255–6)

This emphasis on the temporality of truth is correlated with a kind of eucharistic
literalism. The Eucharist is supposed to be able to 'outwit' the opposition
between absence and presence, death and life, but only because it is practised
within a church that is 'properly the essence and repetition, as both sign and
secret, of that body' which is present in the eucharistic elements (*AW*, p. 254).
The subtlety of Pickstock's meditations on language and meaning is
overshadowed by a massive investment in the Church as the literal and actual
continuation of the Incarnation.

Behind this lies a familiar communitarian strand of modern philosophy and
ethics. Truth-claims and ethical norms, it is typically argued, are tradition-
bound. They do not come from nowhere, or stand on timeless, independent
foundations. They emerge from the practices, the worldviews of living
communities. Applied to Christian faith, this means that talk of Christ outside
the context of the Church and the Eucharist turns him into an ahistorical,
abstract figure, a divine phantom or a mere figure of the past.

Kierkegaard too rejected the claims of reason or romantic irony to step
outside of all contexts in order to pronounce timeless judgements upon reality,
or even to create it *ex nihilo*. However, we have already seen that he would in
all likelihood be intensely critical of any attempt to let Christ be defined and
placed solely within this or that ecclesial tradition.

To her credit, Pickstock is aware of this, as in her conclusion, she belatedly
worries that

> Kierkegaard's covert individualism seems to omit the fact that Christ is always
> already repeated, even in his Eucharistic 'immediacy', by which there is perforce
> a continuation of the incarnation in the sacrament, and the Church and in every
> sign. ... Thus Kierkegaard's stress on the prospectivity of repetition is only
> *sustainable* as such in combination with an account of the Church and sociality. (*AW*,
> p. 272)

In this way, Kierkegaardian repetition is salvaged from the recalcitrant liberal
Protestantism of the man himself.

This should not be allowed to pass by too easily, however. Criticism of
Kierkegaard's individualism has often reared its head, but the issue has
become even more central given the contemporary consensus that relationality
is a 'good thing'. Defences of Kierkegaard have emphasized that he always sets
the self in relationship, and always occupies the public world of
communication, even as he seeks more liberating ways to put that

communication into effect (see Pattison and Shakespeare, 1998, especially the editors' introduction).

Given the validity of all of this, it is nevertheless worth reminding ourselves that Pickstock is right to note the massive presence of the category of the individual in Kierkegaard's works. However, Kierkegaard is not motivated by any abstract desire to solve debates about selfhood or the one and the many. His appeal to the individual – like that to subjectivity – is deliberate and tactical. It is intended to be a gesture of resistance to those world-historical narratives of fall and redemption embedded in the philosophy and theology of his day. The individual was a sticking point, an existential reality who could not be assimilated into any system, be it intellectual or aesthetic. Kierkegaard, by insisting on the relativity of our viewpoint and the incompleteness of any system of existence, secures the necessary space in which alone freedom can operate. The system is a totality of thought, culture and institutions, which denies the possibility of real transcendence, otherness, freedom, relationship and revelation. If Kierkegaard is 'individualistic' it is because he resists this totality, and not because he falls on the wrong side of a debate which has already been decided for us in favour of a heart-warming but vague concept of relatedness.

What then is repetition for Kierkegaard? It makes its most sustained appearance in the book simply entitled *Repetition*. But before jumping in to distil the concept's definition, it's worth examining just what sort of book this is.

Repetition was published in 1843 under the name Constantin Constantius as 'A Venture in Experimenting Psychology'. In it, Constantius describes his friendship with a young man, whom he attempted to help through the break-up of a relationship with a girl. Part of the book consists of letters from the young man, who seeks to use his broken relationship as a springboard to a life of poetry. Constantius' motives are not entirely pure. He has his own interest in observing the psychological development of others, and he uses the opportunity to communicate some of his own autobiographically tinged reflections on the ideas of change, recollection and repetition. He includes a detailed description of a return trip to Berlin, and long reflections on the nature of farce and the performers at his favourite Berlin theatre.

One's suspicions about Constantius gain weight when we discover that he has invented the whole history of the young man as an experiment in thought. The experiment seems to fail, in that Constantius refers to dimensions of the idea of repetition which remain unattainable to the would-be poet of his creation.

Repetition is a fiction wrapped within a fiction. It has no claim to authority or any overarching superior vantage point. The key character of the book, the controlling observer–narrator Constantius, is no more than 'a vanishing person, just like the midwife in relation to the child she has delivered' (Kierkegaard, 1983, p. 230).

It is in this context that we have to read the concept of repetition. At the opening of the book, Constantius writes that repetition will be a key idea for modern philosophy. He contrasts it with recollection, the Greek idea that truth was something we already possessed, and which had to be recalled to mind: 'what is recollected has been, is repeated backward, whereas genuine repetition is recollected forward' (Kierkegaard, 1983, p. 131). This less than helpful definition is amplified as Constantius claims that repetition's love is the only happy one, and that repetition is 'actuality and the earnestness of existence' (ibid., p. 133). This is as much as we get before the narrative of the young man begins.

Some pages later, Constantius reminds us that his whole tale is connected with repetition. He goes on to say:

> The dialectic of repetition is easy, for that which has been repeated has been – otherwise it could not be repeated – but the very fact that it has been makes the repetition into something new ... when one says that life is a repetition, one says: actuality, which has been, now comes into existence. (Ibid., 1983, p. 149)

He further says, somewhat cryptically, that 'repetition is the interest of metaphysics and also the interest upon which metaphysics comes to grief' (ibid.).

One begins to suspect Constantius' grasp of this concept when he describes his attempt to see if there can be a repetition by recreating a previous visit to Berlin. As it turns out, things go wrong. Nothing is quite as it was. His old room, the landlord, the café, the theatre – all let him down in some way. He concludes there is no repetition in life. But his later reflections suggest that this literal understanding of repetition misses the point. Repetition seems to point towards something that goes beyond the capacities of modern philosophy, for which Constantius had such high hopes, indeed beyond what any concepts can express: 'Modern philosophy makes no movement ... and if it makes any movement at all, it is always within immanence, whereas repetition is and remains a transcendence' (ibid., p. 186).

Other works in which repetition is mentioned confirm its connection with transcendence, with the human spirit and freedom and with a collision of the real and the ideal, the temporal and the eternal. Climacus writes that 'For an existing person, the goal of motion is decision and repetition' (Kierkegaard, 1992b, p. 312) as opposed to the static, abstract eternity of idealism.

Milbank is quite right to see repetition and its ilk as 'quasi-categories', since it is clear that they do not have a meaning which can straightforwardly be given and assimilated by the understanding. However, nor can repetition sit easily within *any* bound narrative, whether told by an individual narrator or by the Church.

Repetition brings together some of Kierkegaard's concerns: for doing justice to the temporality of human existence and the limitation of human reason, and for opening out our thinking and living to what cannot be contained by our systems of ideas and concepts. It does not itself define the mode of living which addresses those concerns. It is more like a goad to prick our lazy self-absorbed thinking into motion. To elevate it to the status of a controlling concept, or equate it with the tradition of the Church, is to fall under Constantius' spell, to think that it can be narrated and regulated. But as Constantius reminds us, he is no one. He cannot even guarantee his own presence in the text.

Repetition offers numerous clues to its own absurdity: Constantius' long description of his preference for farce, on which 'Every general esthetic concept runs aground' (Kierkegaard, 1983, p. 159) and whose meaning depends on the self-activity of the viewer, not the correct harmony of its form and content; his description of a brief time of exquisite bliss and transparent satisfaction, which was ended on discovering a piece of grit in his eye (ibid., p. 172); the young man's delusion that he is like Job, receiving everything double from God, when all he has done is become a mediocre poet (ibid., p. 221).

It is because repetition is 'the interest of metaphysics and also the interest upon which metaphysics comes to grief' that Radical Orthodoxy can seize upon it as a resource. It suggests that human existence does not have a meaning which is discoverable by the resources of reason alone. At the same time, repetition seems to affirm the temporality of lived experience, rather than suppressing temporality for the sake of an abstract eternal truth. Repetition thus unites the concepts of transcendence and temporal particularity to offer a new understanding of human identity given and forged through time. It is 'anti-metaphysical' where metaphysics is seen as a self-contained system derived from immanent rational resources.

However, repetition is an inevitably flawed attempt to catch hold of an existential reality, which forever eludes full articulation. Repetition alludes to something we live, to an aspect of our contested subjective freedom, 'suspended above 70,000 fathoms', to use a Kierkegaardian phrase. It is not a panopticon, a theory or viewpoint from which we can narrate the meaning of the whole of existence. This is what the form of Constantius' text makes clear, but this is precisely what is elided by Radical Orthodox appropriations. Repetition is one of the concepts used by Kierkegaard to put our grasp of the narrative of existence into question.

Anonymous Authors and Faithful Idolaters

Even in his religious discourses, Kierkegaard made it clear that he wrote without authority, that he was a poet. That lack of authority did not blunt his criticism of the age, but it did mean that he had to use other methods than that of the knowing dogmatist. Thus he occupies the various worldviews of his time, exposing their incompleteness from within. Ultimately, he challenges them with the religious demand to become nothing before God and the Christian demand to have faith in the paradox of God's incarnation in Christ. Milbank is right to stress Kierkegaard's irreducible and radical Christian critique of secular forms of thought and culture. However, Kierkegaard does not replace secularism with a rehashed Christendom, which appeals to the authority of the Church, the Bible or the metanarrative resources of creed and dogma. Climacus writes:

> No anonymous author can more slyly hide himself, and no maieutic can more carefully recede from a direct relation than God can. He is in the creation, everywhere in the creation, but he is not there directly, and only when the single individual turns inward into himself (consequently only in the inwardness of self-activity) does he become aware and capable of seeing God. The direct relationship to God is simply paganism, and only when the break has taken place, only then can there be a God-relationship. (Kierkegaard, 1992b, p. 243)

This is just the sort of individualism that Pickstock resists in Kierkegaard's texts. But such a judgement is superficial. The *Postscript* is as much about how our individual subjectivity has to be wounded and contested as it is an affirmation of the necessity of subjective appropriation for faith. The analogy here is not the dangerously univocal one implied by Radical Orthodox accounts of participation, but the indirect witness to God's authorship of creation in our own risky and fragile attempts at communication (see Shakespeare, 2001, especially chapter 7).[4]

Kierkegaard's authorship lacks authority, but invites the reader's self-activity, invites a kind of dialogue with the reader's world (see Pattison, 1993, for an exploration of the dialogical nature of these texts). His texts are insistent that Christian categories should not be deprived of their paradoxical offensiveness and scandalous particularity. They also underline just how objectively uncertain and indirect our witness to those categories is, which leads to some surprising results. In the famous parable of the idolater, Climacus writes as follows:

> If someone who lives in the midst of Christianity enters, with knowledge of the true idea of god, the house of God, the house of the true God, and prays, but prays in untruth, and if someone lives in an idolatrous land but prays with all the passion of infinity, although his eyes are resting on the image of an idol – where, then, is there more truth? The one prays in truth to God although he is worshipping an idol, the other prays in untruth to the true God and is therefore in truth worshipping an idol. (Kierkegaard, 1992b, p. 201)

This is an inclusiveness based, not on a lowest rational common denominator, but on the intensity of passion that overcomes the ego's self-containment. It is an opening to dialogue from within the passion of faith's existence, not a refusal based on a metanarrative 'knowledge of the true God'. Climacus says that idolatry is the direct relationship to God characteristic of paganism (ibid., p. 246), but this story makes us pause before presuming we know just how that idolatry manifests itself. Being within the house of God, at the centre of the ecclesial domain of truth, one might still be praying to an idol.

We may begin to suspect that Kierkegaard fits uncomfortably with the implicit system of Radical Orthodoxy, which depends on asserting the ecclesially rooted authority of the Christian story. The problem partly exists because Milbank and Pickstock raid Kierkegaard for concepts which are then deployed out of context. Whilst such creative misreading may in part be unavoidable, this one is especially insidious.

Kierkegaard is insistent that truth, and Christian truth in particular, is not available in the form of a result: a set of beliefs or conclusions which are valid apart from the labour and passion of faith's appropriation. Whilst this may be in accord with some of Radical Orthodoxy's intentions, its use of Kierkegaard suggests that it cannot tolerate the disturbing implications of his approach. The orthodox narrative has to be saved, whether by an idealistic ecclesiology, or by an equally ill-defined set of aesthetic criteria: the 'inherent attractiveness of the picture of God' offered by Christianity (p. 384); the 'dazzling effect' of Jesus on his followers (ibid.); the 'good taste' necessary to ethical judgements (p. 357). Either way, the moment of uncertainty and decision which rupture Kierkegaard's texts is normalized, domesticated into a ritualized system of aesthetics. Repetition becomes another name for ecclesial faith, a tradition whose continuity is affirmed by its own constant renewal.

However, Kierkegaard's emphasis on the individual was an attempt to avoid the temptation of this approach: that faith could somehow be comprehended by a larger set of rational, aesthetic or authority-driven criteria. Repetition thus refers to that never fully understood process whereby meaning is given, and yet its fullness is deferred. It signifies that the meaning which matters to us, existential meaning, the idea for which I can live and die, has to be lived rather than fully comprehended. Even as faith is radically given to us as a gift, it is something that has to be willed and worked out in fear and trembling. Faith is lived in passion and objective uncertainty. There is therefore no viewpoint – not that of the Church, nor that of the rightly attuned theologian – from which the Christian narrative can simply be asserted as a totality in opposition to all other totalities.

This is where Radical Orthodoxy's Hegelian pretensions are exposed. We have seen how a valid emphasis on the social and narrative dimensions of faith becomes the basis for an exclusivist ecclesiology, in which the Church is the sole locus for narrating all reality, realizing true community and judging that 'other religions and social groupings, however virtuous-seeming, were finally on the path of damnation' (p. 388). But from where can such a judgement be made? From what point can such a decisive anticipation of the end of all dialogue be assumed? Only from the claim that the Church gives us access to a world-historical narrative which categorizes and evaluates everything else: a system by any other name. Radical Orthodoxy's genius is to assert that the metanarrative of Christ, as appropriated and repeated by the Church, gives us the key to how things really are and at the same time avoids any atemporal foundation for this truth:

A genuine 'metanarrative realism' does full justice to the internal tension within narrative. In particular, the temporality of the syntagmatic dimension is not betrayed,

> because the metanarrative ceases, as we have just seen, to be *only* a privileged set of events, but rather becomes the whole story of human history which is still being enacted and interpreted in the light of those events. (*TST*, p. 388)

But if this is the movement's genius, it is also its greatest flaw, since it comes at a price. That price is the inability to see any distance between Christ and the Church, for Christ's stubborn historical particularity is transformed into a poem, a metaphor already assimilated by the community of faith.

Consider Pickstock on the Mass, again using Kierkegaard's language but for a very different purpose: 'If the Eucharist repeats what was in the first place a repetition, then it repeats Christ as Himself always nothing other than the gift of the Eucharist' (*AW*, p. 264). If Christ is wholly dispersed in the ecclesial tradition and in the sacrament, he is wholly at our disposal. We are his narrators; or rather, our particularity itself has to be overcome, merged with the all-consuming narrating subject that is the Church (on this idealization of the Church as narrator, see Shakespeare, 2000, especially pp. 171–4).

The unintended result is that Christ's difference is annulled and he becomes another aesthetic category in a story of our devising. The Church becomes a ghost of the speculative philosopher, generating reality out of its own stories. Consider Climacus' criticism of those who try to go beyond the paradox of faith:

> despite the use of Christ's name etc., Christianity has been shoved back into the esthetic (something the superorthodox unwittingly are especially successful in doing), where the incomprehensible is the relatively incomprehensible (relative either with regard to its not yet having been understood or to the need for a seer with an eagle eye to understand it), which in time has its explanation in something higher beyond itself, rather than in Christianity's being an existence-communication that makes existing paradoxical ... (Kierkegaard, 1992b, p. 562)

Ironically, the poet of the paradox is a better witness than the superorthodox theologian to the otherness of the God–Man. One is inclined to ask: what is the ideological distance between the early nineteenth-century 'superorthodox' and today's Radically Orthodox? Is it this: that whereas, for the former, aesthetics is a trap into which they fall unwittingly, for the latter, aesthetics is explicitly celebrated, even as it consumes the substance of orthodoxy?

Milbank's essay on Kierkegaard is among the best short expositions to have appeared in years. It fully acknowledges the indirect and paradoxical form of the texts, and impressively argues that Kierkegaard saw reason itself as inhabited by the paradox. However, even here, the Radical Orthodox agenda attempts to impose a harmony where none exists. Describing his critique of idealism, Milbank claims that Kierkegaard's argument is that reason is in flux, and that 'necessary logical sequences and determinate sets of categories are but formalized and arbitrary abstractions (respectively), from an endless fictioning of possibilities' (Milbank, 1998, p. 135). However, this is to concede too much to a poststructuralist and relativist reading of Kierkegaard. In fact, it is one of

Climacus' chief complaints against Hegel that the latter does *not* respect fixed logical categories, and that he dissolves the paradoxes of existence by illicitly setting logic in motion (see Kierkegaard, 1992b, pp. 109–10; Kierkegaard is in debt to Trendelenberg here). Logic, dialectic and critical reasoning are *not* denied their respective validity by Kierkegaard. Whilst they are inadequate to describe existing reality, they do help us to resist the dissolution of that reality into a fluid morass on to which any pattern of meaning could be imposed. If this is 'anti-foundationalist', it is nevertheless of a different order from those contemporary movements which deny any validity to independent rational reflection. For Kierkegaard, if dialectical thinking is bounded by authority and tradition, it surrenders to superstition. It is reason's own inner passion that drives it to encounter what lies beyond itself (for a defence of the rationality of Kierkegaard's position, see Evans, 1992). Ethical, religious and Christian categories are the grit in the eye of idealism and they are served by forms of reasoning and logic which are not subsumed into a speculatively narrated flux. Radical Orthodoxy is too close to Hegelianism for comfort here. Kierkegaard's problem with idealism was not that it was rationalistic, but that it denied both the specificity of existence and the passion of reason to think what was other than itself (Kierkegaard, 1992b, p. 335). To dissolve all reason and logic into flux is to deny that otherness, and to collude with the idealism Kierkegaard resisted.

Conclusion: On Not Rushing to Conclude

Is Kierkegaard, for Radical Orthodoxy, merely one link in an unbroken chain which hands down the thought of non-identical repetition; or is he in some sense the decisive instigator of a new phase of thinking? The point of the question is not merely to decide on Kierkegaard's place in the history of ideas, but more specifically to discover why he has such an undecided place in Radical Orthodoxy's myth of origins. The answer, I suggest, is that Kierkegaard *does* represent a turning point in Christian thinking, but not one with which Radical Orthodoxy feels wholly comfortable. Specifically, he saw that the reflective nature of the modern age had irretrievably corroded certain forms of authority – notably those of scriptural inspiration and church tradition – to which appeal could no longer be straightforwardly made for assurance of Christian truth-claims. Radically Orthodox writers reject the arbitrary authoritarianism of Protestant biblicism and Roman Catholic claims of papal infallibility. However, they are still left looking for sources of authority with which to back up their refusal of the validity of secular thinking, and their exclusivist stance towards other faith traditions. Their solution is vague. Patristic sources, medieval liturgy, credal statements and scripture itself are all raided, but what holds all this together is far from clear – beyond an aesthetic act of self-assertion.

Kierkegaard is thus used in two ways. On one level, he is a link in a chain, a new apostolic succession of those who kept the true understanding of Christian faith and practice alive. This gives Radical Orthodoxy its link with the origins of Christianity. But second, Kierkegaard is hailed as decisively new, because there does have to be a very different kind of engagement with the challenges to Christian faith thrown up by modernity. Kierkegaard's deep suspicion of free-floating abstract reason, and his teasing, aesthetic mode of writing, are attractive in this changed situation. The question is whether one can have both the Kierkegaard who hands on classic Christian orthodoxy, and the Kierkegaard who is compelled to find radically new forms of communicating Christianity given the absence of any assured 'orthodox' authorities in the modern world.

Kierkegaard's own critique of his contemporary philosophy, society and Church is biting indeed. But it does not offer a secure way of retrieving a lost golden age of patristic truth. Kierkegaard accepts that modern scepticism has moved the goalposts for Christian writing. That is why he writes in the forms he chooses: indirect, poetical, seductive and satirical. Even in their playfulness, these forms in fact acknowledge the unavoidability of dialectical reasoning. They do not simply appeal to the intrinsic authority of the Christian narrative and its metanarrative supports. Surprisingly, therefore, Kierkegaard leaves more room for genuine dialogue than the speculative world-historical narrative of Radical Orthodoxy, which already knows that it has it all. It is that openness, that affirmation of faith without knowing the end of the story, which Radical Orthodoxy cannot abide.

Notes

1 The title for this essay derives from the Shakespearean line used as an epigraph to Kierkegaard's *Philosophical Fragments* (Kierkegaard, 1992a).
2 Paul Janz draws attention to an alternative hagiography in Milbank's work, citing the latter's claims that Hamann and Jacobi constitute the true (if secret) origin of this tradition of counter-modernity (Janz, 2004). Janz makes a compelling case that this fabrication of a secret tradition, allied to a huge misreading of Kant, masks the arbitrariness of Radical Orthodoxy's anti-reason, anti-subject stance.
3 This question of the ecclesial positioning of Radical Orthodoxy is raised by Laurence Paul Hemming in his editor's introduction to *Radical Orthodoxy? A Catholic Enquiry* (Hemming, 2000), the record of a dialogue with Roman Catholic theologians. Hemming points out that the leading lights of the movement are High Church Anglicans, and asks what ecclesial legitimation they have for the assertions they make given they do not submit to the Petrine teaching office. One wonders, wickedly, if this is indeed a particularly Anglo-Catholic temptation: to invoke an ecclesial authority to which one submits only when convenient.
4 Milbank's claim that repetition is Kierkegaard's temporalization of the idea of analogy is an interesting one. However, the move is made without much consideration for the labour and critical questions which such a translation should provoke. Kierkegaard is too easily hitched to Milbank's wagon. See Milbank (1998), p. 148.

CHAPTER 10

After Transubstantiation: Blessing, Memory, Solidarity and Hope

George Pattison

One of the weirdest phenomena of recent theology has been the resurgence of transubstantiation as a topic not merely of confessional disputation but (it is claimed) of fundamental philosophical importance. The weirdness of this development is due not least to the fact that for much of the twentieth century the most influential liturgists (for example Jungmann, Bouyer and Dom Gregory Dix) devoted their best labours to providing alternative accounts of the Eucharistic mystery which, even if they did not lead to an abandonment of transubstantiation, radically refocused the emphasis of Eucharistic teaching, bringing to the fore themes of proclamation and blessing, the offering of the people and setting the sacramental life of the Church within a larger conception of sacramentality, in which the prime sacrament is the whole life of the Church as the Body of Christ. Such revisionist approaches to the Eucharist also often involved a clarification of the deep continuities of early Christian worship with Jewish practices and concepts, where the emphasis lay more on history and community than on metaphysics. As P. J. Fitzpatrick has pointed out, the doctrine of transubstantiation is something of an oddity even in its own terms, since it attempts to interpret a personal, historical and ecclesiastical happening in categories borrowed, ultimately, from physics – categories, that is, developed to explain the relationships between things, not persons (see Fitzpatrick, 1993, especially Chapter One, 'Against Transubstantiation'). Among liberation theologians, criticisms of traditional formulations went even further, with calls for a wholesale, non-hierarchical re-envisioning of the sacramental life of the Church.

And there are other oddities. In writers such as Catherine Pickstock the appeal to transubstantiation has been accompanied by a critique of modernity as supposedly committed to a wholesale project of spatialization, which, following Ong and with a dash of Heidegger, is seen as a kind of technologizing of the Word that enforces the disenchantment of the liturgical world. Yet what doctrine ever did more to bring about the spatialization of sacramental life than transubstantiation? The doctrine and the practices it either gave rise to or endorsed led to the disruption of the narrative and historical integrity of the founding text of Eucharistic life, enacting an understanding of the Church that was ahistorical and hierarchical. Thus it effectively removed the chalice from the public rite, transformed the host into a visual object, reinforced the silencing of the accompanying word and mapped the spatial coordinates of the hierarchization of the Church's life by emphasizing the exclusiveness of the sanctuary and defining public space through a cult of processional liturgies (see especially Rubin, 1992). Not least (and along with other aspects of medieval theology and liturgy such as the emphasis on typology), the new theology of transubstantiation and its liturgical expression sharpened the exclusion of Jews from the social body, as can be seen in legends involving Jews being confounded by their attempts to desecrate the host.

In its own context, the doctrine of transubstantiation was pivotal to the visualization of Christian piety in medieval Europe, a point supremely condensed into the image of the Mass of Saint Gregory. This image was based on a legend of Christ's wounded body appearing on the altar to Saint Gregory at Mass. The story actually originated about the year 1400 and probably incorporated a reference to a Byzantine icon of the Man of Sorrows brought to Rome about 1380 and installed in a church used by the Popes for Good Friday Mass (see references in Belting, 1994). The picture of the miraculous appearance itself, showing both St Gregory and his vision, rapidly became one of the most popular religious images of the time, and prayers said before the image carried with them enormous indulgences. Although the image was reproduced in a variety of visual media, it was at its most powerful when incorporated into the altarpiece, within a sacred space customarily guarded by manifold images defining the hierarchical authority of the Church – apostles, patron saints and the four doctors of the Western Church. To behold (or to 'sacre', to use the medieval English word) the consecrated host (that is, the body of Christ) elevated before an altar bearing the image of the Mass of Saint Gregory was to accede to a visualization and spatialization of the relationship between God and world mapped as a feedback loop of icon–ritual–vision–depiction–authority–icon. Such 'sacring' was the ultimate rite of a theology in which the Church became, literally, the *place* of salvation, outside which God was not to be found. A superb example of the image functioning in this way is in a fresco of the Mass of Saint Gregory in Saint Clement's Cathedral in Aarhus (Denmark). The fresco is divided into the classical three layers of the medieval cosmos. Below is hell, with customarily imaginative scenes of devils torturing their victims. Above is heaven, where Christ and his mother sit flanked by angels. In between is earth, where, reading from left to right, we have a procession of realistically drawn contemporary figures who finally come to rest before the altar at which Gregory (divided from the laity by a phalanx of saints and clergy) is kneeling, celebrating his Mass, before the figure of the Man of Sorrows. Thanks to the efficacy of the Mass, some of those trapped in hell (which is thus shown to be a combination of hell and purgatory) are being lifted out of their torment by angelic hands. The Mass of Saint Gregory (both the imagined event and the image of that event) thus becomes the pivot around which the whole map of the cosmic order turns.

There are, naturally, different responses to this. For many Catholics (but by no means all) this is a supreme expression of the Christian culture of the Middle

Ages in which Church and society, art and doctrine, devotion and cosmology were worked into a harmonious whole. As Eamon Duffy has put it, it was through such visualizations of doctrine and their accompanying dramatizations that the ploughman learned his paternoster (see Duffy, 1992). Protestants, on the other hand (in company with some medieval dissenters, such as the Lollards), see this as a fearful perversion of Christianity, and would rather have had the clergy engaged in teaching the people to read than distracting them with images (Calvin). It is not the business of this essay to get involved with such polemics, since my immediate point is merely to underline how the doctrine of transubstantiation, seen as a historical and cultural event, is indissociable from a hierarchical and visualized spatialization of doctrine and ecclesiastical life. To label modernity (to its discredit) as a culture of spatialization and to do so precisely in order to contrast it to the sacral world centred on the action of transubstantiation is therefore either wilfully misleading or naive. If it is objected that the problem with modern spatialization is not its visual aspect but its mechanical reproducibility, its endless repetition of the same, this does not move the argument on one iota, since it was integral to both the doctrine of transubstantiation and the cult of the image of the Mass of Saint Gregory that it was the same act and the same image, wherever and whenever it was performed or seen. Thus reproductions of the Mass of Saint Gregory were credited with the same power of bestowing indulgences as the original. Only a highly romantic view of the conditions under which medieval art was produced (a view that is actually condescending with regard to the sophistication of the medieval world) could see such images as the spontaneous expression of the simple faith of the common artisan.

Of course, to say that transubstantiation was 'just' about spatialization would be as one-sided as to consign the whole of modernity to spatialization, and that is not my aim. No liturgical or doctrinal idea that has had such an extensive and deep working on Christian history can adequately be dealt with by such taxonomic simplifications. Nor do we necessarily resolve the issue of what transubstantiation 'really' means by delineating the historical context in which the doctrine took shape. The liturgical, artistic and cultural expressions surrounding the doctrine are an important clue and it would be foolish, after Hegel, to believe that we could detach a pure 'idea' from its total historical context. But it by no means follows that the idea is exhausted by its immediate historical appearance. Why should we not allow the idea itself to undergo a kind of transubstantiation or reincarnation and allow it a new life and confront it with new tasks relevant to our historical and intellectual situation?[1] We certainly should not presume that knowing about the doctrine's medieval origins or its role in Reformation polemics means that the whole business is cut and dried. Nevertheless, the historical dimension of the doctrine does point to residual questions that any newly reinvigorated version must confront, including the question as to how far the doctrine can really be separated from a very particular understanding of church order and authority, and whether, even in its post-Heideggerian reworking, it can make any kind of sense outside the form of life of the Roman Catholic communion or, for that matter, outside the language game of Thomistically revised Aristotelian physics. Why, indeed, should anyone who is not caught up in internal Catholic debates want to get involved with transubstantiation any more than contemporary physicists would want to avail themselves of the phlogiston theory – an interesting chapter in the history of ideas but not something in which we find important or trustworthy insight into our contemporary experience? Is not the whole thing a parallel to the kind of preoccupation with internal theoretical issues that wracked Western Marxism in the latter half of the twentieth century – at the very time when Marxism was losing the battle to create societies characterized by prosperity, freedom and justice? Theory is all very well – but what does it *do*, and if the theory is itself about something *done* or *to be done* (as both Marxism and the doctrine of transubstantiation are), how does the theory help us to *do it* better? It was precisely the thrust of the Conciliar liturgists that other theoretical perspectives than that offered by transubstantiation were needed if the Mass was to be rescued from irrelevance and mummification and returned to its role as the common work of the witnessing people of God. But if a theory is theoretically as well worked, as historically well grounded and as systematically rigorous as it can be and nevertheless fails to benefit our practice, it has still failed.

One sign that theory has entered into that zone of vacuity where theoretical formulations become ever more stringent and internally complex while being ever more empty and inapplicable outside the domain of theory itself is that it can be brought into association with just about any state of affairs whatsoever – not so much Flew's death of a thousand qualifications as the death of a thousand reinventions. It could be said that ever since Paul's determination to prove himself all things to all men this has been a perennial problem of Christian theology. Liberalism too is chargeable with having cosied up to the most disparate and incompatible intellectual and social currents, including (most depressingly) Nazism. A theology such as Tillich's theology of correlation seems to give virtual *carte blanche* to such involvements. But if in some sense this is a necessary risk of doctrinal development and central to Christianity's (and not least Roman Catholic Christianity's) proven ability to be a transhistorical, transcultural force, it carries with it the constant possibility of, on the one side, actual corruption and, on the other, empty gestures in the direction of the agenda of the day. And when we revisit doctrinal commonplaces, there is also the question as to whether the driving force is indeed theological, or whether the movement is in fact in the opposite direction: the appropriation by an essentially non-Christian culture or movement in ideas of Christian concepts, vocabulary and images. On what grounds would we distinguish between a truly theological revivification of transubstantiation and a purely postmodern game, in which the term comes to be used at will for whatever purpose the particular theorist concerned wants? Could there be any grounds other than the fact of accepting the Eucharistic practice of the Roman Church itself? But then the whole question would once more become one of purely internal confessional interest, since it would not bother postmodern bricoleurs in the slightest that their usage was excluded by Catholic doctrine.

The evacuation of meaning of the doctrine is illustrated by Laurence Paul Hemming's article 'After Heidegger: Transubstantiation'. Hemming's conclusion makes an odd use both of the doctrine and of Heidegger. Alluding to Heidegger's concept of *Ereignis* (or 'event' – recently and infelicitously translated as 'en-ownment') he writes:

> Theologically thought, this means that the substance of the bread and wine is not strictly speaking at issue (though they are not annihilated): the being of the bread and wine is eventuated (*sich ereignet*) in a particular way which must entail and effect a change in *me*. I am re-*materialized* as 'in Christ' in a way that I did not will, but rather that has enacted me *as* such. *I* am the proper locus, topos, of transubstantiation. The body of Christ in me is a body both within, and outside, its proper place. (Hemming, 2000a, p. 182) [2]

Noting the saturation of this collation of assertions by spatialized conceptions ('in', 'locus', 'topos', 'within', 'outside'), it is hard to read this other than as an utter subjectivization of the doctrine. Not that Hemming wants us to read it this way. Earlier he has stated that 'The real transubstantiation is enacted in the intellect of the believer, yet not in consequence of his or her will, but entirely in consequence of God's power' (ibid.). This 'eventuating' of the being of the bread and wine is not merely a fantasy going on in the mind of the recipient (or beholder?), since the concept of *Ereignis* is itself intended, among other things, to undercut a kind of philosophy of subjectivity that Heidegger himself had been charged with promulgating in *Being and Time*. Heidegger does not allow the human subject, the 'I', to count as the 'subject' of *Ereignis*: rather, the truth of *Ereignis* is a truth disclosed by the world itself in its worlding, the 'event' of Being's simultaneous self-manifestation in beings and self-concealment in its own abyssal depths (yet – n.b.! – 'world' here is not used in the sense of the object of empirical observation and 'Being' is not a concept, not even the highest). Hemming appears at first to follow an analogous line: the subject of the Eucharistic event is, ultimately, not the accidental, everyday 'I' (the you or me who catches the bus and goes to the doctor) but God acting 'in' my intellect in a way that 'I' have not willed.

This, however, is utterly confused. Heidegger was at least consistent enough to recognize that he could not move philosophy on from a subjectivizing conception of truth without abandoning the fundamental structure of a self that is the container of its own experiences. But it is precisely this self that is reaffirmed by Hemming: the locus or place within which the event of the bread and wine becoming the true substance of the body and blood of Christ occurs. Even though it is not my act (but God's – 'entirely'), it is 'within' and only within me that it happens. The very concepts – *Ereignis* itself and the act of God in my intellect – that are supposedly to undo the pretensions of modern subjectivity are converted (substantially or only formally?) into a means of reinstating the most spatially naive view of the subjective self. This self is admittedly not the ghost in the machine exorcized by linguistic philosophy – it is something even more meaningless: an empty container, devoid of intrinsic meaning or value.

Previously, Hemming has taken note of the way in which theologians such as Macquarrie have tried to use the Heideggerian idea of 'the fourfold' (*das Geviert*) of earth, sky, mortals and gods as a way (he says) of revitalizing the doctrine of transubstantiation. Putting it in very summary form, Heidegger's idea is that, since the event (*Ereignis*) of meaning cannot be adequately explained by recourse either to an objective or a subjective source (as if meaning were the impact of 'reality' on the *tabula rasa* of our minds or, alternatively, the imposition of our schematizations of thought onto reality), and in order to resist what he regarded as the near universal prejudice in favour of a conception of truth as the adequation of objective thing and intellectual act, he found it necessary to re-envisage the occurrence of truth as structurally irreducible to any two-term relationship. Instead, in one of Heidegger's expressions, it is a matter of the 'round dance' that joins and articulates the elements of the fourfold such that one is never to be isolated from (nor, on the other hand, reduced to) any of the others. In an image that pervades much of Heidegger's later writing the relationship is not that of a harmonic or sonata-like progression but of a fugal co-positing of elements that interact without ever being resolvable into a final unity. Much of Heidegger's philosophical effort is directed precisely to resisting attempts to reconceptualize this model in terms of linear causality, whether this is done in an objectivizing or subjectivizing way.

Even on this very cursory summary, it is clear that the attempt to exploit the idea of *Ereignis* in an argument in which transubstantiation is an ontological enactment on the part of God 'in' my intellect is to mix oil and vinegar. Indeed, much of Hemming's argument seems to be precisely an attempt to avoid the most obvious (and arguably the most fruitful) thinking through of Heidegger's thought in the context of sacramental theology, namely the undercutting of a schematization that requires us to answer questions of ontological priority. Hemming seems wilfully to row in the opposite direction from Heidegger. This is not in itself an argument against what he is saying, of course – except insofar as he claims to have taken Heidegger seriously and to be writing 'after Heidegger'!

In this connection we may note an almost wilful misrepresentation of Macquarrie. Macquarrie is introduced in a paragraph that begins 'There have been various attempts to reinstate transubstantiation by appeal to Heidegger's elaboration of *das Geviert*, the "fourfold" ' (Hemming, 2000a, p. 176). In the next paragraph, however, we read that Macquarrie's hope that Heidegger will help him avoid a metaphysics of substance 'inevitably commits [him] to a theory of transignification …' (ibid.). But Macquarrie is very clear that this is just what he is intending to produce! Hemming is correct in seeing that Macquarrie wants to hold transignification together in some way with transubstantiation and to this extent his critique of Macquarrie has some purchase. But Macquarrie sees nothing intrinsically wrong with the idea of transignification itself; he merely regards it as only a stepping stone – or, rather, he finds in it precisely a valuable and useful stepping stone. In any case, the problem is only a problem for someone committed in advance to defending a doctrine of transubstantiation. It is by no means an intrinsic objection to transignification to say that it fails to provide adequate grounds for reinstating transubstantiation.[3]

What is it, then, that Hemming is so anxious to avoid? As he makes clear, it is the idea that in some way the sacramental elements have within themselves and prior to the consecratory action an 'originary' 'potential' for sacramental meaning. Transignification, in other words, allows the elements an intrinsic meaning that endows them with a fundamental fittingness for sacramental appropriation and transformation. Potentially, *all* bread has a range of meanings that are conformable to its coming to mean 'the bread of life'. It is just this that Hemming does not want, referring to Aquinas in support of the view that 'all bread is *not* the body of Christ' (Hemming, 2000a, p. 177) – though it is not really clear that transignification is saying that it *is*, only that it has the potential to become that! Why would Hemming not want this? Presumably because it would imperil the unique priority that, on his view, accrues to the special divine act in the Eucharistic mystery.

Clearly, in terms of modern liturgical teaching and practice, there has been an occasionally over-crude emphasis on the material gifts as having a kind of proto-sacramental quality, and, arguably, a misplaced enthusiasm for the thing-ness of the Eucharistic elements that has sometimes manifested itself in a kind of fetishization of the offertory procession to the point where it almost comes to overshadow the central Eucharistic action. But if, here as elsewhere, excessive or inept execution are constant possibilities of liturgy as it is lived, is this possibility itself not the result of key theological insights of the twentieth century? One thinks of Alexander Schmemann's 'world as sacrament', of Tillich's notion of spiritual presence in humanity's pre-verbal life, of Teilhard de Chardin's 'mass on the world'. For all of these, the sacramental realization of the presence of Christ is possible only on the basis of a kind of sacramentality implicit in the created order itself – an idea that could scarcely be strange to Thomism with its conception of what Eco, interpreting Thomas, called 'a structural grace of things' (Eco, 1986, p. 76). Indeed if there is not some such predisposition to bear sacramental meaning within matter and human life (and the elements are – again as the twentieth-century liturgists emphasized – not just matter but human products: 'fruit of the earth *and* work of human hands'), then it is hard to see how sacraments are meaningful at all. In this regard, Heidegger's meditation on a simple earthenware jug as the embodied bearer and revealer of the fourfold can indeed provide a pattern for liturgical reflection. This does not commit Christianity to discover precisely the same world of meanings in the created order as Heidegger believed himself to be engaged in uncovering (and Heidegger, of course, would not have conceded the term 'created order' without strong resistance). However, the argument over whether meditation on the round dance of worldly life discloses the realm of divinity, whether it reveals men as mortals or as made for the glorious liberty of the children of God is not an argument that is precluded by Heidegger's 'method' (if we can still call it that), even though it is clear that Heidegger's own use of this method led to a vision that can only problematically be related to Christianity. But there would be scope here to challenge Heidegger on his own ground, questioning, for example, whether the mediation between mortals and gods offered by the poet, the feast or the demi-gods of the German rivers, does not of itself call out for a deepening in the direction of Christ – as Hölderlin (Heidegger's guide for much of his reflection on the fourfold) seems to have believed. In declining to follow the path of such a constructively critical dialogue, the direction Hemming's argument takes is, bizarrely, towards a kind of Calvinist elevation of God at the expense of the created order and a sectarian hedging off of the Church's sacramental life from the life of the world. It is hard to see what is genuinely 'Catholic' here. These tendencies are, regrettably, typical of Radical Orthodoxy as a whole, though, to her credit, Catherine Pickstock finds herself on the wrong side of Hemming's dividing-line in her assertion that 'all bread is "on the way to becoming the body of Christ"' (Hemming, 2000a, p. 177). At which point one begins to wonder: why bother positioning one's thought as 'after Heidegger' at all?

Why not – and perhaps in conformity with the deep pattern of Heidegger's own path of thinking – leave Heidegger out of it and seek to think through the matter (in both senses) of the Eucharistic presence out of what that matter itself gives us to think? Such a move would not only free us from the obligation to force our thought into the straitjacket of Heideggerian vocabulary (by no means designed for English ears), but would also leave open whether or not we need the assistance of either Aristotle or Thomas!

A Christian meditation on what is given in, with and under a sacramentally mediated experience of the love of God in Christ (through whom, remember, all things were made, including the silent life of earth, sun, seed, flower and fruit) might find itself also speaking of the earth on which it stands and from which it draws its daily bread, of the sky that opens above it as an image of its 'heaven', of the divine world that blesses its mortal wanderings between heaven and earth. Such meditation would find itself in proximity to Heidegger, but would not thereby see itself as either 'Heideggerian' nor, necessarily, as involved in some kind of refutation of Heidegger.

A Christian meditation on the actual experience of Eucharistic life, performed with the discipline of a phenomenological investigation, would probably not find itself reaching or needing to reach the kind of definition enshrined in the doctrine of transubstantiation, though if and as it found itself unable to reach the uttermost parts of its experience other than by image and metaphor, formed under the sign of irresolvable ambiguity, it might find that – *as image and as metaphor* – 'transubstantiation' was no more and no less absurd than any other of the paradoxical formulations it was driven to devise. Yet this meditation would not be tempted to ascribe to this image or metaphor anything more than the most provisional normative value (perhaps for those whose ecclesiastical context 'located' the experience of the Eucharist in the body of institutionally overdetermined practices that provides the doctrine with its *Sitz-im-Leben*).

But, the church theologian might ask, doesn't such a laid-back approach throw Eucharistic experience and Eucharistic teaching into a kind of anarchic free-for-all, where everyone can simply speak as they find?

Those who ask such scare questions betray the fact that for all the grandeur of its claims the insistence on a certain kind of doctrinal adequacy has simply not been prepared to undertake the slow beginner's work of treading the path of actual attention to the phenomenon itself. Of course the Eucharist is not experienced in a hermeneutic void. Not anything or everything can be said of it. It comes to us in concrete and definitive forms. It comes as the gratefully received creatures of bread and wine that are the matter of human offering ('fruit of the earth and work of human hands').[4] It comes as a gift from and the gift of one named in a particular historical context ('our Lord Jesus Christ in the night in which He was betrayed took bread ...'), one whose presence the rite re-enacts in the mode of active remembrance. It comes to us as the sharing of a meal, a communion that is synchronic and diachronic, binding angels and men, saints on earth and those above, and accompanied by prayer for all for whom prayer is appointed. It is thus the nourishing and the increase of Christ's body on earth and therewith a proto-politics of friendship ('with angels and archangels and with all the company of heaven ...').[5] It comes to us as a sign of hope on behalf of the one remembered who is experienced as present in the gifts and in the meal and as one whose life has not been eclipsed in death ('we proclaim the Lord's death until he comes'). And it comes to us as a sign of hope for ourselves and for our world, that what is offered in the creatures of bread and wine was not created for death but for redemption ('looking for the coming of his Kingdom'), and, as the action is fulfilled in the chorus of Trinitarian praise, an affirmation of joy at the last ('by whom, and with whom, and in whom, in the unity of the Holy Spirit, all honour and glory be unto thee, O Father Almighty, world without end').

These remarks are obviously not offered as definitive of a Eucharistic theology, but merely as sketching the rudimentary and inadequate beginnings of a kind of meditative process that is there to be phenomenologically and hermeneutically extended, deepened and enriched. They are intended merely to hint at how the Eucharist has developed its own language – or, rather, has from the beginning had its own language – spoken in the silence of the gifts, in the remembered narrative of institution and in the choral spiral of praise, blessing and thanksgiving in which the gifts are taken, offered and received again and in which the narrative of institution is framed. It is a language that speaks of blessing, memory, solidarity and hope. In it we hear neither of transubstantiation nor, for that matter, of consubstantiation, transignification, real presence or of any other attempt to explain the mystery.

Does it follow that there is no point at all in attempting any kind of doctrinal (that is, any kind of normative) discourse concerning the Eucharist? By no means! The point is merely that there is no obvious reason why that discourse should be couched in the language of Aristotle, Thomas or even Heidegger. Are not the Eucharistic words, the Eucharistic action and the Eucharistic experience their own best interpreters? Is it not the lived reality of an action that is always already articulated as an action of blessing, remembrance, solidarity and hope that gives a measure to doctrinal definition and not vice versa?

These rhetorical questions may seem to be moving me into the same current of thought as Radical Orthodoxy, as if I were saying that Christian truth does not stand in hock to this or that secular current, that ours is 'the language of Canaan' (Bunyan), and the question is one of our own performative competence in this language, a language that is *sui generis*, self-generating and self-regulating. I would be only too happy if the distance were not so great that it could be traversed only by polemics, but I must nevertheless register several points that, I think, make the kind of meditation I am suggesting something slightly different from the self-referential rhetoric and self-sufficient narrativity of Radical Orthodoxy. The first point is that I wish to insist that something is being said *in* the narrative and *through* the action, something that places our exegesis of it on ground where it must both engage with history (and to do so – though by no means in the first instance – with the methods of historical research) and be concerned with the common human task of discerning and accomplishing what we (all of us, and not just 'the Church') take to be our highest good. The second point, and essentially flowing from the first, is that there can therefore be no *a priori* decision as to whether what we find in our Eucharistic experience and reflection will or will not harmonize with any past, present or future body of philosophical reflection or cultural expression. We cannot presume in advance that a future philosophy (or a newly interpreted rendering of a long-familiar philosophy) or a future shift in cultural horizons will not disclose new dimensions of truth in the Eucharistic mystery. What is there in the Christian Gospel that excludes the hope that the best is yet to come?

One further point: if, in all this, we remain concerned to speak rightly, or to speak as best we may about the Eucharistic presence of Jesus Christ in the life of the remembering and hopeful community gathered in his name, we remain ready and open to suspend all our formulations in the light of that primary experience itself, acknowledging always that here and wherever humans turn their minds to divine things we run into a barrage of paradox, equivocation and ambiguity.

A confession of despair? No! Of joy!

All things considered and compared with that success which truth hath hitherto had by so bitter conflicts with errors in this point, shall I wish that men would more give themselves to meditate with silence what we have by the sacrament, and less to dispute of the manner how? If any man suppose that this were too great stupidity and dulness, let us see whether the Apostles of our Lord themselves have not done the like. It appeareth by many examples that they of their own disposition were very scrupulous and inquisitive, yea in other cases of less importance and less difficulty always apt to move questions. How cometh it to pass that so few words of so high a mystery being uttered, they receive with gladness the gift of Christ and make no show of doubt or scruple? The reason hereof is not dark to them which have anything at all observed how the powers of the mind are wont to stir when that which we infinitely long for presenteth itself above and besides expectation. Curious and intricate speculations do hinder, they abate, they quench such inflamed motions of delight and joy as divine graces use to raise when extraordinarily they are present. The mind therefore feeling joy is always marvellous unwilling to admit any other cogitation, and in that case casteth off those disputes whereunto the intellectual part at other times easily draweth ... They had at that time a sea of comfort and joy to wade in, and we by that which they did are taught that this heavenly food is given for the satisfying of our empty souls, and not for the exercising of our curious and subtile wits. (Hooker, 1907, Book Two, LXVII, vol. 2, pp. 320–22)[6]

It must seem crass to add anything to Hooker's words, but, in the light of the argument we have been pursuing, can Christian theologians not say that the Eucharistic presence is not what they need to explain but is itself, in the whole manner of its enactment, the exposition and true interpretation of Christian joy and, in particular, of what it means through blessing, memory, solidarity and hope to find our joy in God?

Notes

1   The relevance of Hegel at this point may be noted by asking the following questions: when Laurence Paul Hemming speaks of transubstantiation as the site of a simultaneous preservation and disruption, is he not simply stating in other words what many have taken Hegel to mean by his concept of *Aufhebung* or, more precisely, is he not positioning the philosophical meaning of transubstantiation on the site of the argument over the understanding of identity and difference implicit in *Aufhebung*? But is this not merely to multiply terms rather than to solve problems? See Hemming (2000a), p. 173.
2   One might make a similar comment about the slogan 'non-identical repetition', which likewise confuses naming a problem with solving it.
3   Which is not to say that there may not be other objections to transignification. See Fitzpatrick (1993), Chapter Two, 'Objections to Transignification'.
4   This far we may find ourselves entirely on ground shared with Heidegger and the fourfold, understanding the latter as one possible interpretation of what this received and offered worldliness might mean. But the actuality of Eucharistic experience, as concretely lived out in even the least liturgical church assembly, is also ineluctably embedded in a narrative in which the historical and personal supervenes upon the material.
5   It is another and telling indication of Hemming's subjectivism that he speaks almost exclusively of the 'I' as the site in which the divine act of transubstantiation is enacted. There is little or no sense that this event is an event inconceivable as anything other than as involving at least two or three gathered together!
6   In finding myself having recourse to Hooker, I cannot help feeling, uncomfortably, just how deeply the views we take on the question of the Eucharist remain under the spell of certain confessional commonplaces. That, however, is less problematic for

the point of view I am advancing (where, for example, we may have a good hope of moving matters on through experiences of shared communion) than for the view that sees a particular doctrinal formulation as metaphysically invincible.

CHAPTER 11

Derrida and Nihilism

Hugh Rayment-Pickard

There are few shades of grey in the writings of Radical Orthodoxy. Philosophers past and present are either given the imprimatur or are treated as heretics. Derrida falls into the latter category. John Milbank denounces Derrida as a 'nihilist' (along with a cohort of fellow 'Nietzschean' perpetrators). Catherine Pickstock characterizes Derrida's 'nihilism' as a form of 'necrophilia'. Milbank and Pickstock stand before Derrida rather as joint prosecuting counsel, concerned to make the charge of 'nihilism' stick. The point here is not to weigh evidence but to present it to maximum effect. Their objective is not primarily to make a contribution to 'Derrida studies' – although they certainly do – but to show how Derrida's philosophy is the wretched end-point of flawed secular thinking.

The use of Derrida as an exemplary culprit means that Derrida's role in Radical Orthodoxy is to illustrate a general theory. Milbank is quite candid about this, saying that he will be treating Derrida as one of 'the major Nietzscheans': 'I deliberately treat the writings of Nietzsche, Heidegger, Deleuze, Lyotard, Foucault and Derrida as elaborations of a single nihilistic philosophy, paying relatively less attention to their divergences of opinion' (*TST*, p. 278). Milbank simply takes as read the existence of a 'single nihilistic philosophy', and concentrates on showing how Derrida is typical of it. Pickstock says that Derrida's 'theory of language as writing, not only sustains modern spatialization but is also driven by the concomitant modern embrace of death' (*AW*, p. 103). Her approach thereafter (as we will see shortly) is to seek out positive evidence to support her claim rather than to discuss possible counter-examples. So we do not get, and perhaps should not expect, a balanced interpretation of Derrida. 'Balance' is not the point. *Theology and Social Theory* and *After Writing* are works of Christian proclamation. *Theology and Social Theory* aims to 'reassert theology as a master discourse' (*TST*, p. 6). *After Writing* is explicitly written as a contribution to 'the new theological imperative of "radical orthodoxy"' (*AW*, p. xii). These books are all about commitment and partiality. They are works of self-conscious 'allegiance' (*TST*, p. 262) to a particular understanding of Christianity.

It is possibly because Milbank and Pickstock both see themselves in the service of a higher mission that they adopt a Nietzschean ethic of intolerance of mere scholarship. The importance of their task authorizes them to adopt an occasionally ruthless critical practice, leaving aside the 'received opinions' on

Derrida. One of the features of their treatment of Derrida is that they refer hardly, if at all, to any existing scholarship on Derrida. So, to give a token example, when Milbank argues controversially in *Theology and Social Theory* that Derrida's infinite ontology of difference is the very opposite of an infinite ontology of harmony, he does not consider Rudolphe Gasché's important essay on Derrida's 'structural infinity' (1986). We need to understand that the voice of Radical Orthodoxy does not speak from *within* the current debates about Derrida's work. Radical Orthodoxy is launched from a platform above and beyond the debates of the academy. Catherine Pickstock opens *After Writing* with the Hegelian claim that her work 'completes and surpasses philosophy' (*AW*, p. xii). Once the apotheosis of philosophy has been achieved, all argument, discussion, dialectics and conversation have (presumably) come to a close. From the vantage point of the completion of philosophy, the task must be to articulate the truth rather than merely to debate it. Thus John Milbank says emphatically that *Theology and Social Theory* is not a work of argument. If we are convinced by his writing, he says, it is the intrinsic persuasiveness of the truth of 'the Christian logos' that will have won us over (*TST*, p. 1).

Nothing that I have just said means that the judgements Milbank and Pickstock make are necessarily inaccurate or unfair. However, Milbank and Pickstock's style does condition their treatment of Derrida. There is little point in looking for a weighing of evidence or an Aristotelian assessment of *endoxa* – this is not their style. The task in this essay will be to consider the truthfulness of the claims made about Derrida – however they are arrived at. The central charge is that Derrida is a nihilist. Milbank argues that Derrida is a 'Nietzschean nihilist' who affirms an ontology of contradiction and discord. Pickstock argues that Derrida's infatuation with death marks him out as an exemplary nihilist. In a final section of the essay, I will argue – against Pickstock – that Derrida does have something useful to contribute to the Christian understanding of the Eucharist.

Milbank's charge against Derrida is simple enough: Derrida's thinking of *différance* is nihilistic because it constantly privileges negation. To a limited extent Derrida would concur with Milbank's analysis: the differential play of the trace in language is marked by the slipping away of meaning, by an absence which always inhabits presence. But Derrida would resist being labelled as a nihilist, because the play of *différance* is always a play of negation *and* position, absence *and* presence, death *and* life. Deconstruction is not *simply* negative. Indeed deconstruction attempts to undermine all *simple* alternatives in favour of undecidable admixtures. The revelation of a certain *complexity* is one of the principal achievements of deconstruction.

What Milbank does is to push uncontroversial observations about Derrida towards a controversial extreme. The undoubted role of the negative in Derrida gets 'hyped' into talk of 'mere negativity', 'ceaseless negativity', a 'total' negation, and 'exact opposition' (*TST*, pp. 310, 313, 315). The role of 'violence' in Derrida's ontology is taken to mean that 'violence is what there is to be known' (*TST*, p. 311). Derrida's problematization of truth becomes a denial 'of absolute truth and value *altogether*' (my italics, *TST*, p. 261). The play of difference is represented as an 'anarchic condition' (*TST*, p. 307) of 'total equivocation' (*WMS*, p. 61) of 'absolute diversity' (*TST*, p. 303) and essentially negative. This hermeneutic of exaggeration serves to position deconstruction as the antithesis of Milbank's Christian ontology. Consigned to this extreme, 'Derrida' can function as the perfect foil for Milbank's theology (*TST*, p. 262).

Whereas Derrida allegedly conceives difference as the perpetual operation of a negative dialectic, an endless and violent dissonance, Milbank conceives difference within an infinitely extensible ontology of presence, which is always harmonious and peaceful. Milbank's fideistic assertion of the absolute harmonics of being is his defence against the deconstructive effects of difference. There can be no deconstruction of presence because there are no hidden contradictions in the harmonic happening of being. The deconstruction of theology can only result in the appreciation of divine harmony, or else precipitate a spiral down into depthless negativity. There can be no dissonance in the divine order and no harmony elsewhere. Milbank asserts an *absolute difference* between ontology and its privation, that is to say the nihil: 'the absolute vision of ontological peace ... provides the only alternative to a nihilistic outlook' (*TST*, p. 434).

If we were to suggest a Derridean rejoinder to Milbank, it might run like this:

> The harmony of being depends upon the absolute difference between being and its privation. This means that the most important difference of all cannot be inscribed within the harmonic order. Therefore the harmonic order rests upon a primary dissonance between harmony and dissonance.

We can perhaps also imagine Milbank's response:

> The difference between being and its privation is not a proper difference because privation is not a condition but the absence of a condition. The harmonic order resounds not against dissonance, but against silence, and is all the more beautiful for it.

In turn Derrida might respond:

> The privation of being as harmony is not silence but being as dissonance. It is the difference between harmony and dissonance that cannot be included in the harmonic order. The exclusion of this difference is what a deconstruction of theology would reveal. This would leave us staring at the primordiality of difference and the impossibility of overcoming it. Theology would have to reconstruct itself from this base. This would not exclude the possibility of an ideal harmony, but the ideal harmonic order – say in the form of a perfect democracy, perfect friendship, perfect forgiveness, perfect generosity and perfect hospitality – would be an article of messianic faith: we would have to await it.

Finally, let us give Milbank the last word:

> Deconstruction will always throw up the possibility of a still more primordial

difference. But this strategy is the very essence of nihilism. The endless positing of differences leads to an abyss of infinite regress that confirms the nihilism of deconstruction. The only way to resist the hopelessness of deconstruction and its empty messianism, is to assert the difference of différance, in other words the presence of the harmonic order. This is a choice without reasons, a basic preference for life that finally cannot be explained but only asserted and celebrated.

Leaving aside this imaginary exchange, let us now retrace some of the same ground again, but this time correcting Milbank's exaggerations.

One of the results of Milbank's assimilation of Derrida into 'Nietzschean nihilism' is the conflation of Nietzsche's thinking of difference with Derrida's in a way that is only partly fair. Certainly, Derrida sees a precedent for deconstruction in the play of forces which operate in Nietzsche's eternal return (*M*, p. 18; *WD*, p. 280). However, Derrida says emphatically that deconstruction does not operate like Nietzschean 'demolition' (*OG*, p. 9; *Psy*, p. 388), but works like Heidegger's *Destruktion* or Husserl's *Abbau* to 'stake out' positive possibilities for philosophy. Milbank's nihilist interpretation of Derrida ignores the interpretation of deconstruction as a positive philosophy.

Two concepts help to clarify the positive way in which deconstruction works: 'solicitation' and 'skepsis'. 'Solicitation' (*OG*, p. 73; *WD*, pp. 6, 152) is a Latin term meaning agitatation or setting in motion. In his early writing Derrida uses 'solicit' to describe how deconstruction works to 'reveal' the 'secret place' in which metaphysics 'is neither construction nor ruin but lability' (*WD*, p. 6). Deconstruction, therefore, is not an anarchic act of vandalism on 'god', 'truth' or 'proper' meaning, but a methodological attempt to get to the secret heart of metaphysics and reveal it as *unstable*. So deconstruction is not just opposed to metaphysics, it wishes to *reveal the truth* about metaphysics. Deconstruction is *revelatory*, a form of phenomenology, and very much committed to the truth; as Derrida has explicitly said, 'truth is not a value one can renounce' (*TS*, p. 10).[1] This is why – despite what Milbank and many others say (*WMS*, p. 61) – Derrida is not a 'sceptic' in the modern sense of someone who *on principle* denies the possibility of positive knowledge: a chronic doubter. Derrida points out that the ancient Greek word *skepsis* was a metaphor of sight and that scepticism can be understood otherwise as an attempt to broaden and intensify our vision by allowing more to be *seen*, more to *happen*, than would be the case in a dogmatic mode of thought. The strategy of the ancient sceptics such as Sextus Empiricus was to suspend judgement in cases where the truth cannot be determined.[2] In the space provided by this suspension (or *epoche*) the sceptics allowed a place in philosophy for incompleteness, contradiction and accident. Sextus tells the story of an artist who, despairing of ever producing the effect he wanted, threw his sponge at the canvas. This arbitrary act produced the image the artist needed. Deconstruction tries to shake (solicit) the rigid structures of metaphysics to provide scope for a more complex and differentiated revelation. Derrida argues that the problem with the metaphysical idea of truth as self-sameness and non-contradiction is that it is simply *not true enough* to the complex world of meanings in which we really do live. Truth, for Derrida, is irreducibly complex – and this is what deconstruction *shows*. Derrida's scepticism means that he refuses to assert the primordial unity of the complex differential nature of life. This refusal is neither a denial of any such unity, nor an affirmation of the primordiality of difference, but a sceptical suspension or *epoche* of judgement. The question of the unity of the world is, in Derrida's terminology, 'undecidable' and he leaves it open. This openness has its uses. The effect of the Derridean *epoche* is prophylactic in its resistance of totalitarianism. There is also an allowance for play, novelty, invention, and a messianic arrival, which has not been pre-judged or determined in advance. Theologically, the deconstructive *epoche* protects against idolatry.

Deconstruction takes place in the name of truth, but a truth that exceeds the constraints of logocentrism. This is a truth that allows for alternatives, for the non-systematic, the excessive. Derrida attempts to deconstruct the idol of the restricted idea of truth as non-contradiction and strict correspondence. In its place appears a more general idea of truth (an 'impossible' truth by logocentric standards), the truth as an unrestricted abundance of meaning. Derrida criticizes western metaphysics for restricting the possibilities of truth, for holding back the plenitude of language and meaning. Deconstruction is not a nihilistic attack upon truth, but an attempt to *protect* truth against the constrictions of metaphysics. The truth about 'truth' is that it is not stable, consistent and logical. The assertion of truth as unstable clearly creates reflexive problems. But this reflexive instability, which means that we can never 'simply' say anything, is the glorious reality of language and meaning. This is not nihilism, but its very opposite: the affirmation of life in all its flux, complexity and ambiguity.

The structural upshot of Derrida's *epoche* is not anarchy or mere arbitrariness, but an organization which is different in kind to the centralized structures of metaphysics. Derrida discusses this other mode of organization in his essay 'Structure, Sign and Play in the Discourse of the Human Sciences', speaking of the need to hold together *both* the quest for structural foundations *and* the affirmation of a play which is not restricted by structure. Elsewhere, Derrida speaks about this structure–play outcome as a 'constellation':

> This absence of both a border and any closure of propriety gives ... [a] galaxic or galactic structure. Galaxy is meant here, at least, as a multiplicity in a perpetually unfolding space, which has no external limit, no outside, no edge, a constellated autonomy which doesn't refer to anything but itself. (*Psy*, p. 99) [3]

How different is Derrida's 'constellation' of difference from Milbank's ontology of harmony? Milbank says that there is no limit to the differences that can be accommodated in the divine polyphony but he does not say *how* this apparently 'impossible' divine harmony is achieved. Milbank's difficulty is that harmony is a cultural concept, mapped out by cultural differences. There is no one understanding of 'harmony' that embraces the range of musical forms across culture and history. Indeed dissonance can itself be harmonic – for example, the suspended 7th, the accident, the blue note, or the mordent – to a *certain* ear and from a *certain* culture. Milbank sees 'baroque music' as the model of perfect harmony because 'individual lines become increasingly distinct and individually ornamented' (*TST*, p. 429). Baroque music also progresses by a continual resolution of suspensions: every tension resolves to a cadence. This may be true for Milbank, given his particular cultural heritage, but we must wonder whether a Christian in Africa or China would agree. Even within the European tradition, not everyone concurs with Milbank's view of baroque music. Edward Holmes (writing in 1828) referred to the 'noise, violent changes of key and that species of modulation which may be termed *baroque*'.[4] (Let us also not forget that the word 'baroque' derives from the French term for an 'irregular pearl'.) To equate the divine harmony with music in the age of Bach is rather like saying that God speaks English or that heaven looks like Grantchester on an autumn morning.

Even if we accept that baroque music is the epitome of harmony, Milbank's assertions about baroque harmony are questionable. First, 'baroque harmony' is not a single, consonant tradition. Early baroque harmony in the hands of Vivaldi is a very different thing from the more adventurous harmonies of Bach. Bach's inventiveness even seemed strange and confusing to some of his contemporaries, accustomed to simpler musical forms. So the progress of baroque harmony from Monteverdi to Bach shows that taste in 'harmony' is historically relative. This applies to the whole history of Western music: the definition of harmony keeps changing. Second, the various forms of baroque harmony are not infinitely extensible but follow strict manners, rules and patterns – all 'extensions' of the music must fit within a pre-given structure. Third, Milbank argues that all dissonances are *included* within baroque harmony. It would be more accurate to say that dissonant forces *compete* with the underlying harmony – they are not so much *incorporated* into the harmony as *defeated* by it. What makes Bach's music so beautiful is the internal warfare between harmonic and dissonant powers: the figured bass on the one hand versus the consonant/dissonant ornamentation on the other. Indeed, Bach's music often employs deliberate musical 'metaphors' of battle: the fugue and counterpoint.

Nietzsche took up this theme in *The Birth of Tragedy*, pointing to the strange truth that dissonance can be intensely pleasurable: 'even ugliness and discord are an artistic game which the will, in the eternal abundance of its pleasure, plays with itself'.[5] Harmony on its own is simply deadening; music needs discord to give it energy, tension and feeling. Nietzsche does not recommend (as Milbank implies) a musical aesthetic of endless dissonance, but an aesthetic of creative interaction between discord and concord: 'an image of the world as ... a harmony produced by conflict'.[6]

The idea of 'harmony' becomes still more problematic when we remember that it is only a *metaphor* for the ontological coherence of *everything*. So 'harmony' is not referring simply to music (baroque or otherwise) but to 'moral harmony', 'social harmony', 'political harmony', 'natural harmony' – indeed any kind of 'harmony' we care to think of. How this harmony works is not clearly explained, and Milbank appears to hold it simply as an article of faith. In itself the appeal to an all-embracing ontological harmony does not say very much, except that all differences somehow 'belong' together. This belonging together of differences in an infinitely extensible structure is what Derrida tries to designate with the term constellation. It would be wrong to force Milbank and Derrida into a false coalition, but the difference between them is not as absolute as John Milbank suggests. There would perhaps be a value in subjecting Derrida to a hermeneutic of fraternity, seeking out mutual points of contact with Milbank and parallel lines of thought.

Catherine Pickstock takes up the baton from John Milbank and in *After Writing* makes a further critique of modern and post-modern nihilism. Instead of trying to anchor theology on 'the void', 'the nothing', 'loss', the 'limit situation' or 'death', Pickstock makes the case for a theology based upon a superabundant idea of life (*pleroma* or fullness) which includes death and the nihil. This all-embracing idea of life is accessible to us only liturgically in the Eucharist where the sacraments make life real and present for us in the body and blood of Christ.

Modernity has erred from the straight path, Pickstock argues, by separating off death from life, both in the practical organization of death – in hospitals, cemeteries and so on – and conceptually by setting up life and death as opposites. Chief among the culprits for this situation is Jacques Derrida, who has a central place in the book. (Indeed the book's title is an oblique reference to the priority that Derrida gives to writing over speech.) The crucial problem with Derrida, Pickstock alleges, is his philosophical separation of life from death, which echoes and reinforces the general cultural trend in modernity to oppose life to death. Only in liturgy, she argues, are life and death integrated into gestures that can properly make sense of human existence. Ironically Derrida's interest in death (his alleged necrophilia) is an indication of an underlying cultural necrophobia that seeks to isolate death.

Derrida certainly does write a great deal about the role of death and Pickstock would appear, *prima facie*, to have a good case. The concept of death plays a role in most of Derrida's writings. Derrida has spoken about death as his 'most difficult ally' (*Cir*, p. 172) and has said that 'only *pure* absence ... can *inspire*' (*WD*, p. 8). The issue is not whether death is crucial to Derrida's philosophy – it clearly is – but whether Derrida's philosophy promotes a *love* of death and the affirmation of death at the expense of life.

Just as Milbank uses exaggeration to make Derrida fit the pattern of 'a single nihilistic philosophy', Pickstock must adapt Derrida's theme of death, to make it fit her general hypothesis about the 'necrophobia' of modernity. She tries to do this by arguing that Derrida's 'exultation of the nihil' is predicated upon a separation of inner life from exterior death. This is not an exaggeration but an inversion of Derrida's philosophy: Derrida uses death to unsettle the logic that life and death are opposites. Deconstruction is a response to what Derrida sees as metaphysical necrophobia: the repression and exclusion of death. By unsettling the metaphysical tradition, Derrida is able to reveal the separation of life and death as the secret feature of metaphysical organization. We find the life/death distinction hidden away in our presuppositions about speech and writing: the spoken word is taken to be more 'alive'. Derrida challenges the life/death binarism by trying to show that all language – spoken and written – is subject to one and the same process of supplementation and delay: *différance*. But *différance* is not on the side of death against life, but belongs to an order in which life and death are held together. So the deployment of death in Derrida's philosophy is not an end in itself, but a strategic move to recast the metaphysical separation of life and death as a unity: 'life–death'. The concern with death that Pickstock labels 'necrophilia' is better expressed by Geoffrey Hartman, who speaks of Derrida's 'thanatopsis' and 'thanatopraxis' (Hartman, 1981, pp. xxv–xxvi).

The way that Pickstock manages to make death and life look like opposites in Derrida's philosophy is to stop Derrida's deconstruction in mid-flow – at the very point that his thanatopraxis raises 'death' as the return of the repressed. At this juncture, Derrida is exploiting the contrast between the pure metaphysical conception of life and its excluded 'other'. As Pickstock keeps our gaze fixed here, Derrida moves on from this confrontation to assert that life is mixed with death. Life takes place as a slipping away of time and meaning, as the transience of presence. This slippage is only a problem if we are still clinging to the metaphysical necessity to exclude death from the system of life. The false impression we get from Pickstock is that Derrida is stuck in a sterile attrition of death against life.

To make her case for Derrida's necrophilia, Pickstock looks at two of Derrida's shorter texts: 'Speech and Phenomena' and 'Aporias'. These texts are well selected for Pickstock's purpose: Derrida's theme of death is prominent in both. Pickstock's first textual example, 'Speech and Phenomena', belongs with a collection of Derrida's early essays in which Husserl is a major focus – *The Problem of Genesis in Husserl's Philosophy*, 'Speech and Phenomena', 'Form and Meaning', 'Genesis and Structure', 'Violence and Metaphysics', *Edmund Husserl's Origin of Geometry* and 'Phenomenology and the Closure of Metaphysics'. The centrepiece of Derrida's writing on Husserl is the argument that Husserl's metaphysics of subjectivity depends upon a conception of phenomenological time as the ongoing present or *lebendige Gegenwart*. Although this concept is mentioned briefly in Husserl's *Cartesian Meditations*, the main source for Derrida's critique is unpublished manuscripts in the Husserl *Nachlass*, where *lebendige Gegenwart* is a key concept. Derrida argues persuasively that *lebendige Gegenwart* is a theological concept, and he does this significantly ahead of others such as David Held, whose *Lebendige Gegenwart* appeared in 1966. Derrida argues that Husserl's phenomenology 'is a philosophy of life ... because the source of sense in general is always determined as an act of *living*, as an act of a living being, as *Lebendigkeit*' (*SP*, p. 10). Human consciousness is always a living intentional act and not just an abstract perspective. Moreover, we think we know we are 'living' because we can hear the meaning of our own living speech. 'The entire Husserlian thematic of the living present' Derrida observes, 'is the profound reassurance of the certainty of meaning' (*WD*, p. 60). In 'Speech and Phenomena' Derrida seeks to show that certainty of meaning is not attainable and that the living present can never abide in the security of its living presentation. Meanings are subject to the linguistic slippage that Derrida calls *différance*. In the course of this deconstruction, Derrida deploys the concept of death as the excluded other of life. Death is, as Derrida puts it elsewhere, a 'crypt – one would have said, of the transcendental or the repressed, of the unthought or the excluded – that organizes the ground to which it does not belong' (*G*, p. 166). The use of death is a strategic move within deconstruction, rather than its goal.

Pickstock summarizes Derrida's deconstruction of Husserl as follows: '(1) life is presence-to-self; (2) there is no presence-to-self; (3) there is only exteriority which is the opposite of presence to self; (4) therefore there "is" only death' (*AW*, p. 107). This summary begins accurately, but immediately veers off to reach a conclusion that supports Pickstock's view of Derrida as a 'necrophiliac'. Pickstock does not provide a reference or quotation to endorse the view that Derrida believes 'there is only death'. (I can think of nowhere that Derrida says this.) What Derrida does say, repeatedly and emphatically, is that there is only the alteration or undecidibility of 'life/death', the 'play of presence and absence' (*SP*, pp. 9–10). He states this conclusion explicitly in 'Speech and Phenomena' when he argues that the logic of Husserl's phonocentrism is an absolute incommensurability of life and death: *'A voice without difference, a voice without writing, is at once absolutely alive and absolutely dead'* (Derrida's italics, *SP*, p. 102).[7] Derrida's argument is in fact more subtle and interesting than the version offered by Pickstock. We could paraphrase it thus: (1) Life, *for Husserl*, is the same thing as presence-to-self, (2) presence-to-self involves an irreducible non-self-presence, (3) the absence or presence of 'self-presence' cannot be 'decided', (4) therefore there is only the undecidibility of life/death.

So Derrida does not seek to replace presence with absence, or life with death. Rather, he seeks to problematize the naïve concept of life – the living present, the living subject, living speech – with the question of death in a variety of forms. This is not an affirmation of death over life, but an attempt to deploy death in order to unsettle the security of a metaphysics conceived as 'life'. Thus Derrida believes that 'the present of self-presence is not *simple*' (*SP*, p. 61) because it is caught in the 'play of life and death' (p. 100). This is not an assertion of the primordiality of death, but it is the assertion of 'the concept of life' as an 'enigma' (p. 6). This play of life–death is the operation of *différance*, which is also not deathly, but 'belongs to no category of being, present or absent' (p. 134).

Having argued that Derrida thinks 'there is only death', Pickstock elaborates the consequences of this 'dismal' and 'miserable' view. Derrida's philosophy is a 'funeral procession', a perverse necrophilia that refers the meaning of everything back to death. Pickstock says that such a philosophy, where everything is contaminated with death, can find no true pleasure in life. This is, as I say, Pickstock's *elaboration* on Derrida's text. Derrida never says anything like this himself. But the religious proclamation of Derrida's nihilism does not require the consideration of counter examples. In fact Derrida says that our response to difference should not be 'grim' or 'morbid' but a joyful affirmation of the play of meanings 'with a certain laughter and with a certain dance' (*Diff*, p. 158). In *Of Grammatology* Derrida says that the breaking out of the play of language from the yoke of metaphysics is a moment of international 'liberation'. In 'Ulysses Gramophone' Derrida applauds the repetitive yes-saying of Molly Bloom in Joyce's *Ulysses* as an instance of the need for an ongoing affirmation of life.

However, Pickstock makes a telling criticism of Derrida's use of death in his ethics. Pickstock questions Derrida's claim that the perfect, disinterested ethical act would be the sacrifice of one's life for another, since the other could never reward the action. She also challenges Derrida's argument that an ethics of mutuality and reciprocation must always be contaminated by self-interest. Against Derrida, Pickstock posits a virtuous reciprocation in which the giver hopes for a return without expecting it in any particular form. This is an intriguing idea. Having said this, there is a difficulty that Pickstock does not tackle. Her ethic of mutuality may be the more interesting view, but (as Derrida points out) Derrida's ethic is arguably nearer to the 'greater love' of the distinctively Christian ideal of martyrdom. Is Pickstock therefore siding with Nietzsche against Derrida in the view that martyrdom is nihilistic? If so, she has inadvertently placed herself on the wrong side of the debate: in attacking the nihilism in Derrida's ethics, she discloses a nihilism within Christianity.

These remarks notwithstanding, Derrida is far from being a nihilist philosopher. Rather, his philosophy is an attempt to overcome a nihilism implicit in the oppressive logic of metaphysics. Metaphysics seeks to control meaning with a delimited idea of truth as self-sameness and non-contradiction. Metaphysics does this in the name of 'life' and 'living', proclaiming life in its purity as that which is present, simple, harmonious, coherent, organized. But Derrida argues that this idea of life breaks down because it must always exclude or repress its own limit, that is to say death. The delimited metaphysical conception of life can never include without contradiction the thought or reality of its own death. In the place of a metaphysics of life, Derrida installs the idea of life–death. Life and death for Derrida belong to a state of 'survival' or 'living on', a progression of life through death and death through life, which makes up our experience of being alive as a series or modulation in which past states and meanings are constantly dying and new ones are coming into life. But human life never comes together into a consummate unity and carries a structural deferral of meaning. The incompleteness of human meaning inspires a 'messianic' longing for human fulfilment and justice.

Pickstock's second focus is Derrida's essay *Aporias*. *Aporias* appeared nearly thirty years after 'Speech and Phenomena' and marks both a point of return to the question of personal mortality raised in 'Speech and Phenomena' and a modification in Derrida's understanding of both Heidegger and death. In *Of Grammatology* (published in the same year as the collection *Speech and Phenomena*) Derrida argues that the Heideggerian understanding of difference must be passed through in order to achieve the 'more originary' ground of *différance* (*OG*, p. 23). In *Aporias*, however, Derrida says that his 'purpose was not to justify a passage ... toward a more radical, originary or fundamental thought' (*A*, p. 79). The prophetic overcoming of Heidegger proclaimed by the young Derrida gives way in the later Derrida to a mystical meditation on the Heideggerian problematic of death. Although in *Aporias* Derrida deconstructs the implicit humanism in Heidegger's being-towards-death, he follows Heidegger in seeing death as an exemplary form of 'impossibility' or aporia. We have no 'access' to death as such, death does not 'appear' in order to become phenomenal (*A*, p. 78), and the word 'death' is 'unassignable' with respect to its 'thingness' (*A*, p. 22). Derrida uses the concept of 'my death' to think through the more general concept of 'impossibility'.

Pickstock's critique fixes upon Derrida's consideration of the non-phenomenal character of death. She immediately says that if death cannot 'appear' it is therefore 'radically unknown and unknowable'. In the following sentence she says that Derrida domesticates 'the unknown' by defining it as "nothing" ' (*AW*, pp. 108–9). Thus we move very swiftly from what Derrida does say (that death is non-phenomenal) to what Pickstock would like Derrida to say (that the unknown is defined as 'nothing'). In fact Derrida neither says that death is 'radically unknowable' nor does he define death or 'the unknown' as 'nothing'. The point about 'death' is that it cannot be 'defined' at all; it is 'the figure' of 'impossibility' (*A*, p. 58). This 'impossibility' is not just the epistemological impossibility of 'knowledge', but the general impossibility of what Derrida calls 'access' to death. We can never 'determine' death (p. 22), close off its meaning, or 'demarcate' its limits (*Ap*, p. 78). This is what Derrida (following Aristotle) calls 'the aporia', the point where the path of philosophy is blocked. Derrida does not push death into a category of any kind – neither 'unknowability' nor 'nothingness'. This is what Derrida elsewhere calls 'the species of the non-species', in other words the attempt to signify that which defies categorization.

Following the fault line of this paradox, Pickstock does make an interesting and telling charge against Derrida's talk of non-phenomenality: surely there must be an effective phenomenology of the non-phenomenon (*AW*, p. 115). Pickstock argues that Derrida could avoid this contradiction with an alternative notion of phenomenology: the appearance of language as *both* living and dead, signifying and dissembling. In fact Derrida does offer an alternative phenomenology, although it is not quite the one that Pickstock recommends. This 'other' phenomenology, 'phenomenology as disappearance', is first hinted at in 'Violence and Metaphysics' (*WD*, p. 129) and has been a key concept in Derrida's writing ever since. In trying to think how disappearance can also be revelatory, Derrida takes his lead from Heidegger's so-called 'privative' interpretation of *Dasein* which 'reveals' by 'taking away'. In *Aporias* – the text

Pickstock considers – Derrida refers to this as phenomenology *not as such* and uses it as a way of asserting the positive value of 'impossibility'.

It is with the concept of 'impossibility' that we come to the real disjunction between Pickstock and Derrida. Pickstock declares Derrida's indeterminacy, aporia, and impossibility to be an empty, abyssal middle realm that confirms deconstruction in its abject nihilism. Derrida takes a more positive approach to 'impossibility', treating it as a meaningful predicate that marks the ambiguous space between all and nothing, life and death, plenitude and emptiness. Derrida's thinking of truth, and the sacred, begins with the experience of the 'impossible' rather than the experience of 'nothing', 'death', 'absence' or emptiness. The concept of 'impossibility' is crucial to Derrida's theology:

> Every time I say: X is neither this nor that, neither the contrary of this nor that, neither the simple neutralization of this nor that with which it has nothing in common, being absolutely heterogeneous to or incommensurable with them, I would start to speak of God. (*H*, p. 76)

In his recent writings Derrida has argued that the 'impossible' inspires us to acts of faith, hope and love.

Derrida's theological remarks hint, again, at the possible fruitfulness of a fraternal dialogue with Radical Orthodoxy. After all, Pickstock argues that Eucharistic liturgy achieves a form of 'openness' in which 'death and life … are no longer held in opposition' (*AW*, p. 266). Is there any analogy here with Derrida's life–death motif? But this dialogue will never take place because Derrida is on the 'other side', one of 'them', a Nietzschean nihilist and a necrophiliac. Derrida's role in Radical Orthodoxy is to serve as a paradigmatic enemy.

In the final paragraphs of this essay, let us give some attention to Pickstock's understanding of Eucharistic liturgy, which models the divine integration of life and death. It is highly significant that Pickstock's reference point for her discussion of the Eucharist is not the Bible but the text of the medieval Roman Rite (*AW*, pp. 223ff.). By contrast with the single narrative of the Roman Rite, the New Testament contains four *significantly different* stories of the Last Supper (in Matthew, Mark, Luke and Paul's first letter to the Corinthians) and Jesus' 'ego' remarks about the 'living bread' in John 6. So Pickstock reduces the open and differentiated pattern of biblical accounts into one text which she calls 'the Institution Narrative' – always with initial capitals and the definite article (*AW*, p. 220).

The naïve assumption that the liturgical texts contain a faithful précis of the various biblical narratives of the Last Supper leads Pickstock to form a radically mistaken picture of the Eucharist. She says that Christ 'lifted' the cup, when this is in fact a liturgical gesture invented by the Church. The biblical accounts make no reference to ritual elevation but record – very definitely – that Jesus made the everyday, non-ritual action of 'taking hold of' the cup. (There are four Greek verbs for lifting, all with strong liturgical resonances, that the New Testament authors could have used to describe Jesus' action with the cup. However, the verb chosen by all four is *lambano* – which is elsewhere used to describe 'taking' lamps, flasks of oil, a spear, palm leaves, and people – and has no special liturgical resonance.) Pickstock also makes much of what she calls 'Christ's ineffable *dicta*': the words 'take *and* eat ... take *and* drink'. This 'coordinating conjunction', she says, is convoluted evidence of God's 'dislocationary reason' over and against all secular models of rationality. The trouble is that the words she discusses are not Christ's *dicta* at all, and the conjunction 'and' simply does not appear anywhere in the biblical accounts of the administration of bread and wine. In Matthew Christ says 'Take, eat'; in Mark he simply instructs the disciples to 'take' the bread without mentioning eating at all. In Luke and Paul he says neither 'take' nor 'eat'. In the case of the cup, the disciples are not instructed to 'take' the wine at all (Jesus alone 'takes' the cup). In Matthew the disciples are instructed to 'drink'; in Mark and Luke they are simply given the cup with no words of instruction; and in 1 Corinthians they are instructed to 'do this as often as you drink it'. The Christ that Pickstock discusses – the one 'lifting the cup', who says 'take *and* eat ... take *and* drink' – is an invention of liturgy, a fictional character who exists neither in scripture nor in history. The anamnesis of liturgy, which should protect against error, becomes a form of false memory syndrome.

Pickstock claims a superordinate authority for the Roman Rite – it is, she says, 'a gift *from* God' – and she uses it in preference to biblical or any other kind of authority. In this way Pickstock effectively turns liturgy into super-scripture, meaning that the Bible (if it is to be read at all) must be read through the lens of liturgy. This is the reduction of scripture to lection, doxology and prayer – a domestication of scripture that reduces its strangeness and capacity to shock. But this approach is not defended and we are left in the position of either accepting or rejecting her personal assurance of the authority of the Roman Rite over scripture. There is something deeply 'radical' about this move, even if it is not obviously 'orthodox'.

The point that Pickstock tries to push home, using a liturgical text as her authority, is that the institution of the Eucharist was essentially 'liturgical' in her particular sense. Naturally, since she is working from a *liturgical* rewriting of the institution narratives, the Last Supper appears intensely ritualized. Things are not so clear cut, however, when one considers the variety and complexity of the biblical material. One particular objection to many of the liturgical versions of the institution narrative is that they exclude reference to Christ's proleptic remarks about the provisional nature of the bread and wine and the importance of awaiting consumption of 'new' wine when the kingdom comes. In all three synoptic accounts Christ says that following the Last Supper, he will abstain from drinking the fruit of the vine until the arrival of the kingdom. If this comment is given prominence in the interpretation of the institution narratives (as I believe it should), the Eucharist takes the form of a feast of deferral, or apocalyptic waiting, whose final meaning and consummation is not ultimately complete in the liturgical act, but depends upon the ethico-religious task of accomplishing the kingdom. The implication of Christ's comment is that the liturgical consumption of bread and wine must be matched by an ethical effort to make real the kingdom of God. Ritual sacrifice must be completed with ethical sacrifice.

An effective theory of the Eucharist, then, needs to explain how the Eucharist works *both* in the present to bind the faithful together as 'the body of Christ' *and* in anticipation of a better social order to come. In the context of this interpretation, Derrida's understanding of the sign as differing/deferring is useful and illuminating. Derrida argues that a proper ethics requires *both* a differential space in which other people can be encountered as 'others' and not merely as modifications of the self, *and* a deferral of truth to protect against totalitarianism. For Derrida, a sign can never be complete, and there is always a remainder or postponement of meaning, a world-to-come, which motivates the ethico-religious quest. Hence the Eucharist nourishes the believer both with a present sign of Christ and with the ethical imperatives of the kingdom. Pickstock's personal selection of the medieval Roman Rite as the authoritative 'Institution Narrative' means that she does not have to take account of Christ's kingdom theology in the words of administration – and she doesn't.

Pickstock's conflation of 'the Institution Narrative' requires a violent reduction of narrative difference. Similarly, Milbank talks about 'the Christian mythos' (*TST*, p. 381) as though there were obviously only one. Yet even within scripture the narrations of the Christian myth are plural, and the subsequent ecclesial re-narrations in liturgy and elsewhere have multiplied that plurality. The question of what constitutes *the* Christian mythos is, and always has been, contested within the Church. So Milbank's 'narration of Christian difference' (*TST*, p. 388) will be constantly hampered by the 'difference of Christian narration'. The Christian myth is not stable and the 'Christian difference' will always be blurred, frayed and open to dispute. The Church is, in part, a *conversation* about the Christian mythos, logos and praxis. The Church has something to lose and nothing to gain from categorically ruling out certain conversational partners.

Notes

1   See also Derrida's scathing remarks about those who say that he is not concerned with truth or reality (*LI*, p. 137).
2   The sceptics called this the *epoche* and Husserl self-consciously borrows this term for the 'bracketing' used in phenomenology. There is not space to elaborate it here, but we can follow the evolution of deconstruction as a radicalization of the Husserlian *epoche*.
3   See also *D*, pp. 257ff., where Derrida refers to 'a constellation of blanks' and 'a tropological structure that circulates infinitely around itself through the incessant supplement of an extra turn'. '*Différance* is not astructural', Derrida asserts in a later text; 'it produces systematic and regulated transformations which are able, at a certain point, to leave room for a structural science' (*Pos*, p. 28).
4   Holmes, Edward, *A Ramble among the Musicians of Germany, giving some account*

  of the Operas of Munich, Dresden, Berlin, etc. By a Musical Professor (London: 1828).

5 Nietzsche, Friedrich, *The Birth of Tragedy*, trans. Shaun Whiteside (London: Penguin, 1995), p. 115.

6 Nietzsche, Friedrich, 'Richard Wagner in Beyreuth', *Untimely Meditations*, trans. Richard Hollingdale (Cambridge: Cambridge University Press, 1983), p. 242.

7 For a selection of other references to the life/death motif, see: *PC*, pp. 259; 46 and 62; *C*, pp. 37, 43 and 69; *Par*, p. 209, *GT*, p. 102; *SM*, p. 51; *D*, pp. 93 and 325; *TP*, p. 159; *G*, pp. 71–2 and 240; *M*, p. 83; *EO*, p. 26; *Dem*, p. 88.

Bibliography

Adorno, T. W. (1979), *Dialectic of Enlightenment*, trans. John Cumming, London: Verso.

Ammonius (1998), *On Aristotle's On Interpretation 9*, trans. David Blank, in Ammonius, *On Aristotle's On Interpretation 9*, trans. David Blank, with Boethius, *On Aristotle's On Interpretation 9*, trans. Norman Kretzmann, Ithaca: Cornell University Press.

Andrews, Floy E. (1998), 'God, the Evil Genius and Eternal Truths: The Structure of the Understanding in the Cartesian Philosophy', *Animus*, **3**, www.swgc.mun.ca/animus.

——— (2000), 'Hegel's Presentation of the Cartesian Philosophy in the *Lectures on the History of Philosophy*', *Animus*, **5**, www.swgc.mun.ca/animus.

——— (2001), 'Amour in Descartes' Thought and Life', *Animus*, **6**, www.swgc.mun.ca/animus.

Aquinas, Thomas (1952–56), *Summa theologiae*, ed. Petrus Caramello, 3 vols, Rome and Turin: Marietti.

——— (1959), *Expositio super librum Boethii De trinitate*, ed. Bruno Decker, 2nd edn, Studien und Texte zur Geistesgeschichte des Mittelalters, 4, Leiden: Brill.

——— (1961–67), *Summa contra gentiles*, ed. Petrus Marc and others, 3 vols, Turin and Rome: Marietti.

——— (1996), *Commentary on the Book of Causes [Super Librum De Causis Expositio]*, trans. V. Guagliardo, C. Hess, R. Taylor, Thomas Aquinas in Translation 1, Washington: The Catholic University of America Press.

Arendt, H. (1954), *Between Past and Future: Eight Exercises in Political Thought*, New York: Viking.

Augustine (1950), *City of God*, trans. Marcus Dods, with an introduction by Thomas Merton, New York: Random House.

Barth, Karl (1982), 'Das Erste Gebot als Theologisches Axiom', in *Theologische Fragen und Antworten Gesammelte Vorträge*, vol. 3, Zürich: Theologischer Verlag, pp. 127–43.

Behren, C. B. A. (1985), *Society, Government and the Enlightenment: The Experience of Eighteenth Century France and Prussia*, New York: Harper and Row.

Beiser, F. (1996), *The Sovereignty of Reason: The Defense of Rationality in the Early English Enlightenment*, Princeton: Princeton University Press.

Belting, Hans (1994), *Likeness and Presence: a History of the Image before the*

Era of Art, trans. E. Jephcott, Chicago: University of Chicago Press.

Berlin, Isaiah (1990), 'Joseph de Maistre and the Origins of Fascism', in Hardy, Henry (ed.), *The Crooked Timber of Humanity: Chapters in the history of ideas*, London: Fontana, pp. 91–174.

Berman, H. (1983), *Law and Revolution: The Formation of the Western Legal Tradition*, Cambridge: Harvard University Press.

Biggemann, Wilhelm Schmidt (2004), *Die Politische Theologie der Gegenaufklärung. Saint-Martin, De Maistre, Kleuker, Baader*, Berlin: Akademie Verlag.

Boethius (1973), *Consolatio Philosophiae*, ed. H. Stewart and E. Rand, Loeb Classical Library, Cambridge: Harvard University Press.

Bonner, G. (1984), 'Christ, God and Man in the Thought of St. Augustine', *Angelicum*, **61**, pp. 268–94.

Boulnois, Olivier (1995), 'Quand commence l'ontothéologie? Aristote, Thomas d'Aquin et Duns Scot', *Revue Thomiste*, **95**, 85–108.

Bowlin, John (2004), 'Parts, Whole and Opposites: John Milbank as Geisteshistoriker', *Journal of Religious Ethics*, **32** (2), 257–69.

Bradley, Owen (1999), *A modern Maistre: the social and political thought of Joseph de Maistre*, Lincoln, NE and London: University of Nebraska Press.

Breyfogle, T. (1996), 'Theology Without Footnotes', *Reviews in Religion and Theology*, Summer, 77–81.

———— (1999a), 'intellectus' in Fitzgerald, A. (ed.), *Augustine Through the Ages: An Encyclopedia*, Grand Rapids: Eerdmans, pp. 452–4.

———— (1999b), 'punishment' in Fitzgerald, A. (ed.), *Augustine Through the Ages: An Encyclopedia*, Grand Rapids: Eerdmans, pp. 688–90.

———— (2004), 'Towards a Contemporary Augustinian Understanding of Politics', in Doody, J. (ed.) (2005), *Augustine and Politics*, Lanham, MD: Lexington Books.

Brisson, Luc (1998), *Plato the Myth Maker*, trans., ed., introduction Gerard Naddaf, Chicago: University of Chicago Press.

Brown, Peter (1964), 'Saint Augustine's Attitude to Religious Coercion', *Journal of Roman Studies,* **54**, 107–16.

Burnaby, J. (1960), *Amor Dei: A Study in the Religion of St. Augustine*, 3rd edn, London: Hodder and Stoughton.

Caputo, J. D. (1982), *Heidegger and Aquinas. An Essay Overcoming Metaphysics*, New York: Fordham University Press.

Cassirer, Ernst (1953), *The Platonic Renaissance in England*, trans. J. P. Pettegrove, Edinburgh: Nelson.

Courtine, Jean-François (1990), *Suarez et le système de la métaphysique*, Épiméthée, Paris: Presses Universitaires de France.

———— (ed.) (1992), *Phénoménologie et théologie*, Paris: Critérion.

Cross, Richard (1999), *Duns Scotus*, Great Medieval Thinkers, New York: Oxford University Press.

———— (2001), 'Where Angels Fear To Tread: Duns Scotus and Radical Orthodoxy', *Antonianum*, **76**, 7–41.

Cudworth, Ralph (1647), *A Sermon Preached before the House of Commons March 31, 1647*, Cambridge: Printed by Roger Daniel.

———— (1664), *A Sermon Preached to the Honourable Society of Lincolnes-Inne*, London: Printed by James Flesher for Richard Royston.

———— (1678), *True Intellectual System of the Universe*, London: Printed for Richard Royston.

———— (1996), *A Treatise Concerning Eternal and Immutable Morality*, ed. Sarah Hutton, Cambridge, Cambridge University Press.

Cunningham, Conor (2002), *Genealogy of Nihilism. Philosophies of nothing and the difference of theology*, Radical Orthodoxy Series, London and New York: Routledge.

Davidson, A. (1995), 'Introduction: Pierre Hadot and the Spiritual Phenomenon of Ancient Philosophy', in Hadot, Pierre, *Philosophy as a way of Life. Spiritual Exercises from Socrates to Foucault*, Oxford: Blackwells.

Deane, H. A. (1963), *The Political and Social Ideas of St. Augustine*, New York: Columbia University Press.

Deleuze, G. (1968), *Différence et répétition*, Paris: Presses Universitaires de France.

Derrida, J. (1967), *L'Écriture et la différence*, Paris: Seuil.

Descartes, René (1984), *The Philosophical Writings of Descartes*, 3 vols, trans. J. Cottingham, R. Stoothoff, D. Murdoch, Cambridge: Cambridge University Press.

Diamond, Eli (2000), 'Hegel on Being and Nothing: Some Contemporary Neoplatonic and Sceptical Responses', *Dionysius*, **18**, 183–216.

———— (2002), 'Understanding and Individuality in the Three Cities: An Interpretation of Plato's *Laws*', *Animus*, **7**, <www.swgc.mun.ca/animus>

Doull, James (1973), 'Hegel and Contemporary Liberalism, Anarchism, Socialism: A Defense of the Rechtsphilosophie Against Marx and His Contemporary Followers', in O'Malley, J. J. (ed.), *The Legacy of Hegel*, The Hague: Nijhoff.

———— (2000), 'Hegel on the English Reform Bill', *Animus*, **5**, <www.swgc.mun.ca/animus>

———— (2003), 'Neoplatonism and the Origins of the Cartesian Subject', in Peddle, D. and Robertson, N. (eds), *Philosophy and Freedom: the Legacy of James Doull*, Toronto: University of Toronto Press, pp. 219–49.

Duffy, Eamon (1992), *Stripping the Altars: Traditional Religion in England 1400–1580*, New Haven: Yale University Press.

Eco, Umberto (1986), *Art and Beauty in the Middle Ages*, New Haven: Yale University Press.

Eriugena, John Scot (1865), *De Divisione Naturae*, ed. H. J. Floss, Patrologia Latina 122.

Evans, C. S. (1992), *Passionate Reason. Making Sense of Kierkegaard's 'Philosophical Fragments'*, Bloomington: Indiana University Press.

Findlay, J. N. (1974), *Plato: The Written and Unwritten Doctrines*, London: Routledge and Kegan Paul.

Fitzpatrick, P. J. (1993), *In Breaking of Bread: Eucharist and Ritual*, Cambridge: Cambridge University Press.

Gardner, Sebastian (1999), *Kant and the Critique of Pure Reason*, Routledge Philosophy Guidebooks, London: Routledge.

Gasché, Rudolphe (1986), 'Nontotalization without Spuriousness', *Journal of the British Society of Phenomenology*, **17** (3), 289–307.

Gascoigne, J. (1989), *Cambridge in the Age of Enlightenment: Science, Religion and Politics from the Restoration to the French Revolution*, Cambridge: Cambridge University Press.

Gilson, Étienne (1947), *Philosophie et incarnation selon saint Augustin*, Montréal: Institut d'études médiévales, Université de Montréal.

——— (1952), *Being and Some Philosophers*, Toronto: Pontifical Institute of Mediaeval Studies.

——— (1962), *L'Être et l'essence*, Paris: Vrin.

Hadot, Pierre (1959), 'Heidegger et Plotin', *Critique*, **15**, 539–56.

——— (1981), 'Exercices spirituels antiques et "philosophie chrétienne"', in idem, *Exercices spirituels et philosophie antique*, Paris: Études augustiniennes, pp. 59–74.

——— (1995), *Philosophy As a Way of Life: Spiritual Exercises from Socrates to Foucault*, ed. A. I. Davidson, trans. M. Chase, Oxford: Blackwell.

——— (1998), 'La Fin du paganisme', reprinted in idem, *Études de philosophie ancienne*, L'âne d'or, Paris: Les Belles Lettres, pp. 341–74.

Hanby, M. (1999), 'Desire: Augustine Beyond Western Subjectivity', in *RO*, pp. 109–26.

——— (2003), *Augustine and Modernity*, London: Routledge.

Hankey, Wayne J. (1987/2002), *God in Himself, Aquinas' Doctrine of God as Expounded in the Summa Theologiae*, Oxford Theological Monographs/ Oxford Scholarly Classics, Oxford: Oxford University Press.

——— (1998a), 'Denys and Aquinas: Antimodern Cold and Postmodern Hot', in Ayres, Lewis and Jones, Gareth (eds), *Christian Origins: Theology, Rhetoric and Community*, Studies in Christian Origins, London and New York: Routledge, pp. 139–84.

——— (1998b), 'From Metaphysics to History, from Exodus to Neoplatonism, from Scholasticism to Pluralism: the fate of Gilsonian Thomism in English-speaking North America', *Dionysius*, **9**, 157–88.

——— (1998c), 'The Postmodern Retrieval of Neoplatonism in Jean-Luc Marion and John Milbank and the Origins of Western Subjectivity in Augustine and Eriugena', *Hermathena*, **165**, Winter, 9–70.

——— (1999a), 'Self-knowledge and God as Other in Augustine: Problems for a Postmodern Retrieval', *Bochumer Philosophisches Jahrbuch für Antike und Mittelalter*, **4**, 83–123.

——— (1999b), '*Theoria versus Poesis*: Neoplatonism and Trinitarian Difference in Aquinas, John Milbank, Jean-Luc Marion and John Zizioulas', *Modern Theology*, **15** (4), July, 387–415.

——— (2001), 'Between and Beyond Augustine and Descartes: More than a

Source of the Self', *Augustinian Studies*, **32** (1), 65–88.

———— (2001a), 'Why Philosophy Abides for Aquinas', *The Heythrop Journal*, **42** (3), July, 329–48.

———— (2002), '*Secundum rei vim vel secundum cognoscentium facultatem*: Knower and Known in the *Consolation of Philosophy* of Boethius and the *Proslogion* of Anselm', in Inglis, John (ed.), *Medieval Philosophy and the Classical Tradition in Islam, Judaism and Christianity*, Richmond: Curzon, pp. 126–50.

———— (2002a), 'Aquinas and the Platonists', in Gersh, Stephen and Hoenen, Maarten J. F. M. (eds), *The Platonic Tradition in the Middle Ages*: *A Doxographic Approach*, Berlin and New York: de Gruyter, pp. 279–324.

———— (2003), '"Knowing As We are Known" in *Confessions* 10 and Other Philosophical, Augustinian and Christian Obedience to the Delphic *Gnothi Seauton* from Socrates to Modernity', *Augustinian Studies*, **34** (1), 23–48.

———— (2003a), 'Philosophy as Way of Life for Christians? Iamblichan and Porphyrian Reflections on Religion, Virtue, and Philosophy in Thomas Aquinas', *Laval Théologique et Philosophique*, **59** (2), June, 193–224.

———— (2004), *Cent Ans De Néoplatonisme En France: Une Brève Histoire Philosophique* in *Lévinas et L'héritage Grec*, by Jean-Marc Narbonne, followed by *Cent Ans De Néoplatonisme En France: Une Brève Histoire Philosophique*, Collection Zêtêsis, Paris and Québec, Librairie Philosophique J. Vrin/Les Presses de l'Université Laval.

———— (2004a), 'Why Heidegger's "History" of Metaphysics is Dead', *American Catholic Philosophical Quarterly*, **78** (3), 425–43.

Hanvey, James (2000), 'Conclusion: Continuing the Conversation', in Hemming, Laurence Paul (ed.), *Radical Orthodoxy? – A Catholic Inquiry*, Aldershot: Ashgate, pp. 149–71.

Harris, Harriet A. (1998), 'Should We Say that Personhood is Relational?', *Scottish Journal of Theology*, **51**, 214–34.

Harrison, J. (1990), *"Religion" and the Religions in the English Enlightenment*, Cambridge: Cambridge University Press.

Hartman, Geoffrey (1981), *Saving The Text*, Baltimore: Johns Hopkins University Press.

Hedley, D. (2000), 'Review of Radical Orthodoxy. A New Thelogy', ed. by John Milbank, Catherine Pickstock and Graham Ward, *Journal of Theological Studies*, **51** (1), 405–8.

———— (2000), 'Should Divinity Overcome Metaphysics? Reflections on John Milbank's Theology beyond Secular Reason and Confessions of a Cambridge Platonist', *Journal of Religion*, **80** (2), 271–98.

Hegel, G. W. F. (1967), *The Philosophy of Right*, trans. T. M. Knox, Oxford: Clarendon Press.

———— (1969), *The Science of Logic*, trans. A. V. Miller, London: Allen and Unwin.

———— (1970), *The Philosophy of Nature*, trans. A. V. Miller, Oxford: Clarendon Press.

————— (1973), *The Philosophy of Mind*, trans. A. V. Miller, Oxford: Clarendon Press.

————— (1988), *Lectures on the Philosophy of Religion*, trans. R. F. Brown, P. C. Hodgson, J. M. Stewart and H. S. Harris, Berkeley: University of California Press.

————— (1991), *The Encyclopaedia Logic*, trans. T. F. Geraets, W. A. Suchting, H. S. Harris, Indianapolis: Hackett Publishing Company.

————— (1998), *Lectures on Fine Art*, vol. II, trans. T. M. Knox, Oxford: Oxford University Press.

Heidegger, M. (1962), *Being and Time*, trans. J. Macquarrie and E. Robinson, New York: Harper and Row.

————— (1969), *Identity and Difference*, trans. J. Stambaugh, New York: Harper and Row.

————— (1972), *On Time and Being*, trans. J. Stambaugh, New York: Harper and Row.

————— (1977), *The Question Concerning Technology and Other Essays*, trans. W. Lovitt, New York: Harper and Row, pp. 53–112.

————— (1982), *Identität und Differenz*, 7th edn, Pfullingen: Neske.

————— (1989), *Beiträge zur Philosophie*, Frankfurt am Main: Klostermann.

————— (1992), *Was ist Metaphysik*, 14th edn, Frankfurt am Main: Klostermann.

Hemming, Laurence Paul (ed.) (2000), *Radical Orthodoxy? – A Catholic Inquiry*, Aldershot: Ashgate.

————— (2000a), 'After Heidegger: Transubstantiation', *The Heythrop Journal*, **40** (2), April, 187–98.

Henle, R. J. (1956), *Saint Thomas and Platonism. A Study of the* Plato *and* Platonici *Texts in the Writings of Saint Thomas*, The Hague: Martinus Nijhoff.

Henry, Michel (1965), *Philosophie et phénoménologie du corps. Essai sur l'ontologie biranienne*, Paris: Presses Universitaires de France.

Hirschman, Albert O. (1977), *The Passions and the Interests*, Princeton: Princeton University Press.

Hobbes, Thomas (1990), *Leviathan*, ed. R. Tuck, Cambridge: Cambridge University Press.

Hollerich, M. (1999), 'John Milbank, Augustine, and the "Secular"', in Vessey, M., Pollmann, K. and Fitzgerald, A. (eds), *History, Apocalypse, and the Secular Imagination: New Essays on the* City of God, Bowling Green: Philosophy Documentation Center.

Hooker, Richard (1907), *Ecclesiastical Polity*, Everyman, London: J. M. Dent.

House, Dennis K. (1981), 'A Commentary on Plato's *Phaedo*', *Dionysius*, **5**, 40–65.

Iamblichus (1989), *Protrepticos*, ed. Édouard Des Places, Collection Budé, Paris: Les Belles Lettres.

————— (2002), *De Anima*, text, trans. and commentary J. F. Finamore and J. M. Dillon, Philosophia Antiqua 92, Leiden: Brill.

———— (2003), *De Mysteriis*, trans, introduction, notes E. C. Clarke, J. M. Dillon, J. P. Hershbell, Atlanta: Society of Biblical Literature.

Inge, William Ralph (1925), *Christian Mysticism*, London: Methuen.

Insole, Christopher J. (2004), *The Politics of Human Frailty: A Theological Defence of Political Liberalism*, London: SCM.

Janicaud, Dominique (1969), *Une généalogie du spiritualisme français. Aux sources du bergsonisme: Ravaisson et la métaphysique*, Archives internationales d'histoire des idées, La Haye: Nijhoff.

———— (1991), *Le tournant théologique de la phénoménologie française*, Paris: Éditions de l'Éclat.

———— (1998), *La phénoménologie éclatée*, Paris: Éditions de l'Eclat.

———— (2001), *Heidegger en France*, 2 vols, Idées, Paris: Albin Michel.

———— et al. (2000), *Phenomenology and the 'Theological Turn': The French Debate*, New York: Fordham University Press.

Janowski, Zbigniew (2000), *Cartesian Theodicy: Descartes's Quest for Certitude*, Dordrecht and Boston: Kluwer.

Janz, P. D. (2004), 'Radical Orthodoxy and the New Culture of Obscurantism', *Modern Theology*, **20** (3), July, 363–405.

Jenkins, John I. (1997), *Knowledge and Faith in Thomas Aquinas*, Cambridge: Cambridge University Press.

Johnston, A. M. (1991), 'Natural Science and Christian Theology', in Harris, S. (ed.), *Replenish the Earth: The Christian Theology of Nature*, Charlottetown: St Peter's, pp. 61–71.

Keating, G. I. (1958), *The Moral Problems of Fraternal, Paternal, and Judicial Correction according to Saint Augustine*, Rome: Pontificia Universitas Gregoriana.

Kierkegaard, S. (1983), *Repetition* (with *Fear and Trembling*), trans. H. Hong and E. Hong, Princeton: Princeton University Press.

———— (1991), *Practice in Christianity*, trans. H. Hong and E. Hong, Princeton: Princeton University Press.

———— (1992a), *Philosophical Fragments*, trans. H. Hong and E. Hong, Princeton: Princeton University Press.

———— (1992b), *Concluding Unscientific Postscript to Philosophical Fragments*, trans. H. Hong and E. Hong, Princeton: Princeton University Press.

Lash, Nicholas (1999), 'Where does Holy Teaching Leave Philosophy? Questions on Milbank's Aquinas', *Modern Theology*, **15** (4), 433–44.

Lemoine, Maël (2000), 'Affectivité et auto-affection: Réflexions sur le "corps subjectif" chez Maine de Biran et M. Henry', *Les Études philosophiques*, Avril–Juin, 242–67.

Levinas, Emmanuel (1996), 'Meaning and Sense', in Peperzak, Adriaan T., Critchley, Simon and Bernasconi, Robert (eds), *Emmanuel Levinas: Basic Philosophical Writings*, Indianapolis: Indiana University Press, pp. 33–64.

Levine, Peter (1995), *Nietzsche and the Modern Crisis of the Humanities*, Albany: SUNY Press.

Lipner, Julius (1994), 'Review of *Christian Uniqueness Reconsidered: The Myth of a Pluralistic Theology of Religions*, ed. Gavin D'Costa (New York: Orbis, 1990), *The Scottish Journal of Theology*, **47** (2), 261–4.

Lipton, D. R. (1978), *Ernst Cassirer — The Dilemma of a Liberal Intellectual in Germany 1914–33*, Toronto: University of Toronto Press.

Lovejoy, A. (1903), 'Kant and the English Platonists', in *Essays Philosophical and Psychological: In honour of William James by his colleagues at Columbia University*, New York: Longmans, pp. 265–302.

Löwith, Karl (1949), *Meaning in History*, Chicago: University of Chicago Press.

Machiavelli, Niccolò (1970), *The Discourses*, trans. L. Walker, Harmondsworth: Penguin.

MacIntyre, Alisdair (1981), *After Virtue*, London: Duckworth.

Maistre, J. de (1884–86), *Œuvres Complètes*, Lyon: Librairie Générale Catholique et Classique, Vitte et Perrussel.

Manent, P. (1994), 'The Contest for Command', in Lilla, M. (ed.), *New French Thought: Political Philosophy*, Princeton: Princeton University Press, pp. 178–85.

———— (1998), *The City of Man*, trans. M. A. LePain, Princeton: Princeton University Press.

Marenbon, John (2000), 'What is Medieval Philosophy?', in idem, *Aristotelian Logic, Platonism and the Context of Early Medieval Philosophy in the West*, Variorum Collected Studies Series 696, Aldershot: Ashgate.

Marion, Jean-Luc (1977), *L'idole et la distance: Cinq études*, Paris: Grasset et Fasquelle.

———— (1980), 'L'instauration de la rupture: Gilson à la lecture de Descartes', in Courtier, M. (ed.), *Étienne Gilson et Nous: La philosophie et son histoire*, Paris: Vrin, pp. 13–34.

———— (1991), *God without Being*, trans. Thomas A. Carlson, Religion and Postmodernism, Chicago: University of Chicago Press (French 1st edn 1982).

———— (1995), 'Saint Thomas d'Aquin et l'onto-théo-logie', *Revue thomiste*, **95** (1), 31–66.

———— (1998), 'The Idea of God', in Garber, D. and Ayers, M. (eds), *The Cambridge History of Seventeenth-Century Philosophy*, Cambridge, vol. 1, pp. 280–83.

———— (1999), *On Descartes' Metaphysical Prism and the Limits of Onto-Theology in Cartesian Thought*, Chicago: University of Chicago Press

Markus, R. (1970), *Saeculum: History and Society in the Theology of St. Augustine*, Cambridge: Cambridge University Press.

Martin, T. (2000), 'Augustine's *Confessions* as Pedagogy: Exercises in Transformation', in Paffenroth, K. and Hughes, K. (eds), *Augustine and Liberal Education*, Burlington, VT: Ashgate, pp. 25–51.

McInerny, Ralph (1961), *The Logic of Analogy: An Interpretation of St Thomas*, The Hague: Martinus Nijhoff.

Milbank, John (1990), 'The End of Dialogue', in Costa, Gavin D' (ed.), *Christian Uniqueness Reconsidered: The Myth of a Pluralistic Theology of Religions*, New York: Orbis, pp. 174–91.

—— (1990), *Theology and Social Theory: Beyond Secular Reason*, Oxford: Basil Blackwell.

—— (1997), 'Sacred Triads: Augustine and the Indo-European Soul', *Modern Theology*, **13**, 451–74.

—— (1997a), 'Pleonasm, Speech and Writing', in *WMS*, pp. 55–83.

—— (1997b), 'A Christological Poetics', in *WMS*, pp. 123–44.

—— (1998), 'The Sublime in Kierkegaard', in Blond, P. (ed.), *Post-secular Philosophy. Between Philosophy and Theology*, London: Routledge, pp. 131–56.

—— (1999), 'Intensities', *Modern Theology*, **15** (4), October, 445–97.

—— (2001a), 'The Soul of Reciprocity, Part One: Reciprocity Refused', *Modern Theology*, **17** (3), July, 335–91.

—— (2001b), 'The Soul of Reciprocity, Part Two: Reciprocity Granted', *Modern Theology*, **17** (4), October, 485–507.

—— (2002), 'Postmodernité', in Lacoste, J.-Y. (ed.), *Dictionnaire critique de théologie*, Paris: Quadrige/Presses Universitaires de France, pp. 924–5.

Miner, Robert (2001), 'Suárez as Founder of Modernity: Reflections on a *topos* in recent historiography', *History of Philosophy Quarterly*, **18** (1), January, 17–36.

Mirandola, Pico della (1965), *Oration on the Dignity of Man*, trans. P. Miller, Indianapolis: Hackett.

Montaigne, Michel de (1987), *The Complete Essays*, trans. M. A. Screech, London: Penguin.

More, Henry (1660), *An explanation of the grand mystery of godliness*, London: printed by J. Flesher for W. Morden.

—— (1708), *The Theological Works*, London: J. Downing.

—— (1712), *A Collection of Several Philosophical Writings*, 4th edn, London: J. Downing.

Morrison, K. (1969), *Tradition and Authority in the Western Church, 300–1140*, Princeton: Princeton University Press.

Narbonne, Jean-Marc (2001), *Hénologie, ontologie et Ereignis (Plotin–Proclus–Heidegger)*, L'âne d'or, Paris: Les Belles Lettres.

Nicholson, Graeme (1998), 'The Ontology of Plato's *Phaedrus*', *Dionysius*, **16**, 9–28.

Niebuhr, Reinhold (1955), *Beyond Tragedy: Essays on the Christian Interpretation of History*, New York: Scribner's.

Noone, Timothy B. (1999), 'The Franciscans and Epistemology: Reflections on the Roles of Bonaventure and Scotus', in Houser, R. E. (ed.), *Medieval Masters: Essays in Memory of Msgr. E. A. Synan*, Houston: Center for Thomistic Studies, pp. 63–90.

O'Daly, G. (1987), *Augustine's Philosophy of Mind*, Berkeley: University of California Press.

O'Donovan, O. M. T. (1982), '"Usus" and "Fruitio" in Augustine, *De Doctrina Christiana* I', *Journal of Theological Studies*, **2**, n.s. (33), 361–97.

———— (1980), *The Problem of Self Love in St. Augustine*, New Haven: Yale University Press.

———— (1987) 'Augustine's *City of God* XIX and Western Political Thought', *Dionysius*, **11**, 89–110.

———— (1996), *The Desire of the Nations: Rediscovering the Roots of Political Theology*, Cambridge: Cambridge University Press.

O'Donovan, O. M. T. and O'Donovan, J. (eds) (1999), *From Irenaeus to Grotius: A Sourcebook in Christian Political Thought*, Grand Rapids: Eerdmans.

Oakeshott, M. (1991), *Rationalism In Politics and Other Essays*, ed. T. Fuller, Indianapolis: Liberty Press.

———— (1996), *The Politics of Faith and the Politics of Scepticism*, ed. T. Fuller, New Haven: Yale University Press.

Pabst, Adrian (2002), 'De la chrétienté à la modernité? Lecture critique des thèses de *Radical Orthodoxy* sur la rupture scotiste et ockhamienne et sur le renouveau de la théologie de saint Thomas d'Aquin', *Revue des sciences théologiques et philosophiques*, **86**, 561–99.

Pailin, D. A. (1984), *Attitudes to other Religions: Comparative Religion in Seventeenth and Eighteenth Century Britain*, Manchester: University of Manchester Press.

Patrick, Simon (1662), *A Brief account of the new sect of Latitude-men. Together with some reflections upon the New Philosophy. By S.P. of Cambridge. In answer to a letter from his friend at Oxford*, London: no printer.

Pattison, G. (1993), '"Who" is the Discourse? A Study in Kierkegaard's Religious Literature', *Kierkegaardiana*, **16**, 28–45.

Pattison, G. and Shakespeare, S. (eds) (1998), *Kierkegaard. The Self in Society*, Basingstoke: Macmillan.

Peddle, David (2000), 'Hegel's Political Ideal: Civil Society, Sittlichkeit and History', *Animus*, **5**, www.swgc.mun.ca/animus.

Petrarch, Francesco (1985), 'The Ascent of Mount Ventoux', in *Selections from the* Canzoniere *and other writings*, ed. M. Musa, Oxford: Oxford University Press, pp. 11–19.

———— (1989), *Secretum*, trans. and ed. D. A. Carozza and H. J. Shey, New York: Lang.

Pickstock, Catherine (1999), 'Soul, city and cosmos after Augustine', in *RO*, pp. 243–77.

———— (2001), 'Reply to David Ford and Guy Collins', *Scottish Journal of Theology*, **54**, 405–22.

Pieper, J. (1999), *Leisure, The Basis of Culture*, trans. A. Dru, Indianapolis: Liberty Fund.

Pouillon, H. (1946), 'La Beauté, propriété transcendentale chez les scolastiques (1220–1270)', *Archives de l'histoire doctrinale et littéraire du moyen âge*,

15, 263–329.

Prouvost, Géry (1996), *Thomas d'Aquin et les thomismes. Essai sur l'histoire des thomismes*, Paris: Cerf.

Reale, Giovanni (1985), *A History of Ancient Philosophy Volume Three: The Systems of the Hellenistic Age*, trans. John R. Catan, Albany: SUNY Press.

———— (1987), *A History of Philosophy Volume One: From the Origins to Socrates*, trans. John R. Catan, Albany: SUNY Press.

Reno, R (2000), 'The Radical Orthodoxy Project', *First Things*, **100**, February, 37–44.

Riedel, Manfred (1984), *Between Reason and Revolution: The Hegelian Transformation of Political Philosophy*, trans. Walter Wright, Cambridge: Cambridge University Press.

Robertson, Neil G. (1998), 'The Closing of the Early Modern Mind: Leo Strauss and Early Modern Political Thought', *Animus*, **3**, www.swgc.mun.ca/animus.

———— (1999), 'The Platonism of Leo Strauss', *Animus*, **4**, www.swgc.mun.ca/animus.

Rose, Gillian (1981), *Hegel contra Sociology*, London: Athlone.

Rousseau, J.-J. (1997), *Second Discourse*, ed. and trans. V. Gourevitch, Cambridge: Cambridge University Press.

Rubin, Miri (1992), *Corpus Christi: the Eucharist in Late Medieval Culture*, Cambridge: Cambridge University Press.

Schmutz, Jacob (1999), 'Escaping the Aristotelian Bond: the Critique of Metaphysics in Twentieth-Century French Philosophy', *Dionysius*, **17**, 169–200.

Scotus, Duns (1639), *Reportatio* (i.e. *Additiones magnae*), in *Opera Omnia*, ed. Luke Wadding, 12 vols, Lyons.

———— (1950–), *Lectura* and *Ordinatio*, in *Opera Omnia*, ed. C. Balić and others, Vatican City: Typis Polyglottis Vaticanis.

———— (1997–), *Quaestiones Subtilissimae in Libros Metaphysicorum Aristotelis*, in *Opera Philosophica*, ed. Girard. J. Etzkorn and others, St Bonaventure, NY: The Franciscan Institute.

Shakespeare, S. (2000), 'The New Romantics. A Critique of Radical Orthodoxy', *Theology*, **103** (813), May/June, 163–77.

———— (2001), *Kierkegaard, Language and the Reality of God*, Aldershot: Ashgate.

Shaw, Gregory (1996), 'After Aporia: Theurgy in Later Platonism', *The Journal of Neoplatonic Studies*, **5** (1), 3–41.

Simon, Y. (1980), *A General Theory of Authority*, Notre Dame: University of Notre Dame Press.

Skinner, Q. (1989), 'The State', in Ball, T., Farr, J. and Hanson, R. (eds), *Political Innovation and Conceptual Change*, Cambridge: Cambridge University Press, 90–131.

Smith, John (1660), *Select Discourses*, London: Printed by J. Flesher for E. Morden.

Strauss, Leo (1950), *Natural Right and History*, Chicago: University of Chicago Press.

———— (1959), *What is Political Philosophy?*, Chicago: University of Chicago Press.

———— (1991), *On Tyranny*, New York: Free Press.

Suárez, (1960-66), *Disputationes metaphysicae* [= *Disp. metaph.*], ed. Sergio Rábade Romeo and others, 7 vols, Biblioteca hispánica de filosofía, Madrid: Editorial Gredos.

Swinburne, Richard (1991), *The Existence of God*, revised edn, Oxford: Clarendon Press.

———— (1993), *The Coherence of Theism*, revised edn, Oxford: Clarendon Press.

Taylor, Charles (1989), *Sources of the Self*, Cambridge: Harvard University Press.

———— (1995), *Philosophical Arguments*, Cambridge: Harvard University Press.

Taylor, Jeremy (1822), *A Discourse of the Liberty of Prophesying*, in *The Whole Works of Jeremy Taylor*, ed. R. Heber, vol. 8, London: J. Moyes.

Tulloch, John (1966), *Rational Theology and Christian Philosophy*, Hildesheim: Georg Olms (repr. of 2nd edn, 1874).

Velde, Rudi te (1995), *Participation and Substantiality in Thomas Aquinas*, Studien und Texte zur Geistesgeschichte des Mittelalters 46, Leiden: Brill.

Voegelin, Eric (1952), *The New Science of Politics*, Chicago: University of Chicago Press.

———— (1987), *In Search of Order* (vol. 5 of *Order in History*), Baton Rouge: Louisiana State University Press.

Westcott, Brooke F. (1891), *Essays in the History of Religious Thought in the West*, London and New York: Macmillan.

Whichcote, Benjamin (1930), *Moral and Religious Aphorisms*, London: Elkin Mathews & Marrot.

Williams, Rowan (1987), 'Politics and the Soul: A Reading of the *City of God*', *Milltown Studies*, **19/20**, 55–72.

———— (1990), '*Sapientia* and the Trinity: Reflections on *De Trinitate*', *Augustiniana*, **40**, 317–32.

Zaganiaris, J. (2001), 'Réflexions sur une "intimate": Joseph de Maistre et Carl Schmitt', *L'Homme et la Société*, **140–41** (2–3), 147–67.

Index

Adorno, Theodore 112
Ailly, Pierre d' 85
analogy 68, 77
Anaxagoras 9, 14
Anglicanism xiv, 18, 99
apophaticism 107–8
appearances 5
Aquinas, Thomas 28, 49–62, 74, 76, 78
Augustine 19, 21, 22, 31–45, 62,
    129–30

Baader, Franz von 122–3
Balthasar, Hans Urs von 99
Barth, Karl 100, 109–10, 112–13
beauty 44, 51–2
being 8, 22, 50, 52, 55–7, 65–74
Bible 32, 118, 138, 172–3
Blondel, Maurice 134
Boethius 27
Bowlin, John xviii
Brisson, Luc 19

Cambridge xiii–xiv, 101, 104, 110
Cambridge Platonists 99–115
Cassirer, Ernst 100–101, 110–11
cause 9 *see also* teleology
Cephalus 3
Christ 102, 134–5, 146, 157, 158, 172–4
Church 41–2, 44, 45, 138–9, 140, 150,
    174
city 1, 4–5 *see also polis*
civil society 42, 121, 122, 125–8
communitarianism 140
community 82, 139, 157
conceptual knowledge 67–9, 71, 73, 76
conscience 124
contemplation 24–5,
Courtine, Jean-François xiii, 56
creation 26, 28, 123
Cudworth, Ralph 99–100, 102–4, 106–7,
    108, 110, 113–14

Dante Alighieri 82
death 167–72
deception, strategy of 29
decisionism 112–13
deconstruction 18, 59, 164–5
Derrida, Jacques 2, 14–16, 18, 26,
    161–74
Descartes, René 26, 85–6, 88–9, 91–3,
    104, 120
desire 33, 36, 43, 91, 126
dialectic 15, 34
dialogue, end of 103, 145
différance xiv, 18, 162, 168–9
difference 9, 12, 13, 14, 35, 61, 163–5,
    174
discipline 94
dissonance 166
distance 8
Donatism 42
doubt 88, 138, 164
doxology *see* liturgy
dualism 1, 9, 19, 58–9, 90–91

Eco, Umberto 155
Enlightenment 2, 3, 7, 31, 109, 111, 114,
    128, 133
etymology 8
Eucharist 54, 102, 109, 139–40, 146,
    149–59, 172–4
eurocentrism 103
evil 81, 91, 95, 124, 129–30
extension 89, 90

faith 59–60
Fall 34, 35–6
fascism 112
fate 81
Faust 88, 95
feeling 6, 44, 159
Findlay, J.N. 2
Foucault, Michel 94